NOTES

County
DURHAM

0 1 2 3 4 5 6 7 8 9 10
Scale of Miles

NORTHUMBERLAND

Ryton
Bradley Hall
Stell
Winlaton
Axwell Pa
Hollins
Gibside
Lintz
R. Tyne
Hamsterley Hall
Ebchester
Tanfie
Medomsley
Pontop H
Shotley Br
Blackhill
Annfield Plai
R. Derwent
Edmondbyers
Muggleswick
Hunstanworth
Lanches
Woodlands Hall

CUMBERLAND

Westgate Eastgate Stanhope
St John's Chapel
Westernhopeburn
Frosterley
Wolsingham
R. Wear
Tow Law
Bradley Hall
Harperley
Helmington H
Hoppyland Hall
Witton le
R. Tees
Hamsterley
Es

St Helen Auckl
Middleton in Teesdale
Stotley Hall
W Auckland
Egglestone
Cockfield
Raby Castle
Staindrop
Streatlam Castle
Headlam H
Westholme Hall
Winston Gainfo
Barnard Castle
Sledwick Hall
Stubb House
Whorlton

WESTMORLAND

YOR

THE BUILDINGS OF ENGLAND
BE 9
COUNTY DURHAM
NIKOLAUS PEVSNER

Map grid labels (top and bottom): 3 · 4 · 5

Right-hand margin (vertical): NORTH SEA

Grid rows (right margin): A · B · C · D · E

Places (north to south, left to right):

SOUTH SHIELDS · Westoe · Hebburn · Jarrow · Marsden
GATESHEAD · Monkton · Cleadon · Whitburn
Winlaton · vell · Whickham · Felling · Heworth
Hollinside · Ravensworth Castle · Usworth · W Boldon · E Boldon · Roker
ibside · Lamesley · Hylton Castle · Monkwearmouth
Causey Arch · Birtley · Washington · Southwick
field · Beamish Hall · Biddick Hall · SUNDERLAND
Pelton · Lambton Castle · Penshaw
Chester le Street · Lumley Castle · Ryhope
Holmside · Houghton le Spring · Seaham
Langley Hall · Sacriston · Dalton le Dale · Seaham Harbour
Finchale Priory · W Rainton le Hole · Hetton · Dawdon
tton Gilbert · Pittington · Murton · Hawthorn
sh · Bearpark · Belmont · Elmore Hall · Easington
Ushaw · Aldin Grange · Sherburn Hospital · Horden Hall
DURHAM · Ludworth · Shotton
tanley · Houghall · Peterlee · Castle Eden · Blackhall
Burn Hall · Butterby · Wingate · Monk Hesleden
rancepeth · Croxdale · Coxhoe · Church Kelloe · Hart
willington · Tudhoe · Trimdon
Newfield · Whitworth · HARTLEPOOL
unwick · Westerton · Bishop Middleham · W HARTLEPOOL
comb · Rirk · Merrington · Mainsforth Hall · Elwick Hall
Bishop Auckland · stranton · Seaton Carew
St Andrew Auckland · Windlestone Hall · Hardwick Hall · Sedgefield · Greatham
St Helen Auckland · Grindon · Wynyard Park · Wolviston
Redworth Hall · Middridge Grange · Blakeston Hall · Cowpen Bewley
Heighington · Aycliffe · Thorpe Thewles · Redmarshall · Billingham · Haverton Hall
Coatham Mundeville · Bishopton · Norton
adlam · Denton · Walworth Castle · STOCKTON ON TEES
ll · Thornton Hall · Whessoe · E Hartburn · Elton
inford · Gt Burdon · Sadberge · Long Newton
ercebridge · Coniscliffe · Haughton le Skerne · Egglescliffe
DARLINGTON
Blackwell · Middleton one Row
Hurworth on Tees · Low Dinsdale
Sockburn

Bottom-left margin: S H I R E

Compass rose: N · W · E · S

THE BUILDINGS OF ENGLAND

County Durham

BY

NIKOLAUS PEVSNER

★

PENGUIN BOOKS
MELBOURNE · LONDON · BALTIMORE

FIRST PUBLISHED 1953

The author and publishers would be grateful
to any user of this book for having any errors
or omissions pointed out to them
in as much detail
as possible

MADE AND PRINTED IN GREAT BRITAIN
FOR PENGUIN BOOKS LTD
BY WILLIAM CLOWES AND SONS LTD
LONDON AND BECCLES

CONTENTS

*

*

The map on pages 2–3 shows all those places, whether towns, villages, or isolated buildings, which are the subject of separate entries in the text. The index on pages 277–279 gives references to the map square in which each place mentioned will be found.

TO THE GENTLE SLIDE-RULERS
OF PORTMAN SQUARE

★

FOREWORD

Preparation of the material on which the following descriptions of buildings and their contents are based was in the hands of Dr R. Schapire. She did most of the extensive preliminary reading and extracting. My own reading was limited, but the travelling and the work 'on the target' was done entirely by me. As for the resulting text I am proud to be able to reiterate, as the title page has already stated, that the entries on Roman antiquities are not by me but by Professor Ian A. Richmond. Entries on prehistory were provided by Mr Jon Manchip White. I am also anxious to thank Colonel Battiscombe, Chapter Clerk of Durham Cathedral, and Mr D. McIntyre, architect to Durham Cathedral, for help in matters connected with that building. I owe a great debt of gratitude to the many rectors and vicars of churches and the many owners and occupiers of houses for the generous help they have given me. The best way in which I can repay those who have opened their houses to me is by saying emphatically that that does not necessarily mean their willingness to open them to others. Public Libraries also have been exceedingly ready to search for information and put it at my disposal, first and foremost the Sunderland Library and its director Mr Crawley.

In addition Mr E. J. Clark, the County Librarian, has patiently answered a large number of awkward questions of mine. On individual problems or buildings I had the benefit of the knowledge of several local and more than local specialists. Amongst these I specially wish to mention the Reverend R. C. D. Jasper of Stillington, Mr C. Ogden, a specialist on the work of Paine, Mr D. H. Burbidge of Durham School and the Reverend S. Z. Edwards of Staindrop.

As in the case of previous volumes the Ministry of Housing and Local Government, who have a statutory duty to compile lists of buildings of architectural or historic interest, have with their customary courtesy given me access to unpublished lists and much other information collected by the Chief Investigator and his staff. Wherever I have relied entirely on these lists I have inserted a reference MHLG. Moreover, Mr H. S. Goodhart-Rendel has once again permitted me to use, and quote from, his manuscript notes on Victorian churches, and Sir Thomas Kendrick his manuscript notes on Victorian glass. My gratitude to both is great. Information based on these notes is marked GR and TK. The National Buildings Record has, as always, been an invaluable source of information and its staff, especially Mr Cecil Farthing and Mrs Parry, untiring in their support of my work. Even with all such help, however, the following pages are bound to be faulty in many ways, and I shall be most grateful to users of this book if they would kindly point out errors and omissions to me.

Winter, 1952–3

INTRODUCTION

THE county of Durham is one of the least-known parts of England. Those in search of the rugged north go to Northumberland and Scotland, those who want moors and dales to the West Riding and Cumberland or the High Peak, those who like to see the waves of the sea break against precipitous cliffs to Devon or Cornwall. Durham Cathedral, it is true, means something to everyone, but how many who have seen it from the train to Scotland appearing suddenly, like a mirage in its improbable splendour, have stopped to spend a day in and around it? And as for the stretches of land between Durham and the dales and Durham and the sea, the impassionate propaganda of the late Ellen Wilkinson in the black early thirties has, it seems, in people's minds, given them an indelible stamp of squalor and desolation.

Wrongly so. The colliery and steel districts are nothing like as grim as some other industrial parts of the country. There are nearly everywhere woods and fields left near the tips, the furnaces, and the mean housing. The county can indeed neither complain of a lack of beauty nor of variety of landscape. The fells of the west and the cliffs between South Shields and Sunderland, High Force, and Marsden Rocks have already been alluded to, but there are in addition the deeply eroded, thickly foliated denes stretching down to the sea and the nicely wooded valleys around Durham.

Landscape expresses geology, and the geology of Durham, structurally very simple, can easily be read, even by the layman. It ranges from the carboniferous limestone and the millstone grit in the west tip adjoining Cumberland and the West Riding, through the coal measures of a broad central strip, to the magnesian limestone which runs in a band of decreasing width from the coast between South Shields and Hartlepool to a line from Piercebridge to Darlington on the Tees, and finally to the sandstone and marls of the SE corner. Both the oldest strata and the youngest are missing. No

granite, no old red sandstone, and none of that oölitic limestone which yields the best building stones of England and
extends from Somerset and Dorset diagonally up, by way of
the Cotswolds, into Northamptonshire and the south of
Yorkshire. On the building stones of Durham literature is
as completely lacking as on those of most other counties. It
must suffice here to say that stone reigns in the north and
west, brick in the south-east, a division reflected to a certain
extent in the fields by that between walls and hedges. As
for stone, the millstone grit of the west is easily enough distinguished from the fine magnesian limestone and the immensely porous sandstone, creating after a time highly
exciting cavernous surfaces, but surfaces which have little
to do with the original masons' work. A speciality from the
dales is called Frosterley marble, a dark, coralline limestone almost saturated with fossilized shells. It takes the
place in County Durham of the Purbeck marble of the
south.

Historically the county begins to assume interest with the
coming of the Romans. Its prehistoric remains are only of
the very slightest interest to the student. Evidence of
settlement in the county before the arrival of the Romans
is extremely exiguous. Early man does not seem to have
been attracted by a district which must always have
appeared remote and inhospitable. A few huntsmen,
fishermen, and strand-loopers strayed along its coastline in
late Old Stone Age and Middle Stone Age times, and the
presence of small communities of villagers is attested in the
Bronze Age. The vigorous Iron Age culture of Parisian
Celts which flourished in nearby Yorkshire appears to have
by-passed Durham altogether.

Roman Durham is a very different story. The activities
of the Romans chiefly between A.D. 86 and their final
departure early in the C5, can only be fully understood in
connexion with Northumberland, and it will indeed be
seen that right through the Middle Ages the architectural
history of Durham cannot be dissociated from the neighbouring county to the N. Hadrian's Wall, the permanent
N border defence is what the works of the Romans in

Durham were focused on. The main roads ran s–n, chiefly Dere Street which entered the county at Piercebridge and went by Binchester near Bishop Auckland (Vinovia), Lanchester and Ebchester to Corbridge and the wall, and another road which branched near Binchester and went by Chester-le-Street to Gateshead with yet another branch to South Shields. The fort at South Shields is being excavated and exposed now and promises to become one of the most interesting sites in the n. The forts of Binchester, Lanchester, and Ebchester have also been excavated to a certain extent, though the remains are not now displayed. But the excavations showed that their history was very different. Ebchester and Binchester were occupied from A.D. 80 until about A.D. 122, when Lanchester was built to take their place. In the reorganization of Severn in A.D. 197 Lanchester was left empty, while Binchester and Ebchester were again restored, Binchester housing a Spanish cavalry regiment. Lanchester was re-established under Gordian III, and its fine inscriptions of the period are to be seen in the Chapter Library at Durham. In the c4 the large ten-acre fort at Piercebridge was added to these defences, to contain a mobile garrison for intercepting sea-raiders. All these precautions imply a civilian population worth protect-ing, and traces of the northernmost *villa* or farming estate in Britain were lately found at Old Durham, 1½ miles E of Durham City. The most impressive visible Roman remains in the county, however, are those at South Shields.

With the Roman departure, the lights of civilization went out in Britain and two centuries of barbarity followed. Meanwhile, however, from obscure Mediterranean, prob-ably Coptic, regions, Christianity had established itself be-yond the boundaries of the Roman world, in Ireland. The beginnings are shrouded in darkness. By the c6 the fervour of the Irish communities of monks which lived in their round huts in kraals under the rulership of bishops had already become so powerful that missionaries started out to conquer heathen lands for this Coptic-Celtic faith. Colum-banus founded Luxueil in France and Bobbio in Lombardy and died in 615, Gallus founded St Gall in 613, and earlier still Columba had settled at Iona in 563 and died there in 597. Then, in 635, Aidan went from Iona to Lindisfarne. He did so at the request of the King of Northumbria, Oswald, a few years after another missionary had been in the north and left again, Paulinus who arrived in 625 from Kent which had been christianized from Rome by St Augustine at the end of the c6. So from the beginning a conflict was outlined between the Roman and the Celtic manners of Christianity, between Monte Cassino and Skellig Michael. Aidan belonged to the latter type. He died as Bishop of Lindisfarne in 651. After his death bishops followed each other quickly until in 685 an Anglian, Cuthbert, was elected. With Cuthbert the beginnings of Durham are closely connected. His shrine which arrived at Durham after the Danish storms in 995 became the foundation and the religious centre of the cathedral.

Now at the time of Cuthbert the conflict between Roman and Celtic traditions had been brought to an end. Cuthbert submitted to Rome in 664. With the Synod of Whitby the Celtic tradition was defeated. Everything was gained in unity, organization, and also in toleration of human nature as it is; what was lost, we can only guess. The miraculous flowering of Northumbria at the end of the seventh and the beginning of the eighth century reflects both. Never was synthesis more successful. Take the Book of Lindisfarne, or take the Ruthwell Cross; the turbulence of the scrolls and interlaces of Irish ornament is still evident, the choice of certain scenes has been proved to be influenced by Coptic precedent, yet the leaf scrolls and the birds playing in them, and the understanding of the human figure are Italian and Kentish. The Book of Lindisfarne and the Ruthwell Cross are both Northumbrian, but the County of Durham was just as much a centre of this renewed, fervent yet humane Christianity. The names here are Benedict Biscop, Ceolfrid, and Bede. Benedict Biscop was of noble Anglian descent. He had become a monk at Lerins in the s of France, then been taken back to England by Theodore of Tarsus, and been put in charge of the monastery of St Peter and Paul at Canterbury. In 674 King Elfrid of Northumbria gave him some land close to the mouth of the river Wear and here he founded Monkwearmouth as a Benedictine monastery, that is a monastery under an abbot governed by the rule of St Benedict and Monte Cassino, not as a community with a bishop and monks living on their own, as Iona and Lindisfarne had been. In 685 he established Jarrow as a sister-monastery to Wearmouth. His successor as abbot of both was Ceolfrid. The two monasteries flourished exceedingly. The Venerable Bede tells us that in 715 they together had 600 monks. Bede lived all his life, from the age of seven, in them, and died at Jarrow in 735. It is immensely fortunate that appreciable remains survive of the foundation buildings on both these holy sites. They are, together with some fragments in Kent and some in France, the earliest remains of Christianity north of the Alps. At Jarrow we may still have walls of the monastery, although not enough to form an idea of its shape and appearance and the tall nave of a small church with some small windows high up survives. At Monkwearmouth the tall, narrow nave is also in existence and the w porch crowned with a later Saxon tower. The porch is particularly interesting. It has as jambs two pairs of squat turned stone balusters and high above on the w face the remains of a large figure of Christ in relief. The balusters seem to have been a favourite motif of decoration in those early days. At Jarrow some twenty of them have been found, and others at Hart and Egglescliffe. The relief of Christ has been pointed out by Clapham to be the earliest piece of large-scale architectural sculpture in any North European country. The proportions of the church at Wearmouth are singularly narrow, and the same quality is perhaps even more noticeable in the amazingly completely preserved contemporary church at Escomb. Others in Northumberland also belong to this group, and in Durham the remaining nave masonry at Seaham, Billingham, and Pittington. Escomb has a straight-headed chancel east of the nave. The connecting arch is narrow and incidentally so well worked that the stones must be from a Roman arch. Narrower still is the arch from the porch into the nave at Wearmouth. There is no suppleness yet in the connecting of rooms, nor does there seem much generosity in the sizes of the churches. That is surprising after what we can read of poetic descriptions of churches of the c8 which no longer survive, and also after what we can see of the art of illuminating manuscripts and carving crosses. The lettering, the ornament, the representation of the human figure are so accomplished and so civilized that a less primitive architecture would be expected. In County Durham this high art of painting and sculpture can now only be studied in the cathedral collection. The most impressive of the crosses still in one of the parish churches, the St Andrew Auckland Cross, is late, of about 800, and indeed no longer as refined as the end of the c7 had been. There is more violence in the figures and a certain barbarity. This is also unmistakable in much later Anglo-Saxon architecture. The most important examples of this are the big crossing tower at Norton on its original supports, the w tower at Billingham with characteristic window surrounds of a kind similar to Barton-on-Humber and Earls Barton, i.e. churches of the c10, and the long-and-short work at Hart. Of details the exceedingly odd 'pre-tracery' above the bell-openings at Billingham should be remembered, and the triangular heads to windows at Hart and Norton.

Just such a triangular head occurs in yet one more place in the county, and that is in a room along the cloister of Durham Cathedral. The room must have been built after the Conquest, but it is likely that it belongs to the earliest Norman structures at Durham, those erected for the monks by Bishop Walcher who was appointed by the Conqueror in 1071 and ruled until 1080. It is quite probable that masons would have worked for him to whom the Saxon idiom was a matter of course. William, besides making Walcher Bishop of Durham, made him Earl of Northumberland, a most unusual act and one which seems to confirm that already at such an early date the Bishops of Durham had a recognized worldly power greater than other bishops. The beginnings of the position of the Bishop of Durham as *comes palatinus* are unknown. His resources and his independence must have grown gradually through the Saxon centuries.

The establishment of the County Palatine as an accepted legal entity belongs only to the late C12 and the C13, but the cathedral, and the castle, as we see the two together to-day, proud and defiant on their rock, are so much the visible symbol of the combination of spiritual and temporal lordship that here, before starting to speak of the architecture of cathedral and castle, something must be said about the peculiar constitutional position of the Bishops of Durham. 'Quicquid rex habet extra, episcopus habet intra.' The King's prerogatives outside are the bishop's inside. The Bishop appointed civil officers and had complete jurisdiction including the right to inflict capital punishment. His subjects served in the Bishop's army and elected representatives to an assembly of the Palatinate. He coined his own money, and all mines of gold and silver as well as of iron, lead, and coal belonged to him. In short, he was like the Prince-Bishops of Germany, not like the other Bishops of England, and so in the Middle Ages his palace was a heavily fortified castle, like the Marienburg of the Bishops of Würzburg.

The Castle at Durham, now occupied by parts of the university, is not sufficiently widely known. It is one of the most impressive and best preserved in the whole country. If one tries to reconstruct from evidence remaining above ground what size it had in Norman times, one will find that it was in area hardly smaller than now. And if one then examines what pieces of architectural value still exist, the poignant contrast will remain in one's memory between the Chapel, built by Bishop Walcher in the 1070s and the spectacular portal and long gallery of Bishop Pudsey (1153–95) of about 1160–70 or thereabouts. Here is the whole development of the Norman style within the century of its life on English soil, from the narrow, clumsily groin-vaulted bays and the barbarously carved capitals of the chapel to the sumptuous three-dimensional decoration of Pudsey's time. Both the gallery and the portal are amongst the most splendid examples of Romanesque domestic architecture in Europe.

To follow the development from the later C11 to the later C12 in greater detail, one has to go across Palace Green from the Castle to the Cathedral. As to the historical significance

and the architectural grandeur of the Cathedral, the reader
will have to turn to the introductory paragraphs on pp. 77
and 78. Here it will be sufficient to recall a few aspects. The
Cathedral was begun in 1093 by Bishop William of St Calais
or St Carileph (1081–96). The E parts were complete and
the nave begun by 1104. The transept vaulting followed
about 1105–10 and the completion of the nave about 1110–
28. All this work belongs to the years of Bishop Ranulph
Flambard (1099–1128). The nave vault was finally closed
between 1123 and 1133. The Chapter House dates from
about 1130–40, and then come the SE portal into the cloister
and the Gatehouse of about 1160–75. The cathedral is the
first building in England to have been vaulted throughout.
It is, moreover, very probably the first building in Europe
to have received rib-vaults. The vaulting of wide spans was
the great problem of Western architecture in the later C11.
It was desirable as a protection against fire but even more as
the completion of the lapidary character of the whole building. The aesthetic unity which the vault gives an interior
can never be obtained by timber ceilings or open roofs. To
the eye they tend to keep the walls apart as two independent
pieces. Only when a stone vault rises from the walls and
joins up above and between them, do we feel that the whole
building has become one. Vaulting on a small scale had
never been wholly forgotten. But when it came to the enterprise of vaulting a nave, much courage and self-confidence
were needed. The earliest major nave vaults were tunnel-
vaults. They were constructed in France about 1075. Shortly
after that in Germany the first groined nave vault was
built, an even bolder enterprise, since a tunnel-vault rests
on the whole side-walls, whereas a groined vault is supported only by four separate piers in the four corners.
Normandy had been comparatively slow in the matter of
vaulting. The great Norman monasteries of the Conqueror,
Jumièges and the two at Caen, had flat ceilings. So had the
great new Norman cathedrals and monasteries in England.
All the more amazing is it, therefore, that Durham was
begun in 1093 to carry not only groined but ribbed and
groined vaults. The vault with cross ribs is a much more

articulate form than the ribless groined vault; and so it goes specially well with the walls of Normandy and Norman England which were punctuated by shafts all the way up and had large arcades, a first floor opening in galleries, and a second floor or clerestory which is split up into two layers in depth by means of a wall-passage in front of the windows. The creation of the rib-vault at Durham is the logical conclusion and the crowning achievement of this systematic work. The chancel aisles still possess their rib-vaults of *c*. 1095. Those in the chancel have been replaced in the C13. But in the transepts, as wide, of course, as the chancel, rib-vaults of *c*. 1104 can still be seen *in situ*.

As regards the development of style, the comparison between the chapel and the gallery in the castle can be amplified by a comparison between the earliest parts of the cathedral and the Galilee. The cathedral was begun about twenty years after the chapel and so has none of the barbarity, though still all the force, of the older design. Indeed what gives it supremity over all other Norman buildings in England or Normandy is this unexpected combination of primeval power, the power of William's conquest and of his bloody conquest of the north, with a consummate mastery of scale and proportion. All the forms used are colossal, but the effect is not cyclopic. They are composed in so noble and harmonious a way that in the end one can well forget for moments their absolute sizes. The most impressive of all motifs is the cylindrical piers which alternate with superordinate compound ones. They are nearly seven feet in diameter, but by the exquisite device of grooved geometrical ornament in large simple motifs their inert mass is made to live. Ornament at Durham (and in the Norman style in England altogether) is almost exclusively geometrical, and it develops from the simplest to the most ornate. At the beginning there are block capitals or single-scalloped capitals only. In the w portal of about 1125–30 the capitals have many fine flutings. The cylindrical piers bring in ornament, first a spiral grooving and then, about 1100, a zigzag groining. It must be the first use anywhere of this favourite Norman motif. One can then follow from ten to ten years how the desire for decorative enrichment grew : zigzags in the ribs of the s transept, then in the nave arcade and other arches, and in the portals. In the portals in addition some sparing use is made of foliage and animals, but never with as much conviction as in France. The Chapter House introduces whole human figures as caryatids below the ribs of the apse. In the end, with the advent of Bishop Pudsey, the geometrical decoration assumes a new degree of plasticity, and rope or battlement or lozenge mouldings fill the extradoses as well as the intradoses of the arches. But in the Galilee, i.e. about 1170–5, something else is at once noticeable which goes beyond more ornamental motifs. The supports of the arcades are extremely slim, or were originally, a pair of completely detached Purbeck marble shafts, the very contrary of the sturdiness of the piers of eighty years before. Elegance, splendour, and sophistication have taken the place of the power, discipline, and directness which were the outstanding features in the design of the cathedral. A hallmark of this phase is the so-called waterleaf capital, very different in its succulent and springy character from the rigidity of earlier capitals. But Bishop Pudsey's importance in the history of architecture in Durham goes beyond those new qualities exhibited by the works planned for him up to about 1175. In his last years it was he who must have been responsible for the introduction of the Gothic style into the county.

However, before that eminently interesting problem can be discussed a few words must be said about minor Norman work in the county. Typical of the elementary and forceful character of the Early Norman style are the remains of St Giles Durham (consecrated in 1112) and the tall central tower at Jarrow, typical of the richest zigzag phase the s Portal at Hartlepool, typical of the Pudsey style at its most boldly three-dimensional the N arcade at Pittington with the snake-like serpentine band round the pier. Of special interest for their plans are the churches of Kirk Merrington and Heighington. At Kirk Merrington the Norman church consists (or consisted ; for what one sees now is a C19 copy) of nave, crossing tower, and chancel. At Heighington a Norman chancel with a narrower also straightheaded Norman apse remains. Norman clerestories are a rarity. Apart from the chancel and nave of the cathedral traces can be seen in the Galilee and at St Helen Auckland. A well-preserved clerestory is in St Margaret Durham.* There are few Norman tympana with sculptural decoration. The names to be mentioned are Coniscliffe and Houghton-le-Spring. Their sculpture is barbaric, whereas the famous bronze Door Knocker of Durham Cathedral though violently stylized has nothing of barbarity. Much more accomplished and elegant are the Cross at Church Kelloe, the panel from the screen of Durham Cathedral (now in the cathedral museum) and the panel in St Mary-the-Less; but these take us to the end of C12 and beyond, that is, to the Transitional and the E.E. styles. As for the Transitional, it is characterized by waterleaf capitals, occasional pointed arches, occasional keeled shafts, and an ornamental motif of little three-sided pyramids. which has been called the nutmeg ornament. It stands evolutionarily between the Norman zigzag and the E.E. nailhead and dogtooth. Transitional remains are at St Oswald Durham, Elwick Hall, Lanchester, and St Helen Auckland. Buildings in the county using this style may be as late as 1200 or so.

By then, however, Bishop Pudsey had turned away from the style of the Galilee and introduced into Durham the Gothic style. This was a moment of great importance; for the Early Gothic, in its English form called Early English, became the style in which the best and the most numerous of the ancient parish churches in the county were to be erected. The C13 is the century of the greatest building activity here, much in contrast to most other counties. That Pudsey was himself responsible for the great innovation can hardly be doubted. The Gothic style appears first in two buildings directly sponsored by him, the truly royal Hall of his palace at Bishop Auckland (palace – for it was apparently never seriously fortified) and the collegiate church at Darlington. Both were probably begun about 1190. The Hall with its elegant shafts and arches of grey Frosterley marble is the most magnificent piece of English domestic architecture

* Norton and Billingham have Transitional clerestories.

of its century. People easily forget that, because the hall has now for nearly three hundred years been a chapel. The Bishop can well be credited with so momentous a decision as the change from the old well-tried to a completely new style. He was a man conversant with many countries, French by birth (his real name was de Puiset), son probably of the Viscount of Chartres, nephew of King Stephen, archdeacon at Winchester, treasurer at York, and then at the age of about thirty or thirty-two Bishop of Durham. We find him innumerable times in attendance at Westminster; we find him at Rouen and at Tours, at Canterbury and in Rome. He might have received the first intimation in France or at Canterbury of how different Gothic churches looked from his. But the style at Auckland and Darlington is certainly neither French nor connected with William of Sens at Canterbury. It is in fact decidedly North English. One may well in addition detect connexions with Lincoln, but Lincoln was only started in 1191. Much closer seem the relations to Ripon, and at Ripon the Gothic building with its typical lancet-shaped arches and blank arcadings and with the motif of a sunk blank quatrefoil in the spandrels (which appears in the s transept at Darlington) was started before the death of Archbishop Roger of Pont l'Evêque in 1191.

After Pudsey's pioneer buildings, others followed rapidly, Finchale Priory, begun in 1196, and Hartlepool being the most ambitious of them. Hartlepool, although of monumental size, was no more than a parish church. Finchale was a Benedictine establishment. But for the *magnum opus* of the Early English style in the county one has again to go to the cathedral. The Chapel of the Nine Altars was begun in 1242 and completed about 1280. It remains one of the most beautifully proportioned monuments in England of the E.E. style at its ripest. The Joseph Window especially with its exquisite double tracery, partly intersected and partly of trefoiled and cinquefoiled circles, is scarcely matched in the C13 and nowhere surpassed.

But this leads almost a century beyond the beginnings. During that century the North of England had a type of

E.E. architecture quite its own, and County Durham shares it. Its chief characteristic is the great liking for extremely elongated lancet windows and the dislike of window tracery. Tracery comes but late and, with the exception of the Joseph Window, achieves little. An interesting example of what might be called pre-tracery is at Houghton-le-Spring, where above two lancets a large pierced quatrefoil is set in, surrounded by an oddly shaped hood-mould. Similarly at Gainford, Low Dinsdale, and Whitburn *vesica*-shaped windows are introduced (cf., for example, Tynemouth, Northumberland). But of bar tracery, i.e. the developed geometrical tracery of the type of Westminster and the Angel Choir at Lincoln, there are less than ten examples in the whole county. On the other hand, one meets time and again E ends marked by groups of three or five slender lancets kept entirely separate from each other but arranged as a stepped-up group with the middle one higher than the others. Inside, such groups are often connected by arches on shafts with or without shaft-rings. Darlington starts all this; it is repeated at Cockfield, Coniscliffe, Dalton, Easington, Gainford, Lanchester, Medomsley, St Helen Auckland, Sockburn, and specially rich in the front of St Edmund's Chapel at Gateshead. Late in the century, when the single lancet was no longer considered to give enough light, Durham preferred to the suavity of foiled circles the harder and more vertical type of window tracery known as intersected, or the yet less luxurious type in which three or five stepped lancet-lights are simply comprised under one containing arch. This form appears at Sedgefield in a window which can be dated as shortly after 1283, a date useful for comparisons.

Now for other elements of the C13 churches. As to towers, West Boldon in all probability possesses a complete C13 broach spire, a rare thing, and doubly rare in a county of few spires altogether.* Sherburn Hospital, which was founded by Pudsey in 1181 and still begun in the Norman

---

* Darlington, Chester-le-Street, Coniscliffe, and Ryton are the only medieval spires besides West Boldon. Houghton-le-Spring and indeed Durham Cathedral formerly possessed lead-covered timber spires.

style, received after 1200 a w tower with fine arcading similar to the upper part of the w towers of the cathedral. To the same group also belongs the proud tower at Hartlepool. This is not strictly a w tower, but rather the centre of a kind of western crossing. The only parallel is Kelso in Scotland. As for real crossing towers in the E.E. style, there is but one in the county, Darlington. c13 aisles are often carried forward to the w face of the towers which would then open into them with arches similar to those leading to the nave. E.E. naves in County Durham have as a rule circular piers or alternating circular and octagonal ones. An ingenious variety (Darlington, Easington) alternates not only from w to e but also from n to s, so that an octagonal pier always faces a circular one and *vice versa*. Piers of richer forms are rare, rarer than in other counties. The most beautiful arcades are no doubt at Bishop Auckland (Bishop Pudsey's Hall) and Sedgefield. Bishop Auckland excels in aristocratic resilience; Sedgefield, with shaftings and gorgeous stiff-leaf capitals, in luxuriance. At Hartlepool there are three different kinds of complex pier sections, one of them repeated at Houghton-le-Spring. Other forms at St Andrew Auckland and Billingham (a more southern type). Keeling of shafts is a favourite device, filleting is rare. c13 clerestoreys survive at Hartlepool and Easington, a completely preserved two-storeyed porch at St Andrew Auckland. Other porches at Bishop Middleham and West Boldon.

Finally c13 Chancels. Only the best can find mention here. They are, apart from the Chapel of the Nine Altars, which is of course in a class to itself, Darlington, what little of original work remains at Hartlepool, and then Houghton-le-Spring and Winston, and the two sister-designs at Lanchester and Medomsley. They have in common the curious motif of small heads set into the wall to hold candles. The style of these heads is clearly that of the Nine Altars. Lanchester has also a mid c13 tympanum with Christ enthroned. It must once have been a very beautiful piece, and it is interesting to compare it with the similar motif carved earlier, about 1215, on a stone slab now at St Mary-the-Less, Durham.

From the hesitation with which the masons of Durham used the more elaborate forms of piers and of geometrical tracery, one can guess that the vagaries of the Dec style, when it came shortly after 1300, did not find a fertile soil here. Indeed there is no early or mid C14 church in the whole county, and the substitution of new windows with flowing tracery for simple and smaller older ones is rare. The best examples by far are the great W and S windows of the cathedral, and the chancel aisle windows on the S and N sides. Others are at Houghton-le-Spring, Sedgefield, Brancepeth, and Easington. At Finchale Priory the aisles were pulled down and the arcade openings filled by windows with ogee-reticulated tracery, a typical Dec motif. One would expect to find a date of about 1330 for this alteration. In fact it took place in 1364–5, and the dates of Prior Fossor at Durham, under whom apparently the Dec windows were put in there, are 1341–74. At the same time in some parish churches arcades were renewed, aisles rebuilt, or chapels added, but amongst all that work there is nothing that calls for special attention.

The same is true of the C15 and early C16, that is the Perp style, and this is for the architectural traveller even more remarkable. For one is used from other counties to find it a rule that of the medieval parish churches one sees the vast majority is Perp, and that nearly all the largest and most expensively built and furnished ones are Perp. In County Durham this is not the case. The list of Perp work of any importance is exceedingly small. The crossing tower of the cathedral (c. 1465–90) has to come first in such a list, then perhaps the S Transept window in the cathedral (c. 1420–40) and the big E windows at Brancepeth, Egglescliffe, and Norton (1495), the big W tower at Sedgefield, the octagon top and spire at Chester-le-Street (c. 1400), and the two porches with transverse ribs at Staindrop and Seaham. The earliest occurrence of Perp forms seems to belong to the later years of Bishop Hatfield (1345–81). A first hint can be seen in the N transept window, fully developed Perp forms in the screen surrounding the Bishop's Throne. This is part of a structure containing below the Bishop's funeral monument. It thus probably belongs to about 1370–80.

This and the stone Reredos and the Sedilia by the High Altar (1372–*c*. 80) are the most ambitious pieces of Gothic church furnishing in the county. They are of stone, as is the Font at Hart, decorated by many figures carved somewhat crudely. Wooden choir stalls are preserved at Staindrop (*c*. 1410), in the chapel of Durham Castle (from Bishop Auckland; early C16), and at St Andrew Auckland and Lanchester. Those at Jarrow are peculiarly flamboyant in their small-scale tracery motifs, a somewhat outlandish characteristic which also occurs in the Pulpit at Heighington, the wall panelling of the Hall of the Deanery at Durham, and the curious Rood Loft (?) at Brancepeth. No Screens of any interest survive. Bede's Chair at Jarrow certainly does not go back to his time, but may well be C14. The equally curious wooden Double Sedilia at St Oswald Durham cannot even be as old as that, in spite of their ancient appearance. The oldest piece of furniture preserved at least in fragments is the throne of Monkwearmouth. Two lions have been proved by Sir Alfred Clapham to form part of a type of throne still existent in a few continental examples. Finally, pre-Reformation Plate is almost absent. The only pieces recorded are at Hamsterley and Heworth.

Medieval Painting is not much more frequent; but what there is deserves close study: some fragments of late C12 work at Pittington, small and not now easily recognized, and some contemporary work in the Galilee at Durham Cathedral which is both well preserved and of great power. There are two Saints in the jambs of a big blank arch, painted hangings against the back-wall of the arch, and broadly treated leaf friezes. Medieval Stained Glass is rare in the county. The most interesting remains are the C13 panels at Lanchester, and they are French. Medieval sculpture is not more abundant. Nor is there anything of outstanding value, except in the Chapel of the Nine Altars. The Font at Hart has been mentioned.* Otherwise there are only Monuments.

---

* There are plenty of other medieval Fonts in Durham churches, but they are all entirely or almost entirely undecorated and are therefore omitted from this volume. Omitted also are church bells and church chests, with few exceptions.

C. H. Hunter Blair has counted sixty altogether. Effigies of the C13 and early C14 are specially frequent, the earliest recognizable by the use of Frosterley marble and by costume, ladies wearing wimples and knights with cylindrical or pot-helmets covering the whole face (earliest knights Pittington, Chester-le-Street;* earliest ladies Easington and Whit-worth†). Only four brasses with figures survive in the county (St Andrew Auckland, the best, late C14; Brancepeth 1403 and 1453; and Billingham 1436). Of all effigies the most valuable are no doubt the Fulthorpe (Blakiston) Monument at Norton and the three Neville Monuments, one at Brancepeth and two at Durham Cathedral. The latter are of alabaster, i.e. were imported into the county, as are also the effigy of Bishop Hatfield at Durham Cathedral and others at Staindrop, Dalton-le-Dale, and Redmarshall. They date from 1367 to 1440. Worth mentioning also are some effigies of oak, one C14 (St Andrew Auckland), one C15 (Brancepeth), and two of a remarkable post-Reformation medievalism (Staindrop 1564 and St Giles Durham 1591). In the light of this so far little acknowledged medievalism (revival rather than survival) the effigies of the Lumley Aisle at Chester-le-Street should be looked at. Lord Lumley in 1594 obtained licence to remove from the Durham Cathedral graveyard certain medieval effigies said to be those of ancestors of his. He supplemented them by others carved deliberately in the same style and this made up a handsome series going right back to Liulph of a distant past.

The scarcity of good late medieval architecture and art is so striking that even the casual tourist will speculate on reasons. They are easily found. While the SW, the Midlands, and East Anglia were having a relatively peaceful time and hence all facilities to develop their staple trades, wool and cloth, Durham and Northumberland were disturbed by never ending Scottish raids and at times by war against the Scots.

The loss to church architecture was a gain to military

---

* Earliest in sandstone Whitworth, c. 1290.

† The monument at Whitworth is of sandstone. The earliest effigies of priests are at Lanchester and Boldon, early C14.

architecture, and no student of medieval castles can afford to leave aside the county of Durham. Of the strength and magnificence of the Bishop's own castle at Durham something has already been said. It had in later medieval days a s and a N Outer Bailey, separated by the very cathedral with its cloisters, and an Inner Bailey, now the castle courtyard. At the NE angle was the high mound crowned by a big polygonal Keep, in its present form a restoration of 1840 of a structure of Bishop Hatfield's time. The fortifications linked up with the town walls and gates of Durham. Of these only short stretches can now be seen, nothing as impressive as the fragment of the Town Walls of Hartlepool with its one surviving Water Gate. But inside Durham Castle Bishop Bek (1283–1311), another of the great builder-bishops of Durham, built a new Great Hall in the w range, and this, with Hatfield's alterations, still exists and is now the proud Dining Hall of University College, Durham, of a size nearly that of the Hall at Christ Church, Oxford. Bishop Fox in 1499 remodelled the Kitchen (therein using brick for the first time in the county). The massive oaken hatches in the Servery are specially impressive. Finally Bishop Tunstall (1530–59) provided a new Chapel and Gallery. He incidentally also added the handsome bay window at Bishop Auckland.

The other major castles in the county are Barnard Castle, Raby, Brancepeth, Lumley Castle, and Witton Castle. Barnard Castle is now a ruin, in a splendid position above the river Tees, with a cylindrical keep-like wall tower and extensive baileys. It is considerably earlier than the others. At Raby parts of the C12 remain, but most of what makes the buildings so impressive is late C14 (licence to crenellate 1378) and early C19. At Brancepeth the C19 has done even more, and the medieval remains are not very eloquent. Raby shows as well as any castle in the country to what size and complexity castles had grown by the time of Richard II. It is built irregularly round an inner courtyard, although the Hall lies still in the familiar position relative to the main gateway. There is a low outer mantled wall as well. Architecturally speaking, however, Witton and especially Lumley are more interesting, in so far as both were built on a plan. Lumley was begun in 1392, Witton before 1410. Both are square, Witton with a curtain wall with symmetrical E and W gateways and an irregular much added-to main living range attached to the keep on the N side, Lumley with ranges of buildings surrounding a nearly square courtyard and four sturdy angle blocks rather than angle towers. The Hall again faces the gateway.

On the battlements of Raby carved figures appear looking down on attackers. This same north country motif (Alnwick, city walls Newcastle) can also be seen at Hylton Castle. Hylton Castle is the most impressive of smaller castles. It was probably built *c.* 1400, a tall, compact structure on a rectangular plan, of a type well known in the North of England and in Scotland in the late Middle Ages and often called tower-houses. No peel-tower survives, though the Keep at Durham was originally one. Ruins of more or less eloquence and picturesqueness exist of Langley Hall, Hollinside, Ludworth Tower, Bradley Hall, and Dalton Tower.* At Witton Tower, Witton-le-Wear, early medieval remains seem to be incorporated with the present dwelling house; at Witton Gilbert just one late C12 twin window with a sunk blank quatrefoil in the spandrel is preserved similar to the arcades at Darlington and Ripon. Interesting evidence of the halls of medieval manor houses can be seen at Crook Hall, Durham, Hurwick (a C15 bay window), and Sacriston Heugh.

Sacriston Heugh was the country residence of the Sacrist of Durham; Muggleswick, quite an impressive ruin, the country seat of the Prior. The Prior had also his house in the immediate proximity of the cathedral cloister. It is now the Deanery. The undercroft and the exterior of the C13 Chapel are still there, remains of the Camera Inferior and the Camera Superior of the Prior, and the Hall made in the C15

* Hollinside, Ludworth, and Bradley have their basements tunnel-vaulted, and such vaults exist indeed in other houses as well. The series begins with the Early Norman tunnel-vaults below the Deanery Hall at Durham and goes on with the Prior's Lodging at Finchale, Sacriston Heugh, and East Deanery.

in what until then had been the dormitory of the monks. There is also a fine early C16 ceiling belonging probably to the Prior's study. A very similar arrangement, in ruins, but more clearly understandable because not adapted by later centuries, is at Finchale Priory.

At Finchale also the refectory and dormitory can still easily be recognized. The buildings are impressive in their clarity and simplicity. At Durham the evidence is more intricate, but the scale much greater. The Dormitory of the monks, of 1398–1404, 194 ft long, with its undercroft and its original timber roof, is one of the most impressive monastic buildings in the country. The Refectory was remodelled as a library in the late C17, but has also still its Early Norman undercroft, and the octagonal Kitchen of 1368–74 with its ingenious star of ribs surrounding an octagonal louvre is one of the most interesting medieval kitchens anywhere in Europe. The star-vault finds its closest parallels in the Muslim architecture of Cordova. Priory Barns still exist, though somewhat altered, on the other side of the river Wear at Hall Garth, just outside medieval Durham. In connexion with these monastic buildings East Deanery, St Andrew Auckland, may also find mention here. It is now a farm but was once the college of priests to serve the church. It was founded by Bishop Bek in 1291.

The other collegiate churches of Durham were Darlington, Norton, Lanchester, Chester-le-Street, Staindrop, and Barnard Castle. Stalls and certain structural alterations made necessary when an older church was made collegiate are the usual reminder of the existence of a college. Monastic houses are exceptionally rare in County Durham. The Benedictine Priory of Durham was too powerful to allow others to establish themselves. Bishop Pudsey's abortive attempt at introducing Augustinian Canons at Baxterwood is an interesting example of how the Prior could veto the Bishop's plans. So the only two medieval monasteries were Benedictine, Finchale which soon became a kind of *dépendance* of, or holiday hostel for, Durham monks, and Neasham, a nunnery, which has entirely disappeared. The famous ancient Benedictine monasteries of Wearmouth and

Jarrow did not, it seems, much outlive the ravages of the Danes. The c7 nunneries of Hartlepool and Ebchester vanished earlier still. Hospitals should perhaps also be mentioned in this context. The only worth-while remains in the county are the gatehouse of Sherburn and the Kepier Hospital near Durham. Now for the Friars. Franciscan houses existed at Hartlepool and Durham, Dominican houses at Hartlepool and Jarrow, and an Austin Friar's house at Barnard Castle. Nothing at all of these is visible to-day. They were the targets of much hatred in the c16 and were consequently more thoroughly destroyed at the time of the Dissolution than other monastic establishments.

The Dissolution, or rather the consistent policy of the Tudors from Henry VII onwards, also deprived the Bishop of most of his territorial privileges, and made the Prior of the monastery of Durham into the Dean of the cathedral. The architectural, like the political, history of the county henceforth was less exceptional than it had been.

Ecclesiastical art altogether lost in importance, as it did everywhere in England. Speaking of the Elizabethan or the Georgian style, one thinks less of churches and church furnishings than of country houses. In the county of Durham there is an exception to this rule, the widespread activity of that remarkable man John Cosin, who was born at Norwich, graduated at Cambridge, became Chaplain to the Bishop of Durham in 1619, in 1624 one of the Prebendaries of the Cathedral, Vicar of Elwick Hall in 1624, of Brancepeth in 1626, Master of Peterhouse at Cambridge in 1635, Vice Chancellor at Cambridge in 1639, had to flee to France when the Civil War started, spent thirteen years abroad, and was made Bishop of Durham in 1662. He died in 1672. He was a High Church man, appreciated by Laud and one to whom the pomp and circumstances of the church building and church service meant much. He did a great deal for the furnishing of his church at Brancepeth, and when he was Bishop saw to it that his Cathedral, his private chapels at the Castle and at Auckland and also the parish churches in the land received the screens and stalls and pews and fonts and font covers due to them. The unmistakable style of the woodwork done for him by local craftsmen, such as *Abraham Smith*, *Robert Barker*, *James Clement*, and *John Brasse* appears, apart from the places already mentioned, especially sumptuously at Sedgefield, and in the font cover at Darlington. Cosin's style is characterized by a mixture of the style of his own day with Gothic, the Gothic being a fully conscious revival. That is the remarkable quality about it, and it would repay further close study. There are clearly two stages of the 'Cosin style', the earlier consisting of strapwork and the balusters of the Jacobean style which was still going strong in English woodwork about 1630 and in addition certain minor Gothic motifs such as poppy-heads, ogee arches, and pendants, the later making a grand show of the crocketed gables of the Dec style and of Perp tracery further enriched in their effect by Baroque scrolls, fat garlands and cherubs' heads.

In the case of the earlier style one might still be doubtful whether the mental process involved should not be called survival rather than revival, in the later works done for Cosin there can be no question. On the strength of this evidence it would be worth while to re-examine C17 Gothic motifs at Oxford and Cambridge. Sir Kenneth Clark has perhaps too readily treated them as survival at Oxford. At Cambridge an attitude of conscious revival can be documentarily proved for the Library of St John's College in 1624 (*see* the Cambridgeshire volume of *The Buildings of England* due for publication in 1954) and stylistically for Peterhouse Chapel of 1628–32. Cosin lived at Cambridge in the late 30s and cannot but have been confirmed in his taste and indeed influenced by what he saw.

For an understanding of this new attitude to the Gothic past much must depend on the dating of C17 Gothic motifs in County Durham. The dates are as follows. The early style with strapwork, etc., is represented by the Gateshead pews of 1633–4 and the ceiling at Brancepeth of *c.* 1638.*

The later, much more sumptuous and self-assured style is that of the woodwork in the Bishop's chapels at Durham and Bishop Auckland, of between 1660 and 1672. The date

* But the style also still appears at Elwick Hall, dated 1665.

1663 at Stanhope corresponds. With these dates in mind one would be inclined to attribute to the 60s rather than the 30s the font cover, choir stalls, and rood screen at Brancepeth, the whole woodwork at Sedgefield, and e.g. the Easington pews. In the latter two cases there is indeed a choice between two dates: At Sedgefield we know that in 1638 the wood carver busy on the Brancepeth ceiling visited Sedgefield from there about the seating, but we also know that Cosin's son-in-law Dennis Granville became vicar in 1667. For Easington there is on the one hand a note referring to the pews as recently made in 1634, on the other the same Dennis Granville was rector of Easington from 1662. The early style is represented, in addition to places referred to above, by the pews and pulpit at Brancepeth and Haughton-le-Skerne, the screen and stalls at Ryton, the stalls at St Helen Auckland, the pews at Aycliffe, Cockfield, Egglescliffe and Redmarshall, the later style by the woodwork of Kirk Merrington, the font cover, stalls and screen at Brancepeth, and the font-cover at Haughton-le-Skerne.

It may be worth adding as a postscript that Cosin's enthusiasm for medieval times went so far as to create even a minor Norman Revival. For thus no doubt must be described his use of polygonal shafts patterned with incised geometrical ornament clearly copied from the Norman piers of the cathedral. Similarly at Auckland in the anteroom to his Chapel, that is Bishop Pudsey's Hall converted into a chapel, Cosin used what was clearly meant to represent Norman capitals. The Chapel at Auckland is one of the few architectural works for which Cosin was responsible. The porch at Brancepeth is another. We know from his correspondence that he was not only keenly interested in all the details of the artistic work ordered and paid for by him, but also quite capable of designing himself. The way in which he discusses the exterior of the chapel with his mason is most professional.

Pre-Cosin woodwork is of little importance (the pulpit at Dalton-le-Dale is typically Elizabethan in style, but woodwork immediately after Cosin, i.e. under Bishop Lord Crewe (1674–1721), sometimes quite splendid. Examples

CD.—2

are in the Cathedral (organ, communion rail, etc.), at St Mary-le-Bow Durham, Bishop Auckland, and Sedgefield (organs). Secular woodwork older than Cosin's splendid staircase with its thick pierced acanthus foliage all along the balustrade is not ample. There is a fine Jacobean staircase at Castle Eden (from Horden), and the fine Jacobean fireplaces in the same house and the Senate Room at Durham Castle; there are very collegiate-looking bookcases in the library, formerly the Refectory, at Durham Cathedral (1684), and there are a few later C17 staircases with thick twisted balusters (Cathedral Library, St Mary's College Durham, etc.).

We must now look for architecture of the same period, from the Reformation to the end of the C17. Not a single church needs mention (St Mary-le-Bow Durham 1685, W tower 1702), but quite a number of country houses. None amongst them are of the very first order, no Hardwicks, no Hatfields (Durham was not popular enough with the richest, and the noble had their castles of old), but there are good, solid, high, four-square houses of moderate size, Walworth of c. 1600 with two thick angle towers and a porch with three superimposed orders of columns, and Gainford of 1603 being perhaps the best. The all-round symmetrical plan of Gainford is reminiscent of the better-known Barlborough in Derbyshire. Stone houses with symmetrical fronts and mullioned windows under hood-moulds are Horden Hall, Gibside, Headlam, and Castle Lodge at Bishop Auckland. The latter is late C17 and has already that hallmark of the coming classical style, the pedimented doorway, but still the mullioned windows of the past. These remained in use for a long time in a county now becoming decidedly provincial. Cosin uses them (Durham Castle) in the 60s and not the more modern upright windows with a mullion-and-transome cross, and they still appear at Little Holmside in 1668, Crook Hall Durham 1671, and Whitfield Place Wolsingham 1677.* Similarly a monument of 1689 at Whitburn church has still a recumbent effigy on a tomb-chest. It looks odd enough in the costume of Pepys's time.

* At Stanhope up in Weardale I noticed a four-centred, that is Perp, doorhead with the date 1693.

After this not a single monument in a church needs recording here, until we come to Bishop Trevor's white marble statue by *Nollekens* (at Bishop Auckland) and *Chantrey's* monument to Bishop Shute Barrington (in the Cathedral), the former of 1775, the latter of 1833. Chantrey also provided a very ambitious memorial to a rector of Sunderland in 1838, and *Gibson* in Rome made the monument to Bishop van Mildert who died in 1836. That is incredibly little compared with other counties.

Yet stately houses of the Georgian century are by no means missing. Again, it must be admitted, there is no Castle Howard or Wentworth Woodhouse, but there is quite enough to enjoy and appreciate. The coming of the Classical style as set up in the s by Inigo Jones and then by Webb, Pratt, and May is first noticed in the county in the introduction of door and window pediments. For door pediments first semicircular or nearly semicircular forms are favoured; then the more normal shallower segment comes (Esh Hall 1657, Helmington Hall 1686, West Boldon Hall 1709, Whickham 1713). The standard type of five-bay, two- or three-storey house with central door, quoins, and hipped roof is perhaps best seen at Heworth and West Boldon. The Baroque reaction against this uneventful type is familiar in the work of Vanbrugh and Hawksmoor. *Vanbrugh* appeared himself in the North (which he preferred to the 'sneaking South') to work for Lord Lumley. The vaulted Library at Lumley Castle with its singular rusticated pillars is unmistakably in his handwriting. His style is also reflected in some buildings at St Helen Auckland. The main building here, done for a Newcastle merchant, is in the grandest and purest Palladianism. Inside are some first-rate stucco ceilings, no doubt the work of itinerant Italians. They can also be found on their wanderings at Bishop Auckland, Bradley Hall, Elemore Hall, and Croxdale. The three last-named buildings belong to the mid c18. Bradley Hall is by *James Paine* who also designed the large mansion of Axwell Park.

Paine is furthermore the architect of the most beautiful, in fact the only architecturally ambitious, church of the c18 in the county, the church in the grounds of George Bowes's mansion at Gibside. Here is a church of the highest aesthetic qualities achieved by any late C18 architect in ecclesiastical work, a domed Greek cross with the projecting apses encased in square walls and with the angles between the arms of the cross filled in by square rooms. It is developed from the scheme used by Wren at St Anne and St Agnes, and presented with a splendour of Imperial Roman detail and a precision of finish not to be found in the City of London. It makes the other C18 churches in the county look homely, and they are indeed jobs done for the little towns along the coast whose commercial and industrial prosperity was begining. St Mary at Stockton is of 1710–12, and *Wren*, oddly enough, had a say in it, Holy Trinity at Sunderland dates from 1719, St John at Sunderland from 1769, and St Hilda at South Shields from 1812.*

In these same towns municipal buildings of some consequence were now put up, the town halls at Stockton (1735), Barnard Castle (1747), and South Shields (1768). Others existed but have since been pulled down. Also the well-to-do began to build houses for themselves, both in the towns and in certain desirable villages close to the towns. Of town houses the best are in Paradise Row, Stockton. They are of brick in the familiar Classical style.† The most accomplished houses in villages are at Norton near Stockton, Westoe near South Shields, and Whitburn.

But it may well be argued that these townish villages are not real villages at all, and that the real villages of County Durham are indeed even more attractive. Their characteristic is the closed green, a large expanse of lawn with trees which may be developed in an infinity of ways, not consciously no doubt, but all the same most gratifying to the eye. Norton, Sedgefield, Heighington, Staindrop, Gainford,

* In addition one charming village church: St John's Chapel of 1752.

† Brick was only then becoming the accepted material in the s and e of the county. Examples of its early, still playful use with courses of diagonally projecting bricks and with shaped gables are the Nag's Head at Darlington of the later C17, the Almshouses at Sedgefield of 1703, and the Vane Inn at Thorpe Thewles.

Wolviston, and many others deserve careful analysis. The planner will derive great benefit from it and the layman much enjoyment. It should be specially noted how a long high street widens into a green, how main roads are conducted along greens tangentially, how vistas are closed, how a cluster of houses or the church and churchyard are allowed to remain as an island in the green, and so on. The first conscious seaside planning is at Seaton Carew near Hartlepool, a neat little late C18 square open to the sea.

From picturesqueness without planning to conscious picturesque planning. The church at Gibside mentioned above is one of several 'exterior furnishings' of the grounds provided, while *Capability Brown* was busy with the grounds themselves. The two outstanding ones are the Column of Liberty, 140 ft high, and the Banqueting House, a very successful effort in a fantastic Rococo-Gothick. Concurrently at Hardwick near Sedgefield, John Burdon, of a rich Stockton family, began in 1750 to put up buildings of a similar character. His architect was *Paine*. The surviving buildings (now derelict) are a round temple, an excellent banqueting house, and a crazy Gothick gatehouse built up partly with genuine bits from Guisborough Priory.

This brings us to the Gothic Revival. So far we have only seen its most playful appearance, in landscaped parks. To these the rather heavy Conduit must be added which was erected in the College Green at Durham in 1751, and the exceedingly pretty Outer Gateway to the Bishop's Palace at Bishop Auckland of 1760. Also very early is the first Gothic Revival church in the county: Castle Eden of 1764 with that remarkable oddity, a Gothic Venetian window. Later in the C18, when, chiefly thanks to Horace Walpole, the Gothic Revival had become universally fashionable for domestic work, the house at Castle Eden was also built with battlements and Gothic windows, and at the Bishop's Palace at Auckland a new wing was added in the same taste (*c.* 1770–5). *James Wyatt*, probably while busy, in 1796, restoring Durham Cathedral rather ruthlessly, helped to remodel the interior of the Bishop's Palace and also gave it its pretty screen wall and Inner Gateway. Now large-scale improvements

in the Gothic taste started in many houses of the
nobility and gentry, and brand-new castles appeared. And
whereas the earlier houses of the Revival had been symmetrical, the new ones are completely irregular, with turrets
and towers and ranges of divers heights, all crenellated. Of
new castles the most conspicuous are Ravensworth by *Nash*
(1808, and now in process of demolition) and Lambton
(begun in 1796 but apparently only disguised as a castle
about 1825). At Brancepeth William Russell, a commoner
and one of the richest men in England, added to and altered
so much of the medieval castle of the Nevilles that it is now
to a large extent a piece of Gothic Revival. His architect
was *Patterson* of Edinburgh. The work started in 1817. At
Gibside also, in 1805, the Jacobean house was more than
doubled in size. The same happened at Witton Castle,
and here as at Brancepeth the domestic apartments
are now almost entirely C19 in appearance. Hoppyland Hall
is said to have been built by the gothicizers of Witton
Castle.

Compared with this sudden outburst of baronial ambi-
tions, the Classical Revival remained on a very modest scale.
The only country house of consequence is Wynyard Park by
Benjamin Wyatt, begun in 1822 and refurnished in a grand
semi-Italian, semi-French Victorian manner in the fifties. A
little later, also with a touch of the French, are Burn Hall
and Windlestone Hall (*c.* 1830). The pure Neo-Greek in the
Smirke taste appears in only two buildings, one the railway
station at Monkwearmouth of 1848, the other the Londonderry Institute at Seaham Harbour of about 1830. Both are
probably by *Dobson* of Newcastle.

Seaham Harbour is a planned town. It was created in
1828 by the third Marquess of Londonderry for the shipping of coal from his collieries. It never developed as it was
meant to and is not a happy sight now. On a larger scale, a
little later, West Hartlepool was begun, also as a new town,
independent of old Hartlepool. This again, although it has
grown into a sizable place, is not gratifying to the eye, in
spite of a Town Improvement Company established in
1854. May the New Towns of the C20, the outcome of a

period of disastrous depression between the two World Wars, and of the programme of a socialist government interested in a sound distribution of population, have a happier fate. At the time of writing they are only just starting: Newton Aycliffe, N of Darlington, planned by *Grenfell Baines*, and Peterlee, near Easington.

A mid-Victorian experiment in planned working class housing must be mentioned at least in passing, because it is hardly known and shows an understanding rare at the time. At Tudhoe Grange, in 1865–70, Mr Salvin instead of putting up the usual terraces of cottages, split them up into semi-detached pairs and set them chessboard-wise with much space between and gardens behind. The result does not look inspired, but is certainly a great step beyond the more famous Saltaire near Leeds of 1853. Also in the category of the planned village belongs Hunstanworth near the Northumberland border, although it is of a very different character. Here, in 1863, the lord of the manor asked a successful London architect, *S. S. Teulon*, to design a church, a vicarage, and a number of houses, tied together by their remarkably original architect's style, but not by a plan.

As to other Victorian church architects of note, they had little opportunity to travel north. *Scott* restored Durham Cathedral, but did not build a single church in the county, *Street* and *Butterfield* did one each, and neither is anything special. *E. B. Lamb's* All Saints West Hartlepool certainly is something special, but for sheer perversity rather than beauty or faithfulness to a medieval idiom. The county mostly employed local architects, first *Pritchett* of Darlington (who designed St Nicholas Durham very competently) and then *Hodgson Fowler* of Durham. But most of the churches they (and some earlier local architects like *Dobson*, *Green*, and *Thompson*) were called upon to design were for colliery villages and colliery towns, as a rule in a minimum E.E. with lancet windows and only a bellcote instead of a tower. According to locality they are of stone or brick.

Nor has the C20 changed this much. With the prosperity of Tyneside and Teesside declining, the quantity of new churches decreased, and only rarely was there much money or much taste where new churches were required. The most noteworthy exceptions are St Andrew Roker and St Michael Bishopwearmouth, Sunderland. St Andrew Roker, 1907, by *E. S. Prior*, is without any doubt one of the half dozen best churches of its time in the country, the time (Europeanly speaking) just before connexions with past styles were entirely broken off, but after the principle of period imitation had at last been given up. The church at Roker is Gothic in feeling, yet wholly original in its spatial solution and its details. It is besides furnished in the most refined taste of the Arts and Crafts, with contributions of *Morris & Co.*, and of *Ernest Gimson*. The church of Bishopwearmouth is by *Caroë*, less robust and less personal, more suave, more tied to the Gothic past, but also designed with sensibility, and incidentally an uncommonly large church.

Victorian church furnishings in the county only very occasionally deserve notice. Two windows have early *Morris* glass, designed by *Ford Madox Brown*. They are at Christ Church Sunderland and at St Oswald Durham. Good glass of the 1870s by *Cottier* is at Birtley and Felling, early *Kempe* glass at Hunstanworth, Durham Castle, and Egglescliffe.

Finally, Victorian and post-Victorian secular architecture. There are no big Victorian mansions worth noting, and few big public buildings. If one wants to compare the Later Victorian and the Edwardian Grand Manner, one should go to the magnificently incongruous Bowes Museum at Barnard Castle of 1869–92 and then the Municipal Buildings at South Shields of 1903. The style of the C20 appeared later and, typically enough first in the pithead baths erected by the Miners' Welfare Committee, a progressive London body financed by the Trades Union. It has built about thirty pithead baths in the county.* Only a few of them can be mentioned in this volume. They have been chosen by what

* They are at Blackhall, Brancepeth, Burnmoor 'D', Dawdon, Easington, East Hetton, Elemore, Fishburn, Harraton, Hylton, Kibblesworth, Mainsforth (Ferry Hill), Morrison Busty, Murton, Ouston, Ravensworth (Betty and Ann), Ravensworth (Shop), Ryhope, Silksworth, South Pelaw, Usworth, Vane Tempest, Washington 'F', Wearmouth, Westoe, Wheatley Hill, Whitburn.

seemed to me their architectural interest. They are all brick-built, and mostly characterized by the dominant group of chimney and water tank, boldly and squarely displayed. Their dates range from 1932 to the present day. The early ones were clearly influenced by the Dutch style of Dudok. Of other modern buildings only a few factories need here find mention; of the new trading estates only the first, the Team Valley Estate near Gateshead. These estates are a departure remarkable both from the social and the visual points of view.

Naturally, in dealing with the more recent monuments, especially those of the last hundred years, a more rigid selection had to be made than for those of the Middle Ages or the Elizabethan age. Completeness was out of the question, and so another principle had to be adopted. It is frankly my own taste. I have endeavoured to see everything myself before deciding whether to put it down in these pages.* Much was thus seen and then discarded. Much of this another critic might have included in preference to what I have. Much also, on the other hand (and that refers to earlier periods as well), will have been omitted simply because I did not know of its existence. Farmhouses of architectural interest especially which are not recorded in the literature available to me and which were by some misfortune not on any of the roads and lanes inspected, will be found to have been left out. Similarly houses of value in back streets of towns may have been overlooked. This is particularly likely to have happened in towns for which none of the Provisional Lists of Buildings of Architectural or Historic Interest yet exist which in the course of the last four or five years have been drawn up by special investigators for the Ministry of Housing and Local Government.

These, when they were in my hands, were the most valuable sources I had. In addition there was Boyle's outstandingly useful *County of Durham*, 1891, and the volume of the *Little Guides*, as always extremely useful too, and Kelly's *Directory*, and a sufficiently old edition of Murray's *Handbook*,

---

* The only exceptions are church plate and a small number of buildings marked by being placed in brackets.

and the handy volume (by W. J. Weston) of the *Cambridge County Geographies*. The *Victoria County History* has so far only covered Durham town and one ward of the county. For places in that ward (Stockton) it is, of course, all round the best source one can wish for. Local archaeological and antiquarian work as far as the medieval and post-medieval centuries go, has on the whole not been of a specially high order or intensity. The chief periodicals are *Archaeologia Aeliana*, the best of them on the whole, the *Transactions of the Durham and Northumberland Archaeological Society*, the *Proceedings of the Society of Antiquaries of Newcastle*, and the *Antiquities of Sunderland*. Some special aspects of the history of art and architecture in the county have been covered in series of articles in these journals: brasses (*Arch. Ael.*, 2nd series, vol. 15), monuments in churches (*Arch. Ael.*, 4th series, vol. 6, 1929), fonts (*Trans.*, vol. 6), church plate (*Arch. Ael.*, New series, vol. 16, republished as a book: R. Blair, *The Communion Plate and Church Bells of Northumberland and Durham*; privately printed, South Shields, 1891), Decorated windows (*Trans.*, vol. 5). Whenever country houses have been treated in *Country Life*, especially during the last twenty-five or thirty years, the information contained in its articles is most valuable.

But on many aspects of Durham architecture no more could be done than to consult the familiar textbooks, books like the late Sir Alfred Clapham's on Anglo-Saxon and Norman architecture, or Sir T. D. Kendrick's on Anglo-Saxon Art, or Collingwood's *Roman Britain*, or Mr A. Gardner's on *Alabaster Tombs*, etc.

On many questions of detail, however, especially as regards the C18 and C19, the most fruitful source is still the county histories and topographies written up to about a hundred years ago, notably Hutchinson (1794), Surtees (1816–40), Mackenzie & Ross (1834), and Fordyce (1837).

DURHAM

*

ALDIN GRANGE
1½ m. WNW of Durham

Medieval one-span stone BRIDGE across the river Browney.

ANNFIELD PLAIN

ST THOMAS, the parish church of Collierley. By *G. Jackson* (GR). 1840, restored and altered 1886. E.E. with bell-cote, the detail, such as hood-moulds and pinnacles, still pre-archaeological.

AXWELL PARK

By *Paine*, 1758. Of fine stone, well worked. The main rooms are on the ground floor; yet this is treated as a basement by means of rustication. The first floor very high up (mezzanine in between at the back), then a half-storey. The house is a block of nine by five bays, the main (E) front with an extensive terrace, a small porch to which steps lead up, and three large rooms, the centre one on the outside emphasized by a large three-bay open pediment crowning the façade. An open pediment also over the centre of the N front. Here, on the first floor, one large arched window on each side of the three-bay centre. In the middle of the house under an oblong lantern was the Grand Staircase, no longer in existence. The plaster-work of the main room Palladian, i.e. in the Inigo Jones tradition, with oblong, oval, etc., panels with broad frames.

DOWER HOUSE. At the N end of the former grounds, on the main road. The garden elevation Gothick.

AYCLIFFE

St Andrew. Part of the nave walls are supposed to be
Saxon; *see* the stones above the first arcade arches from
the w. The present building is mostly c12–c13. Unbuttressed w tower with blocked Norman (?) twin bell-
opening (cf. Heighington). The top part later. Norman
chancel. c13 lancet windows in the chancel s wall close to
the w end, and in tower and s aisle w walls. c13 also the s
doorway with one order of colonnettes and a filleted roll
moulding in the arch. The hood-mould rests on two head
stops. The tower arch inside and the arches to the aisles
which project as far w as the w face of the tower have
responds with thick demi-shafts and double-chamfered
arches, exactly as at Gainford. The n arcade of three bays
with alternatingly octagonal and circular piers with
doubled-chamfered, still rounded arches, and hood-
moulds with nutmeg ornament must be *c.* 1200. The
chancel arch is perhaps a little later, as real nailhead now
appears in the abacus. The s arcade is yet later. The piers
are all circular, the capitals steeper, the arches pointed. –
FONT. Of very primitive shape and entirely undecorated;
Early Norman? – PEWS. *c.* 1630 with very pretty backs
and ends with widely spaced turned balusters, like settles.
– SCULPTURE. Divers Anglo-Saxon fragments, especially
a Cross Shaft on its original base (6 ft of the shaft survive), another with a Crucifixion and frontal figures in
various tiers (w end of s and n aisles). Smaller fragments
and also the foliated cross head of a tomb-lid in the chancel s wall. Another particularly interesting foliated tomb
lid with two birds and oak leaves in the n aisle floor, probably early c14. – PLATE. Chalice, 1641–2; Paten,
London-made, 1727. – MONUMENT. Effigy of a cross-
legged knight; n aisle; sandstone; with mail-coif; *c.* 1300.
Very damaged.

Newton Aycliffe. One of the 'New Towns' of after the
second World War. At the time of writing it consists of a
trading establishment (notably Messrs Bakelite, by *J.
Wilson Hays*, 1946, etc.) and about 800 houses to the n

along the Great North Road, the industrial area. Five neighbourhoods are projected with the Civic Centre in the middle. The master plan was made by the *Grenfell Baines* Group. The architect to the Development Corporation is *Mr G. A. Goldstraw*.

BARNARD CASTLE

St Mary. A low largish building of manifold outline. The w tower of 1874 replaces an earlier one in the same unusual position at the w end of the N aisle. The church is mostly Norman and Transitional, although the outside does not betray much of that. Norman chancel masonry; *see* two windows on the N side (inside). Later Norman the three-order s portal with two rich zigzag bands along the inner voussoirs, but an outer band of nailhead and mouldings characteristic of the coming E.E. rather than of the Norman style. The N aisle arcade of three bays is entirely Transitional, though only the two w bays are original: circular piers with minimum capitals and one-stepped round arches. The s aisle arcade is of four bays* with octagonal piers and double-chamfered pointed arches; full C13. The clerestory and most of the windows Perp, but much of the detail dates from the restoration of 1870, e.g. the E and w windows, the chancel s, and the s transept s windows, etc. The s transept E window, however, is genuine. The best Perp piece is the chancel arch leading into the raised chancel, an impressive and unusual feature. It has responds with embattled abaci, pretty fleurons in one of its concave arch mouldings, and a hood-mould on head-corbels. – PLATE. Chalice, 1670; Chalice, probably 1684; Salver, 1745. – MONUMENTS. Fragments of foliated cross tomb-lids in the N transepts. – Effigy of Robert de Northam, Vicar of Gainford, mid C14. – Late C18 and early C19 epitaphs under the tower, by stone-masons from York and Richmond (Yorks).

* When it was built the N arcade was lengthened on the E side by a narrow fourth arch of the same design as on the s.

Town Hall, Barnard Castle School, Bowes Museum, *see* under Perambulation. Castle, *see* at the end.

The layout of the town is visually extremely successful. From the river the Castle on its hill dominates the view. In the town one does not notice it at all, as it is in its whole length screened by houses. The town has two centres, the Town Hall or Market Cross at the meeting of The Bank from the s, Newgate from the w, and the Market Place from the N, and the HOLY TRINITY METHODIST CHURCH (in an ornate neo-1300 style, 1894 by *Morley* of Leeds) in the *point de vue* at the end of Galgate, where it meets the Horsemarket at r. angles.

The description here starts from the s, where BARNARD CASTLE BRIDGE crosses the river Tees. The bridge is of two slightly pointed segmental arches, built in 1569 and repaired and provided with new parapets after the flood of 1771. BRIDGEGATE from here leads at r. angles towards the town, keeping, however, in the valley. Here are the first examples of the typical stately C18 stone houses of the town, three or five bays wide, two or three storeys high, quoined and with pedimented doorways, on corbels, pilasters, or demi-columns, notably Nos 28 and 17. No. 38 is an earlier type, dated 1705. Its window surrounds are flat bands of smooth rustication. At the end of Bridge-gate THORNGATE, a short street with two lines of trees, leads to a footbridge, continuing the axis of the main streets of the town. In Thorngate the best C18 houses are No. 8, the stateliest in the town, and Nos 10–12. No. 15 has a pretty, curly and thickly foliated door pediment dated 1707. At the end of Thorngate two plain tall mill buildings, one of them dated 1846.

Thorngate is carried on due N in THE BANK, the straight street which leads up the hill towards the Market Cross. In The Bank is the most famous of the houses of Barnard

Castle, BLAGROVES HOUSE, a Tudor house with a 52
gabled bay window of three storeys on the l. The best C18
house No. 28, dated 1742. Nos 40–44 is of the later C17
with elaborate pedimented dormer windows and a doorway with Ionic pilasters, clearly later interfered with.

At the S end of The Bank the MARKET CROSS or TOWN 61a
HALL, an octagon of 1747 surrounded by a Tuscan colonnade with penthouse roof. The ground floor has open
archways on all eight sides, the upper storey alternating
Venetian windows and niches. On the top an open cupola.
From the Market Cross NEWGATE runs W. At its beginning an opening reveals the church set back so that it plays
no part in the visual progress through the town. No houses
of importance in Newgate, but beyond its end to the l.
the sudden apparition of that big, bold incongruity, the
BOWES MUSEUM, looking exactly like the town hall of a
major provincial town in France. In scale it is just as
gloriously inappropriate for the town to which it belongs
(and which it gives some international fame) as in style. It
was designed by *Jules Pellechet* (1829–1903) and begun in
1869. It houses the collections (especially of Spanish art
and of furniture and ceramics) of Mr John Bowes, son of
the tenth Earl of Strathmore, and his wife, the actress
Josephine Benoîte, later Countess of Montalbo. Beyond
the museum the NORTH EASTERN SCHOOL, Neo-
Jacobean of 1886 (probably by *Clark & Moscrop* of Darlington), with a chapel of 1910 by *Caroë*, which is impressive both externally and internally.

Back to the Market Cross, where to the N the Market Place
and HORSEMARKET follow, not straight, but curved so
that at the beginning their end is not visible. Of houses
Nos 15–23 are a nice three-storeyed C18 group, No. 31
Horsemarket is the typical five-bay house with pedimented doorway, and WITHAM HALL of 1854 has a dignified classical front, higher than the others. From the end
of Horsemarket, GALGATE turns W. Here No. 21, a fine
five-bay house, then in KING STREET No. 18, with a recessed Gothick front dated 1825, and back in Galgate the
long rambling front of the house of the Durham historian

W. E. Hutchinson, dated 1760 (Nos 57–59a). At the top of Galgate HARMIRE ROAD with the BEDE KIRK, a small disused medieval chapel, now the W half of a long farmhouse. Remains of the tops of three lancet windows on the upper floor inside.

44b CASTLE. The Castle once covered a very large area, the whole extent between the river and the Market Place and s of the Trinity Methodist church. Its ruins are a spectacular sight above the river. The area consisted of the Outer Ward on the S, through which one now passes on the way from the King's Head yard to the small Middle Bailey and then the Inner Bailey which form the NW corner of the site and is like a large shell keep. To the E of Inner and Middle Bailey lies the Town Ward, a second Outer Bailey. The site has natural defences on the W and N in the form of the river and a ravine, and a quadrant ditch on the other side. Inner ditches ran s of the well between Outer and Town Ward, round the town sides of the Inner Bailey and E of the Middle Bailey. The hub of the defences is the Round Tower in the NW corner. It seems to stand on Norman foundations, but is essentially early C14. Its ground floor has a flat domed vault. On the first floor was the original entrance. There were two more floors above this. In the walls are several garderobes. s of the Keep followed the Great Chamber with a C15–C16 oriel window, then the Great Hall with two-light, transomed C14 windows, and then Mortham's Tower which was originally five-storeyed. Its lower parts are assigned to the C13. The Chapel was in the Outer Ward but only the bottom part of one pier survives now (in a cow-shed). The N wall can best be examined from the Town Gardens N of the Town Ward.

BEAMISH HALL

A stately stone villa of *c.* 1813 forms the SW corner of a house which was twice enlarged in the same style, once in 1897 N and probably E of the old house, and the second time in 1909 E of the previous N extension. The old building is of ashlar, three-storeyed with giant Tuscan angle pilasters and a central bow window to the s. The w porch is no doubt of 1897. A smaller, less dignified recessed range on the s front between the house of 1813 and the extension of 1897 has rainwater-heads dated 1737. The interiors largely altered.

BEARPARK

St Edmund, 1879, by *Hodgson Fowler*. Red brick, E.E. Recently repointed and cleaned and now with its sheer surfaces and unmoulded lancet windows curiously c20 looking, inside and out. The most interesting motif is three tall arches close to the w end.

Less than a mile to the NE, not easily accessible, the scanty fragments of a country residence of the Priors of Durham (Beaurepaire=Bearpark). Ninety years ago, in Murray's *Handbook*, a gable and a mullioned window were still mentioned. They are no longer there.

BELMONT

St Mary Magdalen, 1857, by *Butterfield* (GR), no *chef d'oeuvre* of this remarkable architect. Nave and chancel, no tower, no aisles. Only the restless detail of the timber-roof and perhaps the odd ogee plate tracery of the w, N, and s sides betray the hand of an architect of originality.

BIDDICK HALL
¾ m. s of Washington

Fine early c18 house of brick with stone dressings. Five bays, two storeys, with parapet and quoins. The centre bay is emphasized by giant Ionic pilasters and a pediment on a bulgy frieze.

BILLINGHAM

Billingham now to those who know the name means a vast factory of chemicals of many kinds. They do not know of the church, less than half a mile away, whose tower still faces the open fields.

St Cuthbert. The outstanding feature of the church is
its Saxon W tower, more interesting in its details than any
other in the county. It can, from comparisons with Earls
Barton and Barton-on-Humber, be assigned to the C10.
It is unbuttressed, has on the ground floor no entry, one
S window, and a tiny arch to the nave,* on the first floor
windows with a characteristic surround of raised upright
bands some distance from the jambs and a raised arched
band some distance away from the arch, and above these
the twin bell-openings, with the typical recessed shafts
and outer frames similar to those on the floor below. But
what is most unusual is that in the spandrels there are
openings, a circle on the W, a star-shape on the N and S, as
if they were proto-tracery of the late C12. The nave also
still bears witness to the Saxon building. It may well be
earlier than the tower; for its proportions resemble those
of Escomb and Monkwearmouth. Literary evidence in
fact points to a date c. 860. On the N side a good deal
of this Saxon nave survives. When the late C12 added an
aisle, they kept chunks of the Saxon wall and only slightly
double-chamfered them into piers. There are four of
these, the fourth retaining a wider wall space than the
others. The arches are pointed and also slightly
double-chamfered. The clerestory has small original windows, as widely spaced as the arcades below. The chancel
arch belongs in style to the N arcade. The chancel itself
dates from 1939.‡ The S arcade followed that on the N a
little later, early in the C13, with piers of a rather unusual
shape: circular with four attached shafts in the diagonals
(cf. SE transept, Canterbury), moulded capitals, and
arches with various keeled mouldings. The hood-moulds
have nutmeg ornament. The Perp style completed the
tower and replaced some S clerestory windows. – FONT
COVER. Probably early C17, with the usual short Elizabethan blank arcades, but a steep crocketed polygonal
pyramid above. – SCREEN, near W end. Simple, with

* The ground floor has a C13 rib-vault.
‡ It is by G. E. Charlewood of Newcastle and consists of four bays
with aisles; a new church, as it were, for a new town.

turned balusters, dated 1625, and still without Cosin influence. – SCULPTURE. Insignificant fragments in the S porch. – PLATE. Chalice of 1637; Paten of 1701; three Flagons of 1757 and 1761. – MONUMENT. Brass to Robert Brerley, priest, now headless, 1480.

HAVERTON HILL *see* p. 164

BINCHESTER

ROMAN FORT. Of this large fort (*Vinovium*), little now remains except a hypocaust belonging to the commandant's house and built with tiles stamped N(*umerus*) CON(*cangiensium*). It was occupied A.D. 79 to A.D. 122, but lay vacant until A.D. 197, when it was reconstructed to hold the *ala Vettonum* and later also a squadron of Frisians. An external bath-house and extra mural settlement are also known, but are not now visible.

BIRTLEY

ST JOHN, 1848, by *Pickering* (GR), enlarged 1887–9. The style is Neo-Norman. Two N windows with STAINED GLASS by *Cottier* of Regent Street, 1872, and very Pre-Raphaelite in style (though different in colour).

In the Square the funniest MONUMENT of County Durham, to Col. E. Moseley Perkins, 1874, white marble, as naïve as a Staffordshire figure.

Much planned between-the-wars housing.

BISHOP AUCKLAND

A dull town, if it were not for the Bishop's Palace, but in a fine position on the brow of a hill with the river Wear on one side and the little river Gaunless on another. The river Wear is crossed by the NEWTON CAP BRIDGE of two arches, segmental and pointed-segmental with a cutwater between. It is supposed to go back to the late C14.

The town has no old church. Instead, in the large Market Place and dividing it into an L-shape, is the connected group of the church of ST ANNE (by *Salvin*, 1847)* and the TOWN HALL (1869), both of dark grey stone and restrainedly Gothic, the church of the usual E.E. variety.

* More likely: *W. Thompson* (GR).

In the MARKET PLACE and adjoining streets a few houses
worth noting: On the S side Nos 9–16, a nice C18 group.
In SILVER STREET, just NE of the Town Hall, The
Elms, a detached Georgian brick house of five bays with
a fluted Ionic porch. In KING STREET E of the Town
Hall a row of C17 cottages. King Street runs E into
CASTLE SQUARE, which is also the E continuation of the
Market Place. It is a handsome oblong with, on the N, a
terrace of Georgian cottages. At its E end is the entrance
to the Bishop's Palace.

BISHOP'S PALACE. The Bishops of Durham have had a
residence at Auckland since the C12. Yet the palace, on
approaching it, does not create an impression of venerable
age, though an impression of wishing to create one. The
56b GATEHOUSE is eminently characteristic of the picturesque somewhat nostalgic and somewhat playful
Gothick of the C18. Its date is 1760. Certain features
should be noted as peculiarly typical: the triple shafts in
lieu of columns, obelisks with finials in lieu of pinnacles,
a ribbed cross-vault inside, and a square bell-tower. The
quatrefoils so beloved by the C18 Goths are also present.
The GATEHOUSE adjoins on the S CASTLE LODGE,
later C17 but still essentially in the Elizabethan tradition,
a square tall block of three storeys with a castellated symmetrical N front with a broad pedimented doorway in the
middle and two mullioned and transomed bay windows.
Other windows with mullion-and-transome crosses. At
the back, overlooking the valley, the centre of the house is
marked on all floors by circular windows.

Past the Gatehouse and the Lodge the first impression
of the palace itself is the lush green of lawns, the trees of
the park, and then *James Wyatt*'s screen-wall and inner
gateway. The screen-wall opens in large arches as the
screens of King's and St John's Colleges at Cambridge
were to do later. The wish for a romantic vista was greater
than for the logical use of a wall. Again behind the screen-
wall the first portion of the buildings of the palace to hold
one's attention is exactly like a C18 Gothick villa: three
bays, the centre one developed as a polygonal bay window,

Tudor arches to the large sash windows, thin glazing bars, and top battlements. This part was added to the old palace by Bishop Egerton, i.e. about 1775–80. Behind it extends the irregular group of older buildings. They are from E to W the Chapel, which was originally the Hall, then a connecting wing with Entrance Hall and principal staircase, then projecting L-wise to the S a range with the Great Room, and again further S the principal early C16 rooms. These link up with Bishop Egerton's part. Finally recessed behind this and extending to the W runs a long range with pitched roof of no representational character. It is known as Scotland and probably belongs to the C16. In the basement are some hood-moulds of former mullioned windows. On the upper floor used to be the Bishop's Long Gallery.

Detailed description has to begin with the CHAPEL. It 28 dates back to the last years of Bishop Pudsey. It was then the Great Hall, consisting of nave and aisles like the 50a smaller and slightly earlier Hall at Oakham in Rutland and the ruined Halls of Henry II at Clarendon Palace and of the Bishops of Lincoln at Lincoln. It was altered by Bishop Bek, towards the end of his reign, i.e. in the early C14, and converted into a chapel by Bishop Cosin, i.e. shortly after 1660. With the exception of the Reredos (by *Hodgson Fowler*, 1884), the Stained Glass, and some minor woodwork, it is still in the state of the C17. Many of the craftsmen used in the conversion are known by name from Cosin's correspondence. Architecturally the chapel is the most beautiful work of the late C12 which the county possesses: four tall and wide arcades with arches of perfect resilience. The shafts are quatrefoil with shaft rings, two of the shafts of local grey marble, two of light brown limestone. Of the capitals two (first pier N and S from the W) have still decorated waterleaf capitals, while the others are all moulded, in a decidedly C13 fashion. The W responds rest on pairs of human heads and have stiff-leaf above these. Stiff-leaf also are the little bits of decoration in the exposed fragments of blank pointed tre-foil arcading of the W wall, and the brackets on which the vaulting shafts rest. Placed on these are now late C19 angels. The arches of the arcades are of grey marble as the piers, and that alone singles out the arcade of Bishop Auckland from all others in County Durham. Their mouldings are manifold, with plenty of light and shadow and exquisitely fine, again entirely C13 in style. The windows, on the other hand, belong to the early C14; they range from Late Geometrical forms to ogee reticulation and are nook-shafted inside. The Geometrical forms are surprising in some details and should not be trusted too readily (restored under Bishop van Mildert). When Cosin added the clerestory for his chapel he gave this gothicizing windows, and these have foiled circles remarkably similar to those on the ground floor. In any case the oval right in the middle of the big five-light E window simply cannot be early C14. The S wall of the Chapel was refaced by Cosin with odd, disconnected, regularly placed, raised, diamond-cut blocks on a smooth ashlar surface.

WOODWORK. Most of this is of Cosin's time, amongst the most sumptuous examples of his peculiar, mixed style. Being relatively late in his life, however (cf. Brancepeth, Sedgefield), the imitation Gothic elements recede and the Baroque element is in the forefront. The CEILING is panelled between the main beams. Each division has eight panels except the middle one which has only three. Most of the panels have Cosin's arms, and strangely dry and schematic geometrical patterns.* Above the altar there are cherubs' heads and mitres instead. There is not a touch of the Gothic in all this. Far more splendour is displayed in the SCREEN, the grandest of all Cosin's screens. In it the Gothic style appears, but only in the cusping of the blank arcades of the dado, the polygonal shafts dividing the lights from each other, and the filigree of the Flamboyant tracery between these shafts. The main dividing posts have hanging leaf garlands, the top is a bold entablature with a thick pierced frieze of acanthus foliage and a broad cornice and Baroque cresting on top. The CHANCEL STALLS, as far as they survive, have poly-

* Cosin's STAINED GLASS uses the same pattern, in blue on white.

gonal shafts to form canopies over the two principal seats, and these canopies are patterned in a fashion clearly derived from the Romanesque piers of Durham. The stall ends have coats of arms, mitres, etc., and poppy-heads. PULPIT and READING DESK are identical in design and placed symmetrically against the two middle piers. They are square and again combine Gothic tracery and poppy-heads with hanging leaf garlands and such-like Baroque motifs. The ORGAN is post-Cosin. Its date is 1688. It is a small Father *Smith* instrument said to be in an exceptionally unrefashioned state.

PLATE. A splendid set presented by Cosin, consisting of two Chalices with Covers, three Patens, two Flagons, large Almsdish with the Last Supper in relief, two large Candlesticks. All made in 1651–2 by *Mr Houser* in London. Also a Cup of London make, 1569, and a Paten London-made of 1722–3. – MONUMENTS. Bishop Cosin † 1672, large absolutely plain black marble slab in the middle of the floor with inscription in big letters. – Bishop Trevor † 1771, by *Nollekens*, 1775. Seated, life-size, very naturalistic figure in an oddly Baroque frame with sidepieces coming forward diagonally, and a concave cornice.

The ENTRANCE HALL to the chapel is at the same time the main entrance to the palace. When the Chapel was still a Hall this was the dais end; the Kitchens lay to the E, where now the palace gardens extend. The Entrance Hall has a porch added about 1800 and a doorway provided by Cosin with a door with a fat garland hanging between spiral-coil volutes. Cosin also was responsible, in this doorway and the three doorways inside the Entrance Hall, for the odd variety of fluted capitals which mark another attempt at inspiration from the Romanesque style. From this Entrance Hall opens the main STAIRCASE of *c.* 1800, a spacious but quite plain piece. The balusters are mildly Gothick. This and the other work of the same date for Bishop Barrington is due to *Wyatt*. The staircase leads up to the GREAT ROOM, the date of which is not clear. It is certainly older than its present decoration with thin rib-vaults and cardboardy-looking frontispieces at both ends, one to hold the Bishop's Throne, the other to screen off a lobby which was originally part of the Great Room. The decoration again belongs to the early C19. The windows were then also altered. The outer wall had already been refaced by Cosin (rainwater-head 1664). The basement windows are C15 or early C16, and a row of octagonal piers in the basement seems contemporary. The Great Room may be older, but no evidence now meets the eye to confirm it. It is no doubt that it was the Solar to go with the old Hall. Next to the Great Room is the DINING ROOM. This and the adjoining parts were built by Bishops Ruthall and Tunstall, i.e. in the first half of the C16. Tunstall's handsome bay window remains, oddly enough a half-hexagon, not octagon. The original fenestration (large three-light windows with one transome) can only be seen in the N return wall. The ground floor windows are in better preservation. The Dining Room ceiling is of the Palladio-Inigo-Jones style so fashionable in the second third of the C18. The fine fireplace with caryatid figures of young men with Roman faces is contemporary with the ceiling. The adjoining room nowadays called the CHARLES I ROOM has a much gayer ceiling and fireplace. The ceiling with its Rococo scrolls and faces is no doubt the work of the Italians travelling around England in the 1730s. The same style appears in one smaller back room.

The only other room to be mentioned is Bishop Cosin's STUDY with panelling decorated by one large lozenge in each panel.

BISHOP MIDDLEHAM

The place of one of the favourite castles of the Bishops of Durham. Two of them died here, in 1283 and 1316. The castle has disappeared. It lay a little to the S of the church.

ST MICHAEL. Nave, aisles, and chancel; no tower. On the S side of the chancel near the W end one of the frequent low side windows, lancet-shaped and roundheaded. Otherwise all the original windows are pointed lancets, and the whole church appears indeed as work of the earlier C13 (*see* the chancel lancets, the N aisle W lancet, and the N porch with its outer doorway and its windows). The nave is low and wide, with later clerestory. The aisle arcades are steep, with double-chamfered arches on circular piers with moulded capitals. A little nailhead enrichment. Hood-moulds with head stops. The chancel arch in the same style. – PLATE. Chalice, two Patens, and Flagon, 1818–19, made at York. – MONUMENTS. Foliated cross tomb-lids in the porch.

BISHOP MIDDLEHAM HALL, *c.* 1765.

DUN COW INN. At the foot of Church Street. The inn-sign of stone, above the door, very attractive folk art probably of the C18.

BISHOPTON

ST PETER, 1846, by *Sharpe & Paley* (GR). One late C13 one-light window of the old church re-used just N of the chancel arch. – PLATE. Chalice and Paten inscribed 1680. – Two medieval CHESTS of uncertain date. One of them is attributed to the C13.

BLACKHALL

5 m. NW of West Hartlepool

PITHEAD BATH, 1934, by *F. G. Frizzell*, very Dutch in 63a design, *à la* Dudok.

BLACKHILL

ST AIDAN, 1885, by *Oliver & Leeson* (GR), with a swagger SE tower with ornate, much higher, crocketed stair-turret. The interior disappointing after this display.

BLACKWELL, NR DARLINGTON

BLACKWELL GRANGE. A handsome brick mansion, the product of three building phases. To the first belongs the five-bay, three-storey centre of the long E range. This may be *c.* 1700. In 1722 to its S another five bays were added, of the same height, but two-storeyed and with a parapet with vases. This new range has a seven-bay S façade.

Then about 1900 more was added to the W along the S
front and to the N along the E front. The E porch also *c.*
1900. Much was altered at that time inside too. The finest
room inside is the State Bedroom.

BLACKWELL HALL. Late C18, brick, with two higher castellated bow windows.

BLAKESTON HALL
1½ m. SW of Wynyard Hall

The house, a seven-bay, two-storeyed brick building of the
late C17, at the time of writing, was derelict.

BOLDON *see* EAST BOLDON, WEST BOLDON

BRADLEY HALL
2¼ m. ESE of Wolsingham

Licence to crenellate was given by Bishop Langley in 1431.
From the C15 probably the four tunnel-vaulted chambers
remaining (with fireplaces) in the S range. The E range
Georgianized as a dwelling. A large moat surrounds the
house. Of the curtain-wall hardly any traces survive.

BRADLEY HALL
2¼ m. SW of Ryton

By *Paine, c.* 1750, in his least grandiose manner. Stone,
seven bays by five, with three large S rooms, the entrance
on the E, and a corridor straight on from it behind the
front rooms. On the other side of the corridor by the side
entrance the staircase opens towards the corridor. The
front has the main windows pedimented and a large
open pediment over the central three bays. Inside, two
of the front rooms have fine, delicate Rococo stucco ceilings. The staircase with a delightful Chippendale fretwork
balustrade.

BRANCEPETH

45 CASTLE. The sight of Brancepeth Castle from a distance,
especially from the S, is one of the greatest thrills one can
experience in the county. It seems at first almost as fine as

Haddon. Approaching more closely, however, one sees to one's disappointment that instead of the time-worn mellowness of old walls much of the castle is fresh early C19 work, built of smooth solid ashlar stone tooled diagonally as if it were tweed. This stone also, it is true, will one day weather, but the building will still remain largely operatic scenery. Of the original castle of the Nevilles, earls of Westmorland, quite substantial parts remain all the same, but they are so scattered and so inter-larded with new work as to make their enjoyment almost impossible. On the s one sees first the medieval one-arch BRIDGE, across which the old high road went past the Castle. The Castle itself is entered by a big imitation Norman GATEHOUSE with fat round towers. This is entirely early C19. The inner court is handsomely turfed as are also the grounds close to the Castle outside. The CURTAIN WALL to the r., i.e. on the NW, is original fairly high up. The masonry shows the joint clearly, as it does in other parts of the Castle. The buildings around the Court appear all C19, and one can only recognize by a walk round the outside how much of the masonry of the Westmorland and Constable Towers with the range be-tween (SE) and of the Neville and Bulmer Towers with the range between (SW) is in fact original. The original parts have strong diagonal buttresses. No windows are in their primitive state except one of the late C15 and one of the late C16 on the first floor in the angle at the w side of the Neville Tower. This sw group of buildings has also preserved its tunnel-vaulted basements (round-arched as well as pointed-arched) and its rib-vaulted principal saloons, the Drawing Room, Salon, and Barons' Hall, though the vaulting has been interfered with in the C19.

Altogether the work of the C19 at Brancepeth lacks inspiration. There is not much of the romantic frenzy about it. Ravensworth, though almost completely sham, was much more convincing than Brancepeth. Yet money was lavished on this reconstruction job. The Castle, after changing hands several times in the C17 and C18 had been bought for £75,000 in 1796 by Mr William Russell of

Sunderland, a banker and financier. He made an enormous fortune out of collieries over which he had control and left this to his son Matthew who began rebuilding the castle about 1817. The architect employed was *John Patterson* of Edinburgh. The job cost over £120,000. Patterson had no archaeological knowledge. His is remarkably incorrect work. He was specially fond of the Norman style. Norman windows (with ogee tracery), Norman capitals, inspired by the N doorway of Durham Cathedral, Norman fireplaces are found in many rooms. The Entrance Hall in the SW corner of the court, however, has a Gothic timber roof with pendants. It is of plaster. It is preceded by a Norman porte-cochère and followed by a large staircase hall of a semi-octagonal form. The staircase starts in one arm and then turns round in two towards the upper landing. The room has a circular skylight carried apparently on radial ribs. The CHAPEL was remodelled, it seems, in mid Victorian times in a purer Gothic style, but is also strangely lacking in fervour.

ST BRANDON. In the ample grounds of the Castle and in its own churchyard, with no other house in the neighbourhood but the castle and that not too close either. The church is big and important looking enough to afford such a situation. W tower, nave, and aisles which go as far W as the W face of the tower, transepts, and chancel, all parapetted, no battlements save the very broad ones on the tower which are crowned by tiny obelisk pinnacles. The tower was begun late in the C12, as its small roundheaded windows on the first floor and its plain only slightly double-chamfered arch towards the nave prove. The upper storeys have E.E. pointed twin windows. The nave is tall with its Perp clerestory. The arcades are both E.E., but differ in rhythm. That on the N is of two bays plus a third added later, that on the S has three plus one. On the N the octagonal pier is sturdier than are the piers on the S, and the capitals have broader mouldings. On the N one capital has a little nutmeg decoration, on the S there is nailhead adornment. Double-chamfered arches and hood-moulds on both sides, and a head-stop below one hood-mould also on both sides. The E bays of the nave, the transepts, and chancel arch are all a little later, but still, it seems, C13. The C14 added a number of Dec windows with flowing tracery, especially in the S transept S and N transept N. Most of these were renewed in the C19. After that in the C15 the chancel was rebuilt with three-light Perp N and S windows and a broad five-light E window. They have all still steep two-centred arches. The nave roof is C15, the chancel roof C17 (*see* below). Both have interesting bosses. An unusual enrichment is the N porch, in what can be called the Jacobean style, although of post-Jacobean date. It has pilasters decorated by strapwork with cherubs' heads in the frieze, and a big semi-circular pediment. But the doorways are pointed.

This touch of the Gothic surrounded by C17 motifs is characteristic of the man who was responsible for the porch and also for the glorious WOODWORK inside: John Cosin, Rector of Brancepeth from 1626 onwards, and appointed Bishop of Durham in 1660. The Cosin style with its fully conscious Gothic Revival in the midst of contemporary C17 elements is one of the most remarkable contributions of the county to the history of architecture and decoration in England, and it can nowhere be studied more completely than at Brancepeth. Work seems to fall into two categories, an earlier, represented by pews, pulpit, and ceiling and a later, far more sumptious and self-assured, represented by font cover, rood screen, and choir stalls. For the earlier we have a date: 1638, the year in which timber was being sawn for the ceiling of the 'middle alley'. The craftsman is named: *Robert Barker.** The later work might then belong to the years of Cosin's rule as a bishop. The PEW ENDS have rusticated bases and strapwork decoration above. The same applies to the FAMILY PEWS in the S transept and the pew in the N transept (originally in all probability also provided with doors). In these two, however, there are at least slight bits of acanthus decoration, pierced, in the top friezes.

* Three bells are dated 1632.

The PULPIT, a two-decker, has Jacobean carving too. Its tester is indeed with its tall canopy a piece of pure early C17 style. All the more surprising is after that the FONT COVER, which has a tall crocketed spire and below between full-round Corinthian columns imitation Gothic panels. These are not in the least florid, but have accurate and rather dull tracery. The ROOD SCREEN is the most sumptuous piece in the church, and here the self-consciousness of the Revival is beyond doubt; for the polygonal posts to the l. and r. of the entrance have incised zigzag ornament which is copied from the piers of Durham Cathedral (cf. Sedgefield and Bishop Auckland). The dados with their blank ogee arches and Perp leaves in the spandrels are so accurate that they have deceived Aymer Vallence (in his book on screens). In fact the generous curve of the ogee arches has a decidedly Baroque flavour. The tracery of the screen openings is entirely Gothic, and the three canopies are an incredible *tour de force* of imitation Dec. The CHOIR STALLS have at their ends acanthus poppy-heads and Gothic tracery below (no doubt later than the nave pews) and at their backs thin balusters and cusped depressed arches. The PANELLING of the nave is entirely plain and domestic, of the choir entirely Gothic except for the many cherubs' heads. Finally there is a CLOCK against the E face of the tower towards the nave, surrounded by strapwork, the COMMUNION RAIL, with thick balusters whose upper halves are as their lower halves in mirror image, and a six-leg COMMUNION TABLE. The chancel CEILING has already been mentioned. It is a flat wooden ceiling with ribs and bosses representing angels with spread-out wings. If this work in the chancel with its Gothic borrowings belongs to *c.* 1639, it seems likely that the purely Jacobean work in the nave came before it and was started by Cosin shortly after he took up the living. However the dating may be in detail, Cosin has done his church proud. There is hardly another in the county so completely and so splendidly furnished at his time.

ROOD LOFTS (?). There are in the church two coved

wooded objects which may be the backs of stalls or the undersides of rood lofts. They are both placed above the chancel arch. The upper is in date contemporary with Cosin's work and goes well with it; *see* the Gothic ribs between the panels and the Jacobean cresting. The other is certainly not English. It is of oak, painted white, and consists of small square panels of the most intricate Flamboyant tracery. – CHEST. Flemish; a splendid piece with Flamboyant tracery and monsters in three tiers in the horizontal strips at the sides. – SCULPTURE. A stone panel with Christ in Majesty, in a vesica halo and surrounded by the Symbols of the Evangelists, almost completely defaced, set in the N face of the SE chancel buttress. – MONUMENTS. Robert Neville, the Peacock, † 1319, stone effigy, more than life-size, cross-legged. – Ralph Neville, second Earl of Westmorland, † 1484, and his wife, wooden effigies. The small figures at the head end and the ones at the feet kneeling at prayer-desks are broken off. The monument originally stood in the middle of the chancel. – Ralph Neville, third Earl of Westmorland, † 1523, large stone tomb-chest without effigy, under the tower. On the sides shields in quatrefoils in circles. – Brass to Thomas Claxton † 1403, knight in armour, *c.* 27 in. long. – Brass to Richard Drax † 1456, demi-figure of a priest, *c.* 13 in. long; on the corners of the stone plate the Symbols of the four Evangelists.

There is no real VILLAGE of Brancepeth, but by the Castle gates are two terraces of Georgian cottages, punctuated by showier houses converted or added in the C19, with Tudor gables.

BURN HALL

Built 1821–34 by *Moody*, the Ushaw builder, to the designs of *Bonomi* of Durham. Four bays each to the l. and r. of a four-column giant Ionic portico. The walls are with banded rustication, the roof of mansard shape. At the back a semicircular projection which houses a handsomely shaped staircase starting in one arm and then

opening out and returning in two. The HOME FARM is a
pretty structure with a tall centre pavilion with pediment,
two arms coming forward diagonally, and end pavilions
with pyramid roofs.

BUTTERBY
1 m. N of Croxdale Hall

Of the manor house only the GATEHOUSE survives. It has
a depressed rounded arch above the gateway, and mullioned and hood-moulded windows on two floors above.
The second is in the gable. Inside the gateway a contemporary narrow open stairway leads straight up to the
first floor. The balusters are coarse and of the type in
which the upper half is the mirror image of the lower.
The present farmhouse seems to have little remaining
which could belong to the same date. The main survival
is a panelled bedroom on the upper floor.

CASTLE EDEN

The house of the two Rowland Burdons, the elder † 1786,
the younger (*see* Bridge, Sunderland) † 1838. The house
itself is not dated, but the church is.

ST JAMES, 1764, i.e. a very early example of the Gothic
Revival. W tower (perhaps from the medieval church),
nave, and chancel. The nave divided from the aisles by
two giant Corinthian columns on each side. These aisles
are an addition of *c.* 1800. They have flat ceilings; the
nave ceiling is coved. The windows are pointed, though
too broad to look correct. The E window is of a disarming
variety: pointed Venetian. – FONT. Oval bowl on baluster
shaft. – PLATE. Chalice, 1706; Paten, 1749; Flagon,
1761; saucer-shaped Almsdish, 1765.

CASTLE EDEN. Block of Georgian proportions, but embattled and with depressed-pointed, hood-moulded, i.e.
imitation Late Perp, windows. Built before 1786 but
called 'lately rebuilt' in 1823. C19 additions, especially a

palmhouse at the front. Stables and curtain wall to the N.
In the Entrance Hall Elizabethan fireplace from Horden
Hall.

CASTLE GATES. With asymmetrical Lodge. By one of the
Atkinsons. Late C18 and of course crenellated.

Rowland Burdon also built a COTTON (later sailcloth)
FACTORY (now Brewery) a little to the N of the Gates, a
BLEACHERY, hardly more than a cottage, to the SW, and
a FOUNDRY, one-storeyed, just S of railway station and
inn. All these buildings are of brick. Cotton making began
in 1792, and parts of the original mill seem to be incorporated into the present Brewery. For his workers Burdon
built a terrace of houses, the entrances with Tuscan
pilasters, and the centre marked by a one-bay pediment.
All this is mentioned in a book of 1803.

CAUSEY ARCH

Causey Arch* was built in 1727 to carry the rails for coal-
waggons high across the ravine of the Causey Burn. The
bridge is of a single span, 105 ft long and 80 ft high. The
architect was a local mason, *Ralph Wood*. It can *cum grano
salis* be called the earliest of all railway bridges.

CHESTER-LE-STREET

ST MARY AND ST CUTHBERT. A very picturesque W side,
with the short tower heavily buttressed and with a heavy
W stair-turret, the twin bell-openings E.E., and above an
octagonal storey and a spire, of *c.* 1400. The S aisle projects as far W as the tower W front. The N aisle did the
same originally (*see* the blocked arch inside), but was later
replaced by an ANCHORAGE or ANKER HOUSE. This has
to the street the most curious window, carved all out of
one big slab of stone. It has a mullion-and-transomed
cross on the r. and a narrow single opening to the l. of it.

* On the footpath leading to Tanfield from a house on the W just
S of the Causey Burn Bridge on the A 6076 road.

Towards the s into the church a narrow squint. The tower arches to E and s rest on three-shaft responds with hollows between and typical C13 moulded capitals. The arches are double-chamfered. The aisle arcades were at first three bays and then lengthened by two more towards the W. The piers are circular, the capitals moulded (those towards the W more finely), the arches double-chamfered. On the s side a C13 doorway with one order of colonnettes, on the N side a similar but simpler doorway. The original s aisle windows with reticulated, i.e. early C14 tracery. On the N side further E was the Lumley Chapel, pulled down and replaced by a chapel built by *Bonomi* in 1832. Further W the old vestry. The Sedilia and Piscina in the chancel are E.E., trefoil-headed, and prettily quatrefoil-shafted. – FONT. Octagonal, C15, with shields as sole decoration of the bowl (cf. Staindrop). – SCULPTURE. Interesting Roman inscription and Saxon fragments in the room below the tower and also the s porch, parts of cross-shafts, e.g. one with a horseman, a large slab with figures, etc. In the porch also foliated crosses. – PLATE. Chalice and Paten, 1795–6. – MONUMENTS. Brass to Alice Lambton † 1434, 28 in. long, chancel s wall. – Effigy of a priest, *c.* 1300, close to the font. – A very interesting series of fourteen effigies of members of the Lumley family, placed all in a row along the N aisle wall by John Lord Lumley. Camden in his *Britannia* says they were 'either gotten together out of monasteries that were subverted or caused to be made anew'. As for those ' gotten', our source was the graveyard of Durham Cathedral. In 1594 Lord Lumley obtained licence to remove from it certain effigies. To house all these ancestors Lord Lumley had to cut off the feet of quite a number of them and place the first in double file. He started at the E end, where there is a long explanatory inscription of proud family history, beginning with Liulph at the time of Edward the Confessor. The only medieval effigies are two of Frosterley marble, Nos 3 and 4, which, although not cross-legged, are of *c.* 1310 and No. 10 which is cross-legged, of sandstone, and of *c.* 1310–15. The majority of the monuments are

Elizabethan, but in imitation of the medieval style, an extremely interesting case of early, self-conscious medievalism.

The main street is poor in buildings of interest. The QUEEN'S HEAD is the nicest, C18, six bays, three storeys.

To the S of the town THE HERMITAGE, a pretty Georgian stone house with two symmetrical bay windows at the ends of the façade, Tudorized *c.* 1830 by mullioned and transomed windows and some trim to the doorway.

HARBOUR HOUSE, 2 m. SE. In spite of C15 and C16 traditions now an C18 house. Three bays with flat rustication of the window frames, a pretty Adamish doorway, and a one-bay pediment. Nice lettering indicates the purposes of rooms behind certain windows and also behind two doors of outbuildings: Dairy, Cheeseroom, Repository, and Brasserie.

Chester was the Roman fort of CONCANGIUM, but of this nothing visible remains.

CHURCH KELLOE

ST HELEN. Small, below the road, and not in a village. Norman W tower, heavily buttressed; the tower arch later, but the responds original. The S doorway into the nave also Norman, with shafts with block capitals and an arch too decayed to define its mouldings. On the N side of the nave another Norman doorway; now blocked. Chancel E.E. with a few original lancet windows. E window and chancel S windows Dec, a rarity in County Durham, but unfortunately renewed. The treasure of the church is a CROSS, one of the best pieces of medieval sculpture in 15b the county. The cross head and arms shaped like the high hats of Eastern Orthodox priests. The shaft has three tiers of figurework. Above the announcement to the Empress Helena, the scene in which it was revealed to her where she would find the Holy Cross, then two standing figures, St Helena with the Cross and another, and then the Empress with a drawn sword menacing Judas (with a spade) to make him tell her exactly where to dig for the Cross. The preservation is not very good, yet the style is telling enough. Connexions with the earlier C12 in France are obvious, for example, in the beard of Judas, but the gentle rippling of the folds round the feet of the standing figures is a motif hardly to be expected before the end of the C12; and that is probably the date of the cross. – Heavy tomb-lid with foliated cross, on the floor, next to the Cross. – PLATE. Chalice and Cover inscribed 1681; Paten, 1689.

CLEADON

CLEADON TOWER. Small symmetrical Tudor front to the garden, hood-moulded mullioned windows, doorway with four-centred arch. Inside, four large contemporary fire-places with four-centred arches.

CLEADON HOUSE, 1738, brick, of five bays and two storeys. In the centre of the street front a Venetian window. Behind it a fine staircase with wrought iron balustrade.

COATHAM MUNDEVILLE

(ST MARY MAGDALENE, 1865, by *Withers*.)

(HALL GARTH. Typical C18 limestone façade, but the core of the house and the chimneys older.)

COCKFIELD

ST MARY. E.E. the chancel E wall with three separate stepped lancets, the chancel S lancets, the nave S wall with renewed taller lancets, and the S doorway. All the rest is of 1911. – In the chancel on the floor several foliated cross tomb-lids. – MONUMENT to a girl, probably *c.* 1310–20, badly damaged, in the chancel. – Former PEW BACKS, C17, with sparsely set balusters as at Aycliffe; now used as nave panelling (S wall).

CONISCLIFFE

ST EDWIN. An essentially E.E. church, unusually long. Unbuttressed W tower, E.E. to the corbel-table, then a later, recessed stone spire.* E.E. the chancel with lancet

* Inside the tower a very rough medieval LADDER to reach the upper storeys.

windows, a group of three stepped lancets at the E end, and a chancel arch inside on filleted responds and with a filleted moulding of the arch itself towards the nave. E.E. the five-bay arcade between the nave and N aisle, on low circular piers with single-chamfered arches and chamfered hood-moulds. Only on the S side of the nave close to the W end is a tall roundheaded window, evidence of an earlier, Norman, building phase. To the same phase belongs the N doorway with one order of (missing) colonnettes, a beak-head order of voussoirs in the arch, and, above it, a curious small stone, perhaps once the centre of the tympanum, as it shows the Agnus Dei in a circle. To the l. and r. of the circle severely stylized frontal angel figures in long frocks. At the E end of the N aisle an embattled two-storeyed vestry, built probably in the C15. – CHANCEL STALLS. C15 with poppy-heads with angels. – PLATE. Chalice of London make, 1570.

COWPEN BEWLEY

(IVY HOUSE. Five-bay brick house with interesting decorative treatment of the brickwork: MHLG.) The most likely date is the early C18.

COXHOE

ST MARY, 1868, by *Withers*.

COXHOE HALL. Five-bay, two-and-a-half-storey house of *c.* 1725. Built for John Burdon, father of the elder Rowland Burdon (*see* Castle Eden) and altered *c.* 1749 by *Paine*. Now in ruins. Elizabeth Barrett Browning was born here.

CROXDALE

CROXDALE HALL. A plain, honest house built *c.* 1760 (after 1758) for General Salvin, father of the architect. Stone, two-storeyed. Seven-bay front (W) with central doorway with Tuscan columns and a Venetian window above. Towards the garden (S) five bays with three-bay pediment. Towards the drive (N) an older wing provided by the C18 with two big bows with Venetian windows.

Those on the E were blocked when in 1807 a thinly Gothic private chapel was built in. Of C18 plasterwork the fine staircase ceiling and the ceiling of the Drawing Room remain.

In the grounds just N of the Hall lies the derelict medieval CHURCH. It has a Norman S doorway with a badly weathered tympanum (Tree of Life?), a blocked N doorway probably of the late C12 (the date of the chancel arch, which has keeled demi-piers as its responds), a lancet window near it on the N side, and a Dec three-light E window. – ALTAR PAINTING. Mourning of Christ, by *Maria Cosway*; the style a little reminiscent of Fuseli.

BUTTERBY, *see* p. 64.

DALTON *see* DALTON-LE-DALE

DALTON-LE-DALE

ST ANDREW. N doorway Norman with scalloped capitals and an arch with zigzag in the intrados and extrados. The rest (except for the S porch) is E.E. of the early C13. Nave and chancel without structural division (a Norman chancel arch was removed in the C19). Lancet windows on all sides; at the E end a group of three, stepped, but unconnected. A little later two 'low side windows' with pointed trefoiled heads and one chancel N window: two lights with quatrefoil in circle above, i.e. later C13. – FONT. Round stem and cup-shaped bowl with band of four-petalled flowers round the top (cf. Seaham). – MONUMENT. Knight, *c.* 1400, badly preserved. – Equally badly preserved effigy of a Woman.

NE of the church the old VICARAGE with a four-centred doorhead. Inscribed 'Thomas Sharp, 1670'.

DALTON HALL (or Dawdon Hall) lies higher up the richly wooded dene. It is now a farmhouse. Stepped gables and on the upper floor a room with a piscina. Behind, the ruins of the medieval Hall, called Dalden Tower. One fragment stands high up but is entirely smothered in ivy. The only decorative feature that can be distinguished is an ogee-headed opening with ornamented jambs and tracery.

DARLINGTON

INTRODUCTION

The church lies at the bottom of the town just W of the river Skerne. To its S was the Bishop's Palace or Manor House. The medieval town stretched up the gentle rise W of the church with the Market Place close to the churchyard. The streets named 'gate', such as Skinnergate, North Gate, Bondgate, Blackwellgate, Houndgate, mark the extent of the town, about 2,000 by 2,000 ft. A map of 1826 shows the usual ribbons of houses extending along the main approach roads, but no growth of the compactly built-over area yet. Most of what is Darlington now belongs to the Railway Age which was initiated by the opening of the Stockton–Darlington railway in 1825. The venture was due to the Darlington citizen Edward Pease, and, as all the world knows, to George Stephenson. The population of Darlington in 1801 was 4,700, in 1851 11,600, in 1901 44,500. It is now *c*. 85,000.

CHURCHES AND PUBLIC BUILDINGS

ST CUTHBERT. One of the most important churches in the county (collegiate right through the Middle Ages) and one of the important E.E. churches in the N of England. The church is well preserved and virtually all in the one style. Moreover, it happens to be uncommonly beautiful in its dark grey stone, its external proportions, with the chancel (rebuilt by *Pritchett* in 1864–5) not so excessively long as is common in England, and with a crossing tower and spire (rebuilt in 1752) which seems to possess just the right height. It is a great shame that the visitor usually sees it set against the overwhelming shapes of the cooling towers of the power station further E, and that, when he approaches it nearer, he is surrounded by the uproar of the central bus station of Darlington. – Evidence of a Saxon church preceding the present one exists in some sculptural fragments (*see* below). The present church was probably begun in 1192. Under that year Galfrid of Coldingham reports that Bishop Pudsey in spite of the difficulties with which he was faced did not desist from the building of the church of Dernington ('Inter tam multiplicium tempestatum vicissitudines constructione ecclesie de Derningtona non destitit'). This may sound as if he had started earlier, but the interpretation of the text is not conclusive, and stylistic evidence does not allow for a date earlier than 1190. Then building proceeded, it seems, steadily, and nothing except the aisle windows, which are straightheaded, of two lights and have ogee-reticulated tracery, and the crossing tower whose windows also indicate an early C14 date, can be later than 1250. The proof of that lies in the fact that all windows are lancets and that no C13 tracery occurs anywhere. Fine and typically N English grouping of the lancets in three storeys at the E and W ends, and at the N and S fronts of the transepts. All these four end walls are flanked by broad buttresses with or without turrets. The transepts are aisleless, as is the chancel. The chancel has single lancets on its N and S sides with nook-shafts and moulded capitals. Inside, the windows form part of a tall blank arcade whose shafts are distinguished by crocket and stiff-leaf capitals. Moreover, the middle windows exhibit in the arches some of the 'nutmeg' ornament so characteristic of the late C12 in the county. Sedilia and Piscina are early C14 with ogee arches. The two transepts differ from each other in minor but interesting ways. The S transept carries on the style of the chancel and enriches it by giving the shafts shaft-rings, the capitals dogtooth and a little nailhead decoration, and the spandrels some pretty quatrefoils and eight-petalled stars in circles (derived from Ripon?). In the upper storey stiff-leaf capitals are given up and all capitals are moulded. The N transept has only moulded capitals. The crossing and the E bay of the nave belong together. But the crossing was very clumsily strengthened when the spire was built. The original piers and the first piers of the nave arcade have attached keeled and filleted shafts. Above the nave piers vaulting shafts were carried up. The first arch of the nave is more richly moulded on the S than on the N side. Then a change took place. The plan to vault was given up and the further arcade piers are alternatingly circular and octagonal (alternating also between N and S sides) all the capitals are without stiff-leaf decoration* and the arches are simply treble-chamfered. The clerestory windows are plain, single-chamfered outside, and unshafted. The W doorway has three orders of colonnettes, many-moulded voussoirs, and is crowned by a steep gable. The N portal has two orders and a treble-chamfered arch.

FURNISHINGS. PULPITUM or stone rood screen, a solid arch with three ribs in the intrados like the arch of a bridge. The pulpitum was erected between 1381 and c.1405. – EASTER SEPULCHRE in the chancel, with four-centred arch, the only contribution of the Perp style. – CHANCEL STALLS. C15 or early C16, with poppy-heads and MISERICORDS cords with faces, angels, monsters, figures carrying branches, and (S of the entrance) a king on two birds (Alexander carried into the air). – FONT COVER. A spectacular piece of Cosin-Gothic (*see* Introduction), spire-like and entirely Dec Gothic. – STAINED GLASS. An unusually complete show of mid and later Victorian workmanship. An index may be useful: W end *Clayton & Bell*, N aisle *W. Wallace*, N aisle N from W to E *Burlison & Grylls; Hardman; Clayton & Bell*, N transept N *Clayton & Bell*, E below *Wailes*, above *Atkinson*, chancel N middle designed by *Maclachlan*, NE *Hemming*, E *Baguley*, SE and S middle *Atkinson*, S transept E and S *Clayton & Bell*, W *Atkinson*, S aisle from E to W *Clayton & Bell; Wailes; Atkinson*, S aisle W *Atkinson*. – PLATE. Chalice, London-made, 1762; two Flagons, London-made, 1771; Chalice, Cover, and two Patens, 1774–5. – MONUMENTS. Female effigy, late C13, S transept, very badly preserved, but apparently once of fine quality. – Robert Henry Allan, 1883, by *J. P. Pritchett*, Neo-Gothic epitaph.

ST JOHN THE EVANGELIST, Neasham Road, 1847–8, by

---

* Miss Pamela Wynn-Reeves in her excellent yet unpublished thesis on English stiff-leaf sculpture (Univ. of London, 1952) points out that in many churches the E parts are more richly decorated than the W parts.

John Middleton, in a fine position at the fork of two roads. Dignified E.E. style with w tower and rather tall and narrow nave and aisles.

HOLY TRINITY, 1843, by *Salvin*, but much altered in 1883 and 1890. E.E. with a tower at the E end of the S aisle, and a higher stair-turret with conical roof.

ST HILDA, Parkgate, 1887–8, by *J. L. Pearson*. Red brick, E.E., and of no special merit.

BONDGATE METHODIST CHURCH, Saltyard, 1812, by *W. Sherwood*. Brick, a big parallelogram, with arched windows in two tiers, a three-bay pediment, and a porch on attenuated Tuscan columns.

METHODIST CHURCH, Coniscliffe Road, 1840. Yellow brick, pedimented, windows in two tiers in blank giant arches. Two dignified doorways with Doric pilasters.

FRIENDS MEETING HOUSE, Skinnergate. In existence in 1834. A street façade of five bays, broad centre accentuated by a one-storey Tuscan porch *in antis*.

MARKET AND PUBLIC OFFICES, Market Place, 1864, by *Waterhouse*, but not one of his more ambitious efforts. Yellow brick. The covered market with glass roof and iron outer colonnades separates the Public Offices from the tower with its somewhat bulgy spired top. Inside the market hall stands the former MARKET CROSS, a Tuscan column of 1727.

COUNTY COURT, Coniscliffe Road, 1869, in a quiet Italian Renaissance style.

EDWARD PEASE PUBLIC LIBRARY, East Street, 1884, by *G. G. Hoskins.*

TECHNICAL COLLEGE, Northgate, 1896, by *G. G. Hoskins* in a fancy Perp style, of purple brick with much yellow terra-cotta decoration.

MECHANICS INSTITUTE, Skinnergate, 1853, by *Pritchett*. Red brick, debased classical, and quite stately.

SIR EDWARD WALKER'S HOMES, Coniscliffe Road, 1928, by *Joshua Clayton*. A large group divided up into individual pavilions, in a friendly Neo-Georgian.

NORTH ROAD STATION, Station Road. This building replaced the original terminus of the Stockton–Darlington

Railway. Its date is probably 1842. The building is plain
Late Georgian in character, with a two-storey centre and
one-storey wings. The centre has an attached colonnade
with cast-iron columns. Inside, worth-while cast-iron
details. The train-shed with an open timber roof.

EASTERN REGION STATION, Victoria Road, 1887, probably by *William Bell*. Red brick with a large porte-
cochère and a tall tower between its two entrance arches.
On the platform stands LOCOMOTIVE No. 1, the
original engine of the 1825 railway.

PERAMBULATION

There is too little of note and what there is, is too close
together to make topographical description necessary. In
the centre of the town only one house seems to go back to
the mid C17: the Nag's Head in TUBWELL ROW, red
brick with a gable of stepped quarter-circles and with
superimposed orders of pilaster-strips rather than
pilasters. The brick frieze with the individual bricks sticking out angle-wise is specially characteristic. Of the C18
much more survives than need here be recorded. The best
examples are FEETHAMS, s of the church, a house which
still gives the impression of a pre-urban character in the
area about the church, Nos 10 and adjoining houses in
HOUNDGATE, perhaps the most handsome group still
remaining, Nos 10–18 HIGH ROW as a plain urban group,
and BENNET HALL, Horsemarket, of seven bays with a
high recessed erection on the roof (and a back building of
1846).

Outside the town were villages, some of which have meanwhile become part of the town. That applies particularly
to COCKERTON which has still its pretty green and close
to it COCKERTON HALL, C18, with segmentheaded
windows.

Extension towards these outlying villages began about 1800.
It took the form of terraces as well as detached villas.
Examples of growth up to *c.* 1840 along the main roads
can be seen in BONDGATE (No. 81, ashlar stone, with
Ionic porch; West Lodge, West Crescent, five bays with

three-bay pediment and Tuscan porch, *c.* 1803), Grange Road (HAREWOOD GROVE – centre with Ionic double porch – and HAREWOOD HILL), CONISCLIFFE ROAD (Nos 41–61, a terrace of cottages with Roman Doric doorways; No. 140 with Greek Doric porch; and Nos 98–126 opposite, an irregular group), and NORTHGATE (Education Offices). Of the early C19 also one surviving MILL, originally that of the Peases, a reminder of the woollen industry of Darlington. It lies just across (and partly over) the river in BACKHOUSE STREET. The main block of fourteen bays and four storeys with pediments on the end pavilions dates from 1812. An addition is dated 1818. For Victorian Darlington three examples are sufficient: Barclays Bank in HIGH ROW, 1864, by *Waterhouse* in the Gothic style, No. 37 TUBWELL ROW, of about the same time, in a jolly ornate cast-iron Vernacular, and MOWDEN HALL, Staindrop Road, Cockerton, 1881, by *Waterhouse*, a piece of wealthy domestic architecture with plenty of red terra-cotta. Nothing later than Victorian deserves special mention.

DAWDON

s of Seaham Harbour

ST HILDA AND ST HELEN, 1912; by *W. H. Wood*.

PITHEAD BATH, 1932. An example of the 'Early Modern' of the pithead baths: brick with horizontal brick bands, the pattern a little overdone.

DAWDON *see* DALTON-LE-DALE
DENTON

ST MARY, 1891, by *Pritchett* – Effigy of a member of the Conyers family (vestry, inside a cupboard).

DINSDALE *see* LOW DINSDALE

DUNSTON
2m. sw of Gateshead

POWER STATION, 1933–51 by *Merz & McLellan*. As a group similar to that chain of new power stations in England modelled on the pattern of Battersea, London, but far in advance of all others by encasing most of its machinery in glass rather than solid brick. A power station should look like a vast, complex, yet clean piece of machinery, and Dunston does.

DURHAM

INTRODUCTION

Durham is one of the great experiences of Europe to the eyes of those who appreciate architecture, and to the minds of those who understand architecture. The group of Cathedral, Castle, and Monastery on the rock can only be compared to Avignon and Prague, and (a particularly lucky circumstance) the old town has in no way been spoilt and is still to the same degree the visual foil to the monuments as it must have been two and five hundred years ago. The river Wear forms so close a loop that the town is surrounded by it on three sides. On the land side the two bridges are a bare 900 ft from each other. The position was ideal for a fortress, and it is ideal for the picture of a town. For a cathedral it is as unusual as for a monastery.

The combination of the three at Durham has its historical reasons. The position of the shrine of St Cuthbert in the north and near the Scottish border was an exposed one. To guard the land and to guard the shrine was so much the same that as early as the CII the Bishop was also Earl. Nearly all the temporal privileges which in other counties belonged to the King, in the County Palatine were the

Bishop's. He had his own Parliament (Durham sent no representatives to London) and his own coinage, his subjects were bidden to do military service under him, not under the King, and licences 'to crenellate', that is to build castles, were granted by him. His position was in fact like that of the great episcopal rulers of Germany rather than that of the other English bishops. Moreover, ever since Anglo-Saxon times the religious community of Durham (as of Lindisfarne and many others) had been one of monks under a bishop. So, when the Normans reformed the see, Durham became one of the monastic cathedrals of England, as were Canterbury, Ely, and several others, a complete anomaly from the point of view of Continental episcopal organization, but one familiar in England. Hence the unforgettable group of ecclesiastic, military, and domestic buildings at Durham. Avignon and Prague have been mentioned, but what distinguishes Durham visually from them is again something exceedingly English. The pictures of the buildings on the hill which one remembers have all foregrounds of green. The most moving one, from the Prebends' Bridge, in fact shows the Cathedral rising straight above the tops of the venerable trees up the steep bank, as if it were the vision of a Caspar David Friedrich or Schinkel. Verdure mellows what would otherwise be too domineering, domineering the castle, domineering the site of the cathedral, domineering the architecture of the cathedral, and domineering inside the cathedral the throne of the bishop raised on a higher platform than the shrine of the saint.

THE CATHEDRAL AND THE COLLEGE

INTRODUCTION. There are cathedrals which remain in one's memory as a procession of architecture through the ages

(Canterbury, for instance), and there are others which, whatever later centuries may have added to them, are essentially of one period. Thus it is at Lincoln, thus at Durham. Nothing of Durham Cathedral is earlier than 1093, and with the exception of visually so separate a part as the Nine Altars, with the exception of the great W, N, and S windows and with the exception of the tower over

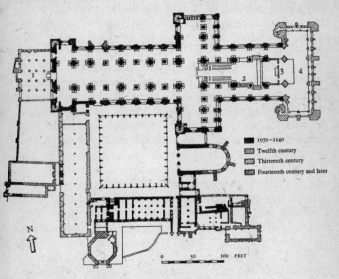

DURHAM CATHEDRAL

1 Galilee
2 Bishop Hatfield's Tomb and Bishop's Throne
3 Neville Screen
4 Chapel of the Nine Altars

the crossing, nothing essential to the general impression is later than the late C12. Most of what makes Durham Durham is of the short space of time between 1093 and 1133, and of that phase, the phase of Vézelay and Laach, it is one of the most perfect and also historically most interesting buildings in Europe. Of its aesthetic perfection more will be said later; as for its historical significance, an introductory remark must be made now. Durham, as far as can be ascertained, possessed the earliest rib-vaults ever ventured upon in the West.* Now rib-vaults are supposed by the layman to be the hallmark of the Gothic style, but the Gothic style was created over thirty years later than the first vaults were closed at Durham, and it was created in France, at St Denis. What is the essential function of the rib-vault? Aesthetically it completes a process which can also be watched in Gothic walls. It is the process by which the inert masses of masonry which constitute a building are made for the eye to disappear. We follow the long shafts up a Gothic wall and see the tall openings of arcades and windows and overlook what is left of solid walls. But a vault must remain completely solid. It cannot be made transparent. So the ribs allow us to go on seeing vigorous, slender lines of action and forget the massive surfaces between. A tunnel-vault or even a groined vault are mass lying heavily on the walls. A rib-vault seems always far lighter, and as a rule really is. For as a rule the transverse arches and the ribs are built separately on their own centering, and the cells are then filled in with less substantial masonry. That is also the case at Durham, and it is almost certain that here this system which is the constructional foundation of Gothic masons, was invented. John Wilson (*Archaeological Journal* 1922) writes this: 'In the course of the repairs of 1915, when the plastering of the cells was stripped, it became possible to ascertain the thickness of the cells in certain places, and the manner of their construction. In the eastern bays their thickness may reach 20 inches or more. I measured it as 18 inches in three places in the second and third bays from the crossing. In the western bays the thickness is less, varying from 12 to 16 inches, and averaging about 14 inches. The cells are built of coursed rubble, with stones

* This is not the place once more to go into the question of the priority of Durham or Lombardy. In any case the early rib-vaults of Lombardy are low and heavy, that is lie on low naves and have broad ribs of plain rectangular section. They do not aspire to the Gothic effect of effortless growth which is heralded in the Durham vaults.

of irregular length up to about 18 inches, and generally from $2\frac{1}{2}$ to 3 inches thick on the soffit, with some thicker courses (about 4 inches) in the lower parts of the cells. Between the tops of the ogives and doubleaux and the cell, there is always a wide joint (of 2 inches or so) which received the boards of the centering on which the cells were built, and some fragments of oak boards were found in the course of the repairs.'

However, these observations refer to the nave, vaulted *c.* 1130 and to the earlier chancel. But John Bilson has proved beyond doubt that the chancel also was rib-vaulted from the beginning, that is *c.* 1104, as indeed the chancel aisles still are. The designer of the Durham chancel was thus probably as great a technical inventor as he was an architect. But to call Durham Cathedral a Gothic building, because it is the first to use Gothic methods and a Gothic motif, the rib-vault, would be manifestly wrong. In spirit Durham is still entirely Romanesque, and it is spirit that determines architecture, not technique.

EXTERIOR. Durham Cathedral on its rock is so overwhelming an apparition that no one will regret the time spent on obtaining the best general views of the whole building before studying its details. The best views are, in my opinion, from Prebends' Bridge to see the towers above the trees, from South Street to see the w front dead on, from Gilesgate to see the whole N side above the town, from the s end of Church Street for the corresponding view from the s, and from Palace Green to get a close yet complete picture. It is here we shall begin to examine the exterior.

Medieval churches were usually started at the chancel end. Durham was no exception. But the E end was altered in the C13. So we shall open the book of the cathedral at the junction between that *novum opus* and the original work and then follow it to the w (taking N and s sides together, which will be tiresome to the visitor) and end by the Galilee, before turning to the Gothic E end.

The foundation stone of the Cathedral was laid by the

Bishop on August 11, 1093. The bishop was William of St Calais or St Carileph, as they anglicized his name here. He was a Frenchman, had been a secular priest at Rouen, then became a monk at St Calais in Maine and abbot of St Vincent at Le Mans. William the Conqueror called him to Durham in 1081. In 1088 he had to flee the land and spent three years in Normandy before returning. He must have been familiar with the great abbeys of Normandy, St Étienne and the Trinité at Caen and Jumièges, as well as much in other parts of France. Yet his building was not French, not indeed entirely Normandy-Norman. It has from the beginning Anglo-Norman features, which is perhaps not to be wondered at, as Durham came late amongst the great cathedrals and abbeys of William's new Kingdom. Canterbury and St Augustine's at Canterbury, Battle, Old Sarum, St Albans, Winchester, Lincoln, Ely, Worcester, London, Gloucester, Rochester, Chester, all had been begun before Durham.

The chancel is divided into bays by broad flat buttresses. The thin horizontal courses separating the inner storeys from each other are taken round the buttresses. The ground floor has large blank arcades, two for each interior bay. They have columns with block capitals (the most elementary form the Romanesque style had conceived) but arches with quite articulated mouldings.* The aisle windows above this dado are amongst the most playful of Dec designs in the county, every one on the s as well as the n side different in the tracery from the others. They were put in about 1350–60, it seems. Unfortunately they are now entirely renewed. Above these windows

---

* On the N side these have been interfered with, apparently in the c18 (see the large shallow curve); on the s side they seem trustworthy in their details. More than this one should not say. Right into the middle of the c19 drawings and engravings show the aisle gallery and elementary windows all with tracery. Many other things also which we are inclined to regard as strictly original belong to *Sir George Gilbert Scott's* restoration. As a rule he restored the original state, but we cannot always rely on him, especially where *Wyatt's* earlier restoration had too thoroughly obscured the evidence.

those of the gallery are of the earliest design again, very small twins each in a larger blank arched panel and the two together in a joint panel with a depressed rounded arch, all very primitive looking. Perhaps the smallness of these windows and the amount of solid wall left finds its explanation in the thought that the temerity of the vaulting inside called for the greatest solidity of abutment. On the s side the tympanum of these gallery panels has flat lozenge decoration, the earliest piece of geometrical surface decoration in the cathedral. As to its date, this question must be postponed for a short while. The clerestory has one sizable window per bay, with nook-shafts and a moulded arch. A corbel-table finishes the elevation.* The Norman roofs were higher than they are now, as can be seen from their waterline against the crossing tower.

The present CROSSING TOWER is Norman only in its lowest stage. How high it went up beyond that, no one can say. That a tower existed is known from medieval inferences. About 1465 a new crossing tower was built. It is of two stages, the higher one being an addition of about 1490 (in different stone). Both masons are probably known by name. The master-mason to the Cathedral from 1465 was *Thomas Barton*. He was succeeded in 1488 by *John Bell*. The lower stage has on each side two very long two-light windows with one transome each and simple Perp tracery. They are set close together. Above them is a broad band of panelled crenellations meant to be the crowning motif of the tower. Then, when the third stage was put on, the same kind of window was used, but not so long. The real battlements are pierced. The tower is strengthened by set-back buttresses, decorated with three tiers of statues under canopies and with pinnacles where they end. It is a sound and robust design, even if out of keeping with the Norman work. It adds a decisive accent in a place where William of St Carileph and his great mason would not have wanted it. But the Perp style

---

* Some of the grotesque corbel-heads have been re-used in the C13 E bay of the chancel. They can there be examined at ease.

adored big and tall single towers, be they at the W end of a parish church as at Boston or Louth, or above the crossing of a cathedral as Bell Harry at Canterbury and our Durham tower. The earlier medieval feeling for a hierarchical order was going.

The TRANSEPTS on their E sides now give the most complete picture of the character of the earliest work, strong and forbidding, though a little mellowed by the beautiful, almost Pentelic light brown of the stone. The system is the same as in the chancel, except that instead of the Dec windows, the aisle windows here (for the transepts have an E aisle) are large Norman windows with nook-shafts. The transept fronts are both not in their pristine state. On the N side, under Bishop Hatfield, a very large Dec window of six lights was put in. The date seems to be *c.* 1360, and it is, therefore, interesting to note that in the two vertical bars to the l. and r. of the big upper six-lobed star a first sign of Perp feeling appears. On the S side the monastic buildings abut against the transept. The disposition must, therefore, be different. The first floor is now blocked by the Song School (*see* Cloister), but inside the transept a very large centrally placed blocked Norman window can be recognized. Above this is a large Perp window of six lights, probably put in between 1420 and 1440. To return now to the Norman evidence, at the top of the aisle ends of both transepts is a blank arcade of intersecting arches; at the top of the transept 'nave' end, above the Hatfield window, the same motif is used. On the S side the decoration of the gable is a little different. An all-over lozenge pattern, larger and more distinctive than above the gallery windows appears. The N gable is C13. Both the transepts have flanking turrets decorated with blank arcading. Those at the W ends, housing spiral staircases, are bigger and end in octagonal tops.

We must now proceed to the nave. But before doing so it is well to recall some dates. William of St Carileph began in 1093. He must have had plenty of funds accumulated, for building went on so rapidly that by the time he had been dead three years and a successor was at last appointed (that is in 1099), this successor, Ranulph Flambard, known in political history more than in architectural history, found the church 'usque navem . . . jam factam'. So by then chancel, transepts, and crossing and as much of the nave as had to be put up to help abutting the crossing, were already complete. It will be shown below that five years later the chancel must also have been vaulted. The NAVE was built by Flambard who died in 1128. He, Symeon, our chief source, tells us, erected 'navem circumdatis parietibus usque testudinem'. The *testudo*, i.e. the vault, was put in between 1128 and 1133. Flambard's mason was content to follow in William's footsteps. The ground floor arcades are unchanged, and the aisle windows unchanged. Only above these, for the gallery, he permitted himself one larger window instead of the two minute ones, and only in the clerestory did he begin to use what was to become the standard motif of C12 decoration in England, the zigzag.* Both sides of the nave are identical, though the S side has lost much of its character by a thorough C19 refacing. On the N side near the W end, in the place usual for the principal porches of English churches, is the main PORTAL. It projects in front of the wall to gain space for its five orders of shafts, but it does not form a porch. It has capitals of a design not otherwise occurring in the cathedral or the county; they are block capitals with the receding part below the upper segment closely fluted. The arches have several friezes of grouped zigzags. The surround with polygonal turrets and an ogee gable, all decorated by blank panelling, is Perp, but is said to have been much renewed. Affixed to the oaken door of this portal is the celebrated C12 DOOR KNOCKER, one of the greatest ex- 32a amples of the power which the Romanesque style could achieve by stylization. It stands in the front rank of metalwork of the century, together with the Brunswick Lion.

* On its earliest appearance at Durham, *see* Interior.

The different way in which hair and flesh are interpreted
in terms of parallel lines should be noted. The fleshy nose
is a system of convex flutings, like rope, the wildly flicker-
ing curls of incised lines. The eyes were of course of
coloured enamel.

The W TOWERS were probably begun together with the
nave. They have nothing of the slightly more ornate
character which we find in the upper parts of the nave.
This is, however, present in the GREAT WEST PORTAL
now blocked by the Galilee. It will therefore be referred
to under Interior. But it must already here be said that,
though it is ornate, its ornateness is also essentially obtained by a multiplication of zigzags. The towers have
three Norman stages; only on one does zigzag occur in the
windows. The broad stair-turrets are completely plain,
opened only in the narrowest slits. Between the towers
and above the W doorway was once a large Norman window whose outline can still be seen. But this was replaced about 1360 by a huge seven-light window still
entirely in the Dec style. The tracery cannot easily be
described, but should be memorized a little; for its forms
will be found to have stimulated much of a minor nature
in the county. Above this runs a narrow Norman blank
arcade in which jambs and arches are all one display
of zigzag. Above this the Norman style is replaced by
the E.E., though when these additions were made is not
known. The forms are early C13 anyway, and go with
similar work at Darlington, Hartlepool, Gateshead, and
Sherburn Hospital. The tower tops and the gable have
lancet windows and blank shafted lancet arcades. On the
towers there are four tiers, two high, two low. The pierced
parapets with their battlements were added about 1801.
Up to the Commonwealth the W towers had lead spires
(an odd idea to the present admirer of the cathedral).
They were probably put on in the C14. And although they
were certainly not in harmony with the Norman design, it
must not be forgotten that, to reconstruct in one's mind a
Norman cathedral, one must think in terms, if not of

spires, of pyramid roofs on W towers and crossing tower. What makes, however, an even approximate reconstruction impossible is the fact that, quite apart from the roofs, we do not know at all how high Carileph and Flambard wanted their towers and in what relation of height they wanted them to each other.

The GALILEE is Pudsey's chief contribution to the cathedral. It remains a strange idea that he should have wanted his Lady Chapel at the W end. We are told, and evidence has confirmed it, that he actually began at the E end, where one would expect to find the chapel, and then went to the W instead, where he had not only no reasonable central wall-space inside for his Lady Altar (because of the W portal, which remained open) but also had to go so close to the ravine that he could not have a W entrance into the chapel at all. Its general appearance can therefore to-day only be appreciated from the other side of the river, and that can never have been otherwise. The chapel consists of nave and inner and outer aisles, all embattled at a later date. The height of the five parts steps down gently in two stages. The whole Galilee is not high, and so, seen from the W, appears to the eye no more than an offering at the feet of the cathedral. Of Pudsey's exterior only the patterning of the W front and the N doorway remain. The W front has against the substructure a tier of blank, corbel-like arches, then a tier of blank intersected arches, and then a large lozenge pattern, different from the earlier lozenges in that these were slightly raised like scales or tiles, whereas Pudsey's is a diagonal trellis of thick rope.* The N doorway is externally redone by *Wyatt*. In that form it has three orders with zigzag and crenellation motifs in the arches, nothing like as rich as Pudsey's portals at the castle and in the cloister. The windows of the Galilee are all of a late date, partly of Bek's time, intersected and cusped or of the type with three lancet lights under one two-centred arch. The three

* It can best be seen inside a little chamber in the W wall of the Galilee to which access is from the Galilee itself.

main W windows were replaced in the early C 15. The new ones have depressed pointed heads, one transome each, and minimum Perp panel tracery.

We now come to the great *novum opus* of the cathedral, the E TRANSEPT or CHAPEL OF THE NINE ALTARS. This replaced the apsidal E end of Carileph's church. It was planned, it seems, as early as 1235, when an indulgence was granted for contributions to the 'novum opus ... apud orientalem ecclesiae partem', and begun in 1242 ('Anno Domini MCCXLII incipit Thomas * novam fabricam ecclesiae'). In 1253 already it was in a state which made it possible for the monks to move in ('Eodem anno intraverunt monachi novum chorum') but had at that time no doubt only some temporary roof at a comparatively low level. It was not yet completed in 1278, when another indulgence tried to produce donations 'at reparacionem novae fabricae Dunelm ecclesiae celerius consummandam'. The conception of an E end stretching out to the N and S just like a transept is most unusual. The only parallel in England, and indeed the immediate predecessor of the Nine Altars, is the E end of Fountains Abbey in the North Riding, completed by an abbot who ruled from 1220 to 1247. This is a N country parallel, and, although much has been made of the fact that in 1235 the Bishop of Durham was Richard Poore who as Bishop of Salisbury had begun the cathedral there, there really are no architectural relations between Salisbury and Durham.‡

Yet the fact remains that the Nine Altars, especially in the interior, are essentially in the North country style. The show front is the E side, and this has unfortunately greatly been interfered with. *Wyatt* restored it with much licence, inserting the deplorably thin rose window. He

* De Melsanby, the then Prior.

‡ Elias de Derham is sometimes also brought into discussion of the authorship of the Nine Altars. However, his name was de Dereham rather than Durham although he was in charge of the building funds of Salisbury Cathedral from *c.* 1220 to *c.* 1245, he did not accompany Bishop Poore to the north and appears at Durham only once, in 1229, as a witness together with the Bishops of Wells and Carlisle and others who evidently had travelled to Durham for the purpose.

replaced one of the C15, and so we do not know at all what the great architect's original design was. One has to be careful not to use the present-day term architect too freely in dealing with the master masons of the Middle Ages, but in the case of the Nine Altars is it known that at that time one *Richard of Farnham* was 'architector novae fabricae'.* The E end is so wide that it looks like a whole English 'screen façade' of the C13. It is divided into three times three parts. The angles and the two main inner divisions are marked by broad and strong buttresses, the angles being in addition crowned by turrets whose detail, however, is far from reliable.‡ The turrets, of course, repeat at the NW and SW angles of the transept. The three outer bays of the E front on the l. and the r. have three long lancet windows each with smaller lancets above. The windows are separated by buttresses not as heavy as those making the main division. The centre instead of the buttresses has projecting uprights without any setbacks. They form hoods to the three main lancets giving them deep shadow. Above that is the rose window. The S front of the Nine Altars is divided into two bays by a heavy middle buttress. Each bay has two tiers of two lancet windows (provided with delicate Perp tracery in the early C15), a curiously even composition without any gradation to a climax. The master who, after all this had been done or begun, designed the N front must have felt that. The front 24 had been started in the same way as that on the S; *see* the foundations of the central buttress. But the new master (aware no doubt of the glorious E window of the Angel Choir at Lincoln, put in about 1275) decided to give the Nine Altars another such window, far larger than any Durham (or the whole North) had seen before. The JOSEPH WINDOW is of six lights, with a three-light

* In another document he is called a mason, *caementarius*. In addition, on the corner stone of one of the central buttresses at the E end is an inscription: 'Posuit hanc petram *Thomas Moises*.'

‡ The N turrets are due to *Wyatt*. The S pinnacles are earlier, but it is not clear from illustrations whether they have not also been adjusted.

intersecting pattern as the main feature and with eleven foiled circles to enliven the spaces between the main intersecting bars. Lincoln also operates entirely with such simple forms, but the motif of intersection is more characteristic of the Late than of the High Early English style. It marks the very moment when England left the French pattern of Amiens and set out on her own voyage of discoveries which led her so far away from France and to all the enchantments of the Dec style. The Nine Altars is a very early example of this, and the interior will show how conscious the designer was of its importance. It is less classical than the Westminster-Lincoln system of tracery, as it makes the positions and sizes of the foiled circles a little less logical. At Lincoln you could not alter any size or any location without upsetting the whole composition; here richness begins to have precedence over clarity.

After 1200 the only additions were the C14 and C15 windows mentioned in passing and the crossing tower, until we come to the restorations, first of *James Wyatt* in 1795, then in 1845 and 1850 (crossing tower), and then in 1870–6 by *Sir George Gilbert Scott*.

11 INTERIOR. The character of the work at Durham changed so little between its inception in 1093 and the completion of the nave in 1133 that the visitor, after entering the church by the N portal and sitting down in the nave to abandon himself to his first impressions, can be certain that it is essentially the design of the first great master that he is looking.

The impression is overpowering. The forms which surround him are domineering to the utmost, without, however, being brutal. The force of the impact is conducted with a supreme mastery. The size of Durham is not greater than that of our other Norman cathedrals. The nave is 201 ft long by 39 ft wide and 73 ft high. That compares, for instance, with the 248 by 40 by 72 ft of Ely or the 174 by 34 by 68 ft of Gloucester. Yet the effect is quite different. That has chiefly two reasons: one the design and proportions of the elevations, the other the shape of the chief members used. As for the elevation, it consists of nave arcade, gallery, and clerestory, as in nearly all major Norman churches of England and Normandy. But it could be interpreted in two ways in the direction from w to e and in two ways in the direction from floor to roof. Concerning the first, all piers could be identical or nearly so as at St Étienne in Caen and Ely, in which case a rapid and uninterrupted progress towards the altar is symbolized, or they could be of alternating shapes, every second pier being superordinate in design and every second subordinate. This was done in Normandy at Jumièges, c. 1035–65, and it is done at Durham, whose compound piers alternate with circular ones. In this case progress towards the e is slower, every two bays being felt as one square major bay. One is inclined to halt in the middle of each of these major bays and take them in centrally. This experience can be had at Jumièges as at Durham, but whereas at Jumièges the subordinate columns are indeed subordinate, at Durham they are given an enormity of size which in the end remains the distinctive feature of the whole cathedral. These columns or round piers are 27 ft high and nearly 7 ft in diameter. The monument to James Britton in the nave, with the deceased reclining comfortably on a mattress on which he has placed an open book, could be put inside one of the piers, and if he had a moderator lamp he could continue reading and musing in that circular cell. Moreover, the piers are patterned in nobly scaled grooved designs. So everything is done to give them the utmost importance, and it is the mighty impact of the piers from left and right which makes one feel so utterly overwhelmed. But there is nothing savage in this attack. The proportions are actually handled with a sense of balance rarely achieved in the Norman style. One has to study the elevation to appreciate that. At Ely arcade and gallery are nearly of the same height. Hence the same sense of uniform movement which is present in the w–e direction prevails in the upward movement as well. At Gloucester, on the other hand, the gallery is so low and its openings are so small that its effect on the eye is hardly more than that of a band above the arcade. At Durham the gallery is neither too large nor too small. It is there in its own right, yet can never compete with the cyclopic arcade. The actual proportion of gallery to arcade is 5 : 2. Niceness of proportions is so rarely aimed at in early medieval buildings on such a large scale that, if one has not been to Durham for a long time and has only seen the cathedral in the meantime in occasional postcards or illustrations, one is every time shocked by the sheer bigness of everything, starting from the blank arcading along the outer walls of the aisles which is no more than an enrichment of the dado of the walls and yet has columns of more than the height of a man.

The nave, where most visitors will experience their first impressions of the interior design, is not the earliest part of the Norman church. It was begun at the E end, as has been said before, and here then must our detailed examination start. William of St Carileph's CHANCEL was built with a large apse terminating the chancel nave and two subsidiary apses (encased in square walls) terminating the chancel aisles, a type of E end usual in Normandy, not unusual in Norman England, and derived from the great monastic church at Cluny as it was built in the later C10. The foundation of the apse at Durham has been excavated and can be seen.* The apses and the chancel with its aisles were complete by 1104, when the shrine of St Cuthbert was transferred to the new church. The chancel is not as easily seen as the nave, because of the stalls, organ, Bishop's Throne, etc. The system is of two double bays E of the crossing, and then originally a long piece of solid wall behind which lay the aisle apses with their thick E walls. At the E end of that wall the main apse followed. The aisles have the blank arcading already referred to. It has coupled columns with block capitals and intersected arches of quite a multiform moulding, a surprisingly early occurrence of the Norman motif of intersecting arches and altogether of a certain *finesse* of detailing. The aisle windows are C14 (*see* above). The vaulting of the aisles is

* Trapdoor in the Feretory behind the High Altar, also s of the main N pillar at the entry to the Nine Altars.

done by means of cross-ribs, the earliest surviving ribs in 13a the cathedral. The European importance of these ribs has already been discussed. Their mouldings again are remarkably refined. They and the transverse arches rest on tripartite shafts against the outer walls and against the nave piers.

These piers, to say it again, alternate between compound and circular. The two circular piers on each side are spiral-grooved on a wonderfully bold scale. The painting of Romanesque piers in spiral, lozenge, and other geometrical patterns was of course not at all unusual. Notre-Dame-le-Grande at Poitiers has preserved a specially complete display of such painted piers. Other examples are St Savin, also in Poitou, and St Mary-in-Capitol at Cologne. But to do the same thing sculpturally may well have been an innovation of the great Durham designer who was so clearly out to combine force and splendour. The innovation caught on at once in Britain, and examples are found as far N as Dumfermline and as far S as Norwich and Waltham Abbey near London, apart from Selby and the Crypt at York Minster.* The only slight disappointment in the original design at Durham is the way in which at the back, towards the aisles, the cylindrical piers suddenly become tripartite to hold arches and ribs of the aisle vaults, an indication perhaps of how new the idea of diagonal ribs altogether was.

The circular piers have low circular capitals in which the plain segments characteristic of block capitals are simply multiplied. Multi-scalloped capitals are a later stage than that of Durham East. The superordinate piers are really large chunks of solid wall enriched by three groups of three demi-shafts. The middle ones go right up to the vault, the others support the arcade arches, which have again got quite refined mouldings. The capitals are

* That deeply carved ornamentation of Romanesque columns may not have been confined to Britain can perhaps be deduced from the surviving small columns in the crypts of the churches of St Peter at Utrecht and St Lebuinus at Deventer in Holland and also from *Robert Campin's* painting at the Prado in Madrid.

single-scalloped, an elementary form of scalloping developed immediately from the block capital.* The gallery has a twin opening under one containing arch for each arch of the arcade below. The capitals are again single-scalloped. The gallery can be used, although its outer windows are very small. The visitor will notice that it is crossed by transverse arches. These are neither decoration nor adornment, but part of the provisions regarded as necessary by the architect who planned to give the Durham chancel its vaults. It must be repeated again that there was, as far as we know, no precedent whatever for the rib-vaulting of naves. In fact the vaulting of the wide expanses of nave was at the end of the C11 still a new experience altogether. The earliest nave vaults belong to France and the C11. They are all tunnel-vaults. The more difficult task of groin-vaulting, where the weight of the vault is carried by four corner points instead of the whole side wall, as in the case of tunnel-vaults, had only been faced at the end of the C11 in the Rhineland (Speier) and probably also in Normandy. But Durham is not later than these and yet adds the refinement of ribs. As to accurate dates, if the beginning at Durham was in 1093 and the whole chancel was complete by 1104, the aisle vaults must certainly belong to about 1095 and the main vault to *c*. 1103–4. The latter date is confirmed by a legend re-told soon after, according to which St Cuthbert one night, immediately before the date assigned to the solemn transfer of his shrine, was so perturbed by the remaining muddle of wooden centerings inside that he came along and knocked down thoroughly but gently 'materia lignorum quae recentem presbiterii testudinem sustruebat' (William of Malmesbury). These chancel vaults were replaced by new ones in the C13 (*see* below), because they were already in 1235 'plenae fissuris et rimis'. This perhaps is additional confirmation of their experimental character. The existence of Norman vaults prior to the present ones can be deduced as well as seen. The deduc-

* In the Winchester transept in the 1070s both forms occur side by side.

tion, carried out in a masterly fashion by Bilson, can point to the fact that to the l. and r. of the triple shafts of the main pier which were to support the triple transverse arch there rises from the gallery cill yet one more shaft on each side. What can they have been meant to perform? Moreover, between the two gallery openings, i.e. above each circular pier, there rise from the same level another three shafts. The only explanation is that the middle one of these was intended to carry a subordinate transverse arch, whereas the lateral ones together with the lateral shafts of the compound piers were supports of ribs. As a confirmation of this, Bilson could point to marks on the clerestory wall facing the chancel, which were left by the original vault close to the present vault, when it was hacked down in the C13. These marks are unmistakable, and they give a shape of vault identical with that of the N transept.

The CROSSING rests on four arches each carried on three big demi-shafts like the transverse arches of the chancel. In addition there is in each corner one more shaft reaching right up into the tower masonry. This no doubt was meant to help in carrying the beams of the ceiling inside the tower. With the addition of the C15 crossing tower the ceiling was removed and the whole height of 155 ft opened. The C15 design has at its foot a gallery on corbels, then a zone of tall, slim, twin arches with crocketed canopies, and then the huge twin two-light windows with transomes and Perp tracery. The vault is star-shaped with tiercerons and liernes. The wonderful thing about this tower is the suddenness with which its quite un-Norman height meets the eye, after one has felt, in Norman terms, the nave itself to be so splendidly high.

The TRANSEPTS also were built between 1093 and 1104. Their aisled E side is indeed entirely a continuation of the system of the chancel except that when the outer circular pier was reached on the S side a broad horizontal zigzag pattern was substituted for the spiral pattern used so far. It seems to be the earliest instance in England of the Norman use of zigzags. Otherwise the E sides of the N and s transepts are identical to the top of the gallery. Then some puzzling disturbances seem to occur, proof of another uncertainty in conducting building which may be explained by the death of William in 1096, or perhaps of his master mason. The last bays on the N in the N transept and on the s in the s transept have one shaft reaching to the vault without any capital and without any function. It can perhaps be assumed that a minor transverse arch was here projected, it was then felt that the bays would become too narrow, one wide quadripartite vault was substituted, and the shaft allowed to run to waste. Alternatively the shaft may be an indication that the monks, left without guidance and perhaps without funds after William's death, had decided to give up his hazardous idea of major vaults. There are indeed other indications pointing in the same direction. To appreciate them the upper parts of the transepts must be examined in some further detail. On the E sides between the gallery openings above the inner circular piers there are two demi-shafts instead of the three of the chancel. In the chancel they supported transverse arch and ribs. Here they were meant to support ribs only. That would result in a composition of two cross-ribbed bays without transverse arch between, a somewhat unsatisfactory arrangement but one which was indeed executed and continued in the nave. Then we come to the clerestory. This differs in the transepts from the chancel and in both from each other. In the chancel there simply was one window with solid wall to the l. and r. In the N transept there is the much more handsome arrangement of a tripartite stepped group of arches with the window in the higher middle one and with a wall passage. This composition appears a litttle earlier at the N transept of Winchester. In the s transept at Durham we find a much odder arrangement, though it is now obscured. On the W it can be seen more clearly than on the E side. There is also a tripartite composition. But the side arches are as high as the middle arch, and that, it will at once be realized, makes vaulting impossible. The vaults, as finally put on, indeed cut into the side arches.

So here is proof that between 1096 and 1099, when the monks were in charge, the adventurous spirit of William went and flat ceilings were preferred to vaults. The W sides of both transepts even at gallery level look in fact much cruder and heavier in all their details (quite probably the work of an in-between phase with no architect of vision on the spot). Then, perhaps with the election of Flambard in 1099, things changed again. The N transept received its Normandy-Norman tripartite clerestory and its vaults, and after this had been completed the S transept was also vaulted, in disregard of the timid clerestory design. And as the year 1110 was probably now reached, the ribs were adorned with zigzag work.

The zigzag became the one distinguishing feature of the NAVE. The blank arcades of the outer aisle walls indeed continue so unchanged right round the church that perhaps their outer walls had already been set out to a height of ten feet or so in the very early days. In addition the easternmost parts of the newer arcades and galleries must have been started; for they are a necessary abutment of the W crossing arch and the crossing tower. In fact we find the very first gallery openings identical with the E parts, and it is quite instructive to trace the joint between the old and the new work in detail. The most interesting thing is that there are no vaulting shafts at all between the twin openings of the galleries. That must mean that this stage in the easternmost bay was reached before Flambard's new master began. He accepted the design, and we do not know what he intended to do about vaulting. For the vault was only put on after 1128, and then it was placed simply on corbels in the spandrels between the gallery openings. The nave vaults are like those of the inner bays of the transepts, i.e. oblong and cross-ribbed with transverse arches stuck only above the main piers and not above the circular subordinate piers. Such oblong rib-vaults may be evolutionarily particularly interesting, as the High Gothic style of the C13 used them without exception, but they are visually not as satisfactory as those of the chancel must have been. The vaults call for
CD.—4

transverse supports on both sides. As it is, they seem to
limp or sag a little where the arches are lacking. In the detail the zigzag now appears everywhere; in the aisle vaults
and the main vault, in the arcade arches and gallery arches,
and in the clerestory. Other modifications of the original
scheme (to which however, by and large, the C12 architect remained remarkably faithful) are no doubt improvements. He introduced two more and equally successful
patterns for the circular piers, one of lozenges, the other
of close vertical flutings, and he did not stick to the back
of his circular piers tripartite bits for the support of the
aisle vaults, but, on the contrary, made the wall supports
of these vaults also semicircular or rather segmental.

Finally the C12 master introduced two more new
features, and these are of special interest, considering the
date of the vaults (the nave was completed in 1128 and
vaulted between 1128 and 1135). Inside the galleries, the
transverse arches are no longer semicircles as in the chancel but quarter-circles, and a quarter-circle struck from the
clerestory wall to the outer aisle wall is for all intents
and purposes a flying buttress and had been used as such
by the French already in the C11 to abut tunnel-vaults
(Nevers, Clermont Ferrand, etc.). Secondly the transverse
arches across the nave itself (and this influences its
appearance considerably) are pointed and no longer semicircular. This also has of course its technical advantages.
The thrust of a heavy vault will be carried down more
safely along the steeper curve of a pointed arch than along
the flatter curve of a semicircle. This again was understood in France at the same time or probably a little earlier
(at Cluny in the new building begun in 1089 and then at
Autun, also in Burgundy). But Durham is certainly
amongst the earliest buildings making use of pointed arches
for vaults.

The w end of the nave is disturbed a little in its elevation by the two towers. They need strong corner supports,
and so instead of a fourth pair of circular piers, as one
would expect them, the superordinate, compound piers
are here repeated, and in the vaults two oblong bays ap-

pear with a proper transverse arch between. In the vaulted
chambers beneath the towers the staircases are an ugly,
unintegrated interference (as they are in the W corners of
the transept). The W wall must be imagined with the big
original W portal. This has, facing the nave, only one
order of columns and one zigzag frieze in the arch, but in
addition an outer frieze of foliage embracing medallions
with animals and monsters, an innovation for Durham.
The outer, originally exterior side of this portal is much
grander. It must be mentioned in conjunction with the
Galilee. But there are two more PORTALS in the nave, and
these have now to be examined. They both lead from the
S aisle to the cloister. The more easterly one is interesting
as the earliest of the Durham portals. It must belong to
the work complete by 1104. The order of columns here
has capitals, different from all others at Durham, except
those in the Castle Chapel, but similar to late CII capitals in other places in England. They have the crudest
of volutes and just a few lancet-like leaves rising up to
them. The arch is moulded like the blank arches of the
walls. The other S portal, on the other hand, has three
orders of columns, the outer ones being decorated with
zigzag, the inner with a lozenge pattern and a tiny leaf
design in each lozenge, a playful small-scale repetition of
the grooving of the cylindrical piers. The arches have zigzag but also foliage with medallions. It can perhaps be
assumed that the appearance of foliage and human figures
in the W and S portals (and also the N portal; *see* above
under Exterior)* belongs to the years, when the nave was
being completed, about 1130. This tendency towards increased luxury and elegance is one noticeable in other
major churches of the second third of the century as well.

At Durham it reached its climax with the buildings for
which Hugh de Puiset or Pudsey (1151–95) was responsible. It was he, as we have seen, who, about 1170–5,
placed in front of the W portal the GALILEE or Lady 14
Chapel, inspired probably by the aisled narthexes of

* Its interior face has two orders and again zigzag as well as medallions.

French, especially Burgundian and Cluniac churches. Attention has already been drawn to the fact how unusual is a Lady Chapel at the W end, and the story deserves telling that Pudsey was so disgusted by the idea of having to admit women to the E parts of his church that he rather placed the chapel as far W as could be done. It is true anyway that a line in grey local marble in the floor of the nave just E of the main N doorway marks how far women were allowed to penetrate into the church. The Galilee is still entirely Norman in style, but this Late Norman is in its character very different from the earlier work, and one can well understand that the Bishop in his late years showed so much appreciation of the arriving Gothic style. In the Galilee all is lightness. The nave is four bays long and divided from the inner aisles and then from the outer aisles by thin coupled but detached shafts of Purbeck marble (the only occurrence of this southern material at Durham) carrying waterleaf capitals and arches elaborately enriched by zigzag. The pairs of shafts placed at right angles to the main direction of the Galilee were later found too flimsy a support, and early in the C15 were strengthened by two sandstone shafts for each pair, with capitals remarkably faithfully copied from the old ones. The idea was taken from the Great Hall at Bishop Auckland, where the piers looked from the beginning like the present ones in the Galilee. The Galilee was originally lit by upper side windows in the inner aisles. These are blocked but remain easily visible. They had no nook-shafts but roll-mouldings all round. The main W PORTAL of the cathedral can here be admired in its size and details. It has four (originally five) orders and generous zigzag ornamentation, with again an outer frieze of medallions with leaves. It was blocked early in the C15, when Cardinal Langley here erected an altar and a monument for himself (*see* Furnishings, below).* The windows are all of later centuries. With their clear glass they make Pudsey's room much too light. One feels in it as though outdoors, an impression certainly misleading

* The timber roofs are also no doubt of his time.

After the completion of the Galilee nothing important was done for sixty years at least. Then the decision was taken to replace the apses of William of St Carileph's church by a far more ambitious and spacious E end. The old E end had allowed the placing of three altars into the three apses. Now, behind the remaining High Altar, another NINE ALTARS were to be provided. The peculiar 23 conception of an E transept has been commented on above. We must now describe it and try to analyse its aesthetic effect. If that of the Norman cathedral is essentially one of colossal forces held in balance, the Nine Altars neither operate with forces of such weight nor want to achieve balance. The effect aimed at is one of sustainedly stressed verticals at the expense of the horizontals, and one of forces compressed into shafts of extreme slenderness. To achieve extreme height the designer (as has been said, he probably was *Richard of Farnham*) even went to the expedient of lowering the floor below that of the chancel aisles and even more of the chancel, and the Feretory behind. The Feretory, i.e. the space behind the altar where the shrine was going to repose, is at chancel level and thus a good 5 ft 9 in. above the new transept. The transept and the E parts of the chancel aisles which had to be adapted to connect the old work with the new continue the blank arcading introduced by William of St Carileph's mason. But instead of coupled colonnettes, these are now single, and they are in addition slimmer and taller and made of grey Frosterley marble (the Durham substitute for Purbeck) to emphasize their linear thinness. This is symptomatic. On a large scale it is taken up by the very tall lancet windows of the transept, by the extreme multiplication of shafts between them, and by making every second in each cluster of shafts of Frosterley so as to stress once more the thin uprightness of them.

The E side of the Nine Altars is divided into nine bays, inside like outside. They are separated by compound piers and each has two lancet windows above each other. The lancets are tall, even if not as excessively tall as those of Yorkshire. The shafts lie well ahead of the windows allowing

for a wall passage at cill level of the lower as well as
the upper tier, and this two-layer arrangement adds
greatly to the transparency and lightness of the composition. The piers are of nine shafts plus two on each
side which are the nook-shafts of the adjoining windows.
The three middle bays, of a width exactly corresponding
to the Norman nave, are treated as one unity, as they are
in the exterior. This is done by giving the wall-piers between the three middle windows only five shafts each, but
the wall-piers flanking the middle bays thirteen each. The
dominance of this centre of the E wall is yet further
stressed by the rose window above, and although the rose
as we see it is entirely *Wyatt's*, we can well believe that a
rose window has always existed in this place. The rose
window, it is true, has never been a favourite with the
British, but it could be seen, for example, at Lincoln (*c.*
1225).

So much for the general composition of the E wall. The
S wall is simpler but in harmony. The same wall-arcading
is followed by the same two tiers of lancets, though they
are here indeed of Yorkshire slenderness. Curiously
enough there are not three or five but four of them. The
four are grouped in two pairs with a big central outer buttress taking the middle. The tracery, as has already been
said, is C15.

In detail the blank arcades have lively stiff-leaf capitals
and carry trefoiled pointed arches. In the spandrels are
head-stops (as far as one can still see exceedingly well
carved), and above these blank sunk pointed quatrefoils.
The forms almost crowd each other out, with a tendency
to overdo things which can often be noticed in the E.E.
style. Higher up the heads of the principal tier of windows
are enriched by dog-tooth, friezes of separate stylized
flowers, and head-stops. Finally the vaults are reached.
They are set out in an interesting way. The outer bays are
quadripartite and relatively narrow. The next bays of the
vaults comprise two of the elevation. The designer here,
instead of using two quadripartite vaults, preferred one
sexpartite one, i.e. a type popular in France up to the end

of the C12, in Early Gothic days, and taken over in England only very occasionally, at Canterbury in 1175, in the Lincoln transepts about 1210, etc. At Durham the reason was no doubt that the perfect symmetries of his E bays had made the designer unaware of the fact that the chancel aisles, when he opened them out towards his *novum opus*, would be wider than his bays opposite the aisles. It must be remembered that, according to medieval custom, the old building would have been left complete and usable as long as possible and the new walls built up around it. So the E, S, and N walls may well have gone up and even the return walls on the W sides begun, before the old aisle and nave apses were finally demolished. Then the irregularity was noticed and the sexpartite vaults designed so that the transverse ribs ran askew. This is not very nice, especially in relation to the bosses, but more tolerable than it would have been in two quadripartite vaults. The centre finally has a vault of a form invented, it seems, by the Durham architect. From the main piers in the corners spring eight instead of four ribs. They slightly diverge so that in the centre the eight are just far enough from each other to contain a large ring. Bent into the ring are the seated figures of the four Evangelists, pieces of exquisite carving, clearly of the same style as the bosses of the Angel Choir at Lincoln, begun in 1256 and 26 completed about 1280. The foliage and figures in the other bosses are of the same style and the same quality. One should have a good field-glass ready to examine them and wait for a sunny morning.

Now Lincoln, as has been pointed out when the exterior was discussed, is also responsible for the Joseph Window, i.e. the N window of the Nine Altars and without any doubt the finest piece of Gothic design at Durham. The composition need not be described again, but what strikes one immediately when looking N is the tremendous and at first inexplicable depth of the intersected tracery. Such vigorous relief is just what one would expect the master of the vault sculptures to have wanted. And so he took a hint from the clerestory of the Angel Choir at

Lincoln, where the tracery is duplicated in two layers to allow for a wall passage to pass through, and did the same here. The mullions and the main intersecting arches are inside as well as outside the wall passage, the trefoiled and cinquefoiled circles are only in the outer wall. The effect is one of breath-taking vigour and splendour.

Only when the Chapel of the Nine Altars was nearing completion was the joining up with the Norman work carried out. It was a bigger job than had probably at first been contemplated. The Norman chancel vaults, it will be remembered, had as early as 1235 been badly cracked. They were now taken down and rebuilt in the style of the mature C13, with transverse arches and ribs richly decorated. The Norman vaulting-shafts at the same time were given new, thick foliage capitals, and little, rather ugly, Frosterley shafts were added high up for the wall-arches. Between the last Norman pier and the main apse there had been a broad strip of bare wall. This must have looked too solid to the Gothic builders, and so shafts, again alternately of sandstone and Frosterley marble, were placed in front of it. Beyond them another bay of the arcade was opened and thus the Nine Altars reached. The new bay is rather makeshift in its composition, a none too happy compromise between what the old style necessitated and the new style demanded. The elevation of arcade, gallery, clerestory is kept. But the arcade has most oddly shaped arches starting with a vertical piece and then breaking round into the curve. The gallery has a wide tripartite opening with steeply pointed arches which, however, to have a containing arch, like the Norman work, are placed beneath a depressed arch, the only motif of the C13 at Durham to compare immediately with Salisbury. The clerestory has two shafted lancet windows with a shaft between, but they are not placed centrally above the gallery. And the vault is sexpartite with the transverse rib running almost horizontally along the N-S ridge. However, these discrepancies are remedied by a display of decoration so luxuriant that it clearly shows the mood of the end of the century and the approaching Dec style.

Foliage in the blank arcading on the ground floor level had been entirely of stiff-leaf type. These capitals indeed must have been carved shortly after the beginning of the work, i.e. *c.* 1250. The capitals of the arches between chancel aisles and E transept, on the other hand, bring in beasts, birds, harpies, and other monstrous combinations of man and beast.* The shafts along the blank piece of wall to the N and S of the altar space rest on demi-figures. They end in capitals again with human and animal forms as well as foliage, and carry trefoiled arches under steep crocketed gables. In other capitals one can see a fight between a lion and a gryphon, and a fox stealing geese.

Even the string-courses below the gallery and below the clerestory have their leaves and beasts and birds and little men. And so it goes on into the gallery capitals and the clerestory capitals. The very lintel in the clerestory which connects the shaft between the twin openings with the outer wall has figure carving. Finally high up, on each side of the E end of the chancel, are two much larger figures of angels. They are again of the very best quality and clearly derived from the Angel Choir at Lincoln. One hesitates to date them and the capitals with their rich fauna before 1280.

FURNISHINGS (from W to E). GALILEE: WALL PAINTINGS. St Oswald and St Cuthbert, in the jambs of the arched recess N of the former portal, and decoration with painted hangings against the back wall of the recess. These are most valuable survivals of Bishop Pudsey's time, *c.* 1170-5. The bold leaf-frieze also deserves study. The dominant colours are yellow, red, and green. – PAINTING. Triptych of the Crucifixion with Christ carrying the Cross and the Virgin mourning Christ, said to be Westphalian, *c.* 1500; given by Viscount Gort in 1935. – STAINED GLASS. Some figures in the Perp tracery at the W end, and a jumble of small fragments; all of Langley's time. – MONUMENTS. It is owing to Cardinal Langley (1406–37) that the W portal of the cathedral was blocked. He wished to place a new altar here and his own tomb. It

* Miss Wynn Reeves compares them with the N transept at York.

is an impressive composition, with the very large tomb-chest, without any effigy, in the middle and steps to the l. and r., leading up to the altar. A wooden reredos originally stood behind it. – The Venerable Bede: also a plain big tomb-chest, with black marble top; no effigy. Erected in 1542. The remains of Bede had been transferred to the Galilee in 1370. The inscription was carved in 1830.

NAVE AND AISLES: FONT, 1663. A beautifully simple, yet elegant example of the baluster type. – The FONT CANOPY is one of the most gorgeous of the many pieces of elaborate woodwork made for Bishop Cosin during the eleven years that he held the see of Durham. It stands more than 40 ft high and is at the base about 9 ft across. It is octagonal with fluted composite columns and a bold acanthus frieze at ground floor level. That kind of decoration goes well with the shape of the font itself. But above, between the next tier of columns, Gothic tracery and Gothic crocketed gables appear, and from there it goes on entirely Gothic with tier after tier of traceried and gabled canopies. – ORGAN. The organ case is of 1683 and was made for one of the first of the Father Smith instruments. It was removed from its original position in 1846 and reassembled as adequately as could still be done in 1905. It is wholly in the Baroque vein with no more of Cosin's Gothic reminiscences. Scrolly pediments, thick garlands, terms ending in the heads of young angels the size of live young girls or boys. – DOOR. Door towards the cloister near the w end of the aisle with a splendid display of iron scrolls; original C12 work. – DOOR KNOCKER. N doorway outside; *see* p. 85 – WALL PAINTINGS. Remains in the s aisle have allowed the reconstruction in one bay of the blank arcading of the painted wall decoration as it originally was. Small-size ashlar imitated by painted joints, and in the middle of each stone a many-petalled flower. A frieze of scrolly tendrils with small crocket-like leaves above. The colours are buff, black, and red. – STAINED GLASS. N aisle, 'Good Shepherd' by *Wailes*. – w window, Tree of Jesse, uncommonly good, rather sombre work of *Clayton & Bell*, 1867. – MONU-

35,a
and
b

32a

MENTS. At the E end of the S aisle was the Neville Chantry. It occupied two bays. Of the effigies erected here two now stand in two bays of the arcade, sadly damaged: John Lord Neville † 1388 and his wife, alabaster, on a fine 39b tomb-chest with shields and mutilated but still elegant figures of mourners, and Ralph Lord Neville † 1367 and his wife, also alabaster, hopelessly badly preserved. – MINERS' MEMORIAL, S aisle. Made up of four cherubs preserved at the cathedral from some big Cosin piece, and fragments from a Baroque (Spanish?) altar used as a fireplace at Ramside Hall. – Sir George Wheler †1724, S aisle. Standing wall monument with bust against a reredos background; not big. – James Britton, by *C. Smith*, 1839, comfortably semi-reclining on a mattress rolled up to give support to his elbow, a scheme usual about 1700, but unusual in the C19.

CROSSING AND TRANSEPTS. A pulpit given to the cathedral by Bishop Lord Crewe (1674–1721) was replaced by one in 1876 which *Sir George Gilbert Scott* designed ill-advisedly in the Italian Cosmati style of the Shrine of the Confessor at Westminster Abbey. – The LECTERN which stands opposite the pulpit is still more recent. It was designed by *D. McIntyre* about 1934 in the style of 1700. – The ROOD SCREEN also by *Scott* and with its three wide arches and its polished granite columns just as much out of sympathy with the C12 as with the C13 cathedral. It should be replaced. – SCREENS to the chancel aisles, Cosin work, round arch with Gothic tracery spandrels between fluted pilasters supporting an acanthus frieze. – PRAYER-DESK, right under the crossing, also Cosin work, with poppy-head ends. – CLOCK. Originally erected by Prior Castell (1494–1519), rebuilt and much altered by Dean Hunt in 1630, recently reconstructed in the S transept. It is a huge contraption in a mixed Gothic and Jacobean style, and one would like to know, whether Dean Hunt, when he re-used the Perp polygonal turrets at the corners of his openwork dome with its pinnacles, thought already in terms of a playful revival. After all, Hunt's was the time, when Cosin, as

Vicar of Brancepeth, started refurnishing the church there. The doors below are painted with a pretty church interior with little figures, no doubt by a Dutchman. – – STAINED GLASS. S transept S window, by *Clayton & Bell*. – MONUMENTS. Matthew Woodifield † 1826, E aisle N transept, a very self-assertive Grecian monument of white marble. Absurdly short Greek Doric columns on a big plinth. Entablature above with segmental top and acroteria, a large urn or ball on top. – Bishop Shute Barrington, by *Chantrey*, 1833, standing wall monument of white marble, with the kneeling figure of the Bishop in profile.

CHANCEL AND CHANCEL AISLES: REREDOS (NEVILLE SCREEN) and SEDILIA, both of stone, given by John Lord Neville and made in London of 'French peere'.* It was begun in 1372 and consecrated in 1380. It had originally 107 figures of alabaster. Even deprived of these, it remains precious. The style, as also that of the sedilia (four on each side of the chancel) is not really Perp yet. Perp tracery occurs only in very inferior places (on the pedestals of statues), and the term can only be applied if by Perp one really means perpendicular. For the verticals are indeed here emphasized to the almost complete exclusion of horizontals, but that is just what the new style, inaugurated at Gloucester before 1350, never does. Here there are five major canopies and four subordinate canopies between, and all of them have hardly anything but long thin parallel uprights. The sky-line is as spiky as that of Edward II's Monument or other such masterpieces of the Dec style, though admittedly it is harder and drier. – ROOD SCREEN: *see* Crossing. The rood screen of Cosin's time has been dismantled, but fragments have been re-used. – CHOIR STALLS, 1665, that is under Cosin. His style is unmistakable, only the close ornamentation of the stall-ends is surprising. Otherwise there are the long, alternating columns and the high Gothic canopies and the backs with Gothic tracery and cherubs' heads. The first stalls on the l. and r. are distinguished by backs with thick garlands. The carver was *John Clement*. – STALL FRONTS.

* That is 'pierre'. But Boyle says it is of Dorset clunch.

One made up of parts of the same (Spanish?) altar which provided parts of the Miners' Memorial. Others with a very thick, oversized acanthus frieze. – COMMUNION RAIL, with fine pierced acanthus work, 1940, in the style of 1700. By *W. Hollis*. – PARCLOSE SCREENS to the aisles. Again Cosin work, and remarkably exact in the imitation of Perp screen tracery. In this case one is tempted to believe that the Bishop insisted on the actual copying of some surviving screen. – LECTERN. In the N chancel aisle. Metal, by *Scott*, laboriously ornate and highly dangerous to the reader's shins. – BISHOP'S THRONE. This forms part of the funeral monument which Bishop Hatfield erected for himself. – MONUMENTS. Bishop Hatfield, who died in 1381, built a chantry chapel for his tomb, and on the platform above this a new Bishop's Throne as part of a stone screen. As a composition it is unique, as a work of art it lacks imagination. The chapel is rather a solid and heavy piece with a segmental arch, cusped, with angels at the tips of the cusps flying upside down. The walls are panelled, each panel with an ogee-head. The effigy lies on a tomb-chest and is of alabaster. The interior vault has foliage bosses. The platform is reached by a staircase whose balustrade has C17 acanthus work. The balustrade of the platform itself seems earlier. The Throne is the centre of a screen with tall canopies originally no doubt meant for sculpture. The bottom part to the l. and r. of the throne proper has pierced panelling in an entirely Perp fashion. It is probably the earliest appearance of the Perp style in the county. – Bishop Skirlaw † 1405. Of his chantry chapel in the N chancel aisle only a bench along the wall with a display of heraldic shields remains. – Bishop Lightfoot † 1891. Recumbent effigy of white marble, by *Sir E. Boehm*, on a tomb-chest and placed under one of the Cosin screens. – Sixth Marquess of Londonderry † 1915 and his wife † 1919, bronze relief with kneeling figures, by *Tweed*. N chancel aisle.

NINE ALTARS: BALUSTRADE behind the feretory. Elizabethan, but mostly a C20 reconstruction, in the main from surviving parts, the cresting from a drawing of the time before it was renewed (1844). – SCULPTURE. Cross head from Neasham Abbey, C13, with stiff-leaf decoration and on one side the Crucifixion, on the other Christ in Majesty. – Saint, carrying his head in his hand, C15, on the feretory floor. – STAINED GLASS. N and central E windows by *Clayton & Bell*, 1877. – MONUMENTS. Epitaph to Dean Spencer Cowper † 1774, son of Earl Cowper. Unsigned, but exceedingly delicately done. Probably not a provincial workshop production. – Bishop van Mildert † 1836, seated white statue on circular base; carved by *John Gibson* in Rome.

PLATE. Paten, presented by Bishop Cosin. – Chalice, German or Dutch, C17. – Two Chalices, two Patens, two large Patens, two Flagons, two Loving Cups, three Almsdishes, all by *Butty & Dumée*, London, 1766. – Two Candlesticks, 1767.

THE CLOISTER AND THE BUILDINGS ROUND THE CLOISTER. Bishop Walcher (1071–80), we are told by Symeon, 'coepit aedificare habitacula monachorum'. There is indeed one part of the buildings round the cloister which seems in style to precede William of St Carileph and rather to harmonize with the chapel in the castle. It is the UNDERCROFT OF THE REFECTORY to the S of the cloister with rude groined vaults on piers only 3 ft high and tiny windows to the S with their heads cut out of stone, more Saxon than Norman looking, the PASSAGE to its E with short, unmoulded wall arcades and a tunnel-vault, the UNDERCROFT of the original Dormitory, now the DEANERY DRAWING ROOM (*see* below), with two tunnel-vaulted aisles divided by arches on short unmoulded piers, the masonry outside towards the cloister (the S part of the E range) which is very different from the neighbouring early C12 parts, and a triangular-headed recess in that wall immediately S of the Chapter House. Such a Saxon feature may well have been used by a native workman ten years or so after the Conquest.

In its present size the CLOISTER belongs, however, to

the great Norman building period of the cathedral. It seems to have been begun at the same time as the nave and built parallel with it. It has undergone many changes and is more profitably described topographically. The cloister arcades themselves were rebuilt by Bishops Skirlaw and Langley. They were completed in 1418. The tracery of the three-light openings is an odd, somewhat bleak invention of *c*. 1773. The timber ceilings with shields on the bosses are C15 but much restored in 1828.

The cloister is entered from the nave by one of two DOORWAYS. The one to the W is of the time of the lower stages of the nave, with three orders of shafts with block capitals. A comparison with the E doorway, clearly of Pudsey's time (*cf*. the castle doorway), is illuminating. Pudsey's doorway has also three orders of shafts, but the capitals are either scalloped with decoration, or of the water-leaf type. The arches are ornamented with rope and battlement friezes in the highest relief. A frieze of small petalled flowers also occurs. Zigzag is only used for minor purposes. The tendency to luxury and rather ostentatious display which had come into the Norman style in its latest stages is at once evident.

The EAST RANGE of the cloisters starts at the N end with a blocked doorway into the transept which must be of the same date as the transept. S of the transept follows the PARLOUR and the CHAPTER HOUSE. The Chapter House has, as was usual, a central entrance flanked by two windows. These have twin openings. All the arches here are enriched by zigzag in the style characteristic of the last stage in the building of the nave. The Chapter House was indeed completed by Bishop Rufus, i.e. between 1130 and 1140. The Parlour is tunnel-vaulted and has against its walls arcades of intersected arches. Above the arches runs a zigzag frieze. The same elevation is used for the Chapter House. This is a rib-vaulted room of ample and satisfying proportions. It has two square bays and an apse of equal width. The transverse arches rest on triple shafts, the ribs on corbels, as in the cathedral. The ribs are accompanied by fine zigzag friezes. The E end was pulled down in 1796, but rebuilt close to the original plan in 1895. Only the setting-out of the apse ribs was not copied, and Norman windows were put in for which there was no authority.

15a The apse ribs rest on caryatids, the originals of which are preserved in the Dormitory (*see* p. 114). They are a motif unique in England, but comparable to contemporary work in North Italy of the style of Niccolo, and in the South of France. The W window, tall, of five lights, with a fine two-centred arch was inserted in the C15.* Above the Parlour, a little earlier, a Library had been built. The room is the SONG SCHOOL now and recognizable by its five-light depressed pointed E and W windows. It was built in 1414–15. S of the Chapter House are three small chambers, used as the PRISON for light offences. The Usher's Door S of this connects with the Prior's Hall, i.e. the present Deanery.

The WEST RANGE starts at the N end with yet another Norman doorway. This, however, leads into the later 38a DORMITORY. The Dormitory is one of the most impressive parts of the monastic buildings of Durham. It is 194 ft long and 39 ft wide. It was built by Bishop Skirlaw in 1398–1404, instead of the original dormitory in the E range which was then reconditioned and made into the Prior's Hall (*see* Deanery). The masons of the work are known, *John Middleton* and *Peter Dryng*, but not the carpenter of the big, solid timber roof, cusped along the underside of the ridge-beam. The Dormitory has tall Perp two-light windows with two-centred heads. Below is a tier of small straightheaded windows of double the number of the upper ones. The Dormitory rests on an UNDERCROFT which seems to belong to the C13. It is divided along the middle by short circular piers and has heavy, simply chamfered arches and ribs.

The Dormitory now serves as the cathedral MUSEUM, and though it is not the job of these volumes to discuss the contents of museums, many of the objects here are too closely connected with the cathedral and its history to

* The STAINED GLASS in this window consists of C15 bits; the E windows have recent glass by *Hugh Easton*.

be omitted entirely. When the grave of St Cuthbert was opened in 1827, in it were found the coffin of the saint, his pectoral cross and his comb, and amongst other objects 4a parts of a stole and a maniple. The COFFIN was made at Lindisfarne in 698. It is of oak and has incised figures of Christ, the Virgin, saints and angels. They are a convincing rendering in two dimensions of the style of the early sculptured crosses of the North. The STOLE and the MANIPLE were embroidered for Aelflaed, queen of 8b Alfred the Great's successor, as a present to Bishop Frithestan of Winchester. They must thus be dated between 910 and 930. How they reached the North and were presented to the shrine of St Cuthbert is not certain. They show the art of drawing or painting of the early C10 at a height not to be presumed from any other surviving English work of contemporary date. There is nothing barbaric or violent about the figures or the ornament. In the Museum are also displayed the outstanding illuminated MANUSCRIPTS of the chapter library, and here again the figures in such a book as the *Cassiodorus In Psalmos*, Northumbrian, mid C8 (closely related to the more famous and more accomplished Lindisfarne Gospels at the British Museum) are clearly related to the style of the crosses. The writing of these C8 manuscripts is remarkable too (*see*, for example, the Bede Gospels). It is of a clarity, evenness, and beauty of proportion that makes all contemporary manuscripts of France or Italy look barbaric. No wonder that it was here that Charlemagne went to find a head for his schools. The collection of CROSSES at Durham is unique. It is true they are all fragmentary, and to tell their story need the plaster casts of the Bewcastle and Ruthwell Crosses and Acca's Cross at Hexham which are also exhibited. But with their help the various types of decoration can be studied ideally, the surprisingly antique and genuinely felt foliage scrolls and birds of some of the early ones, the figure style from the breadth and understanding of Bewcastle and Ruthwell to the dolls and dummies of some of the late pieces. Also displayed are some Saxon hogs-back GRAVESTONES, the originals of the Norman CARYATIDS which once carried the ribs of the Chapter House apse (*see* p. 112) and a panel said to come from the former Chancel Screen of the Cathedral and showing, one above the other, wo appearances of Christ after the Resurrection. In style these are Late Norman, and may date from about 1175. They are the most important pieces of sculpture of their date in the county.

The Undercroft in the SOUTH RANGE has already been mentioned as one of the earliest pieces of Norman architecture in the county. Above it was the REFECTORY, as was usual in Benedictine monasteries. This was, however, converted in 1684 into the CHAPTER LIBRARY. The high and low bookpresses, very much like those in contemporary Oxford and Cambridge libraries, remain, and the staircase leading up to the library (with heavy twisted balusters) and the restrainedly classical doorway from the cloister, with Tuscan pilasters. The anteroom into which this doorway leads and where the staircase is, has in its SW corner two straightheaded doorways of C14 form. These connect with the KITCHEN, in its way one of the most remarkable medieval buildings of England. It was built in 1366–70, and its ingenious designer is known to us by name. He was *John Lewyn*. The room is square, but made octagonal by having four big fireplaces in the four corners. The louvre is carried on broad ribs arranged so that they form a perfect eight-cornered star. Ribs are thrown from corner one to four and six, two to five and seven, three to six and eight, four to seven (and one), and five to eight (and two). By doing this a smaller octagon is left in the middle at the intersection of the ribs, and this carries the louvre. This delightful method of vaulting has no parallel in England and may either be *John Lewyn's* invention or due to inspiration that had come to him from Mohamedan vaults in Spain (Mosque Cordova). The layman is as a rule not sufficiently aware of the wide international knowledge which by travel or by clients' travel the master mason of the Middle Ages could possess.

THE COLLEGE GREEN AND THE BUILDINGS ROUND
THE COLLEGE GREEN. THE DEANERY (former
PRIOR'S LODGINGS). The Deanery is the link between
Cloister and College Green. It belongs to both. Its s side
overlooks the Green, but its Great Hall has Early Norman
walls built as part of Bishop Walcher's monastic accommodation round the Cloister (see p.110). The main apartment was the Hall, now Hall and Dining Room. This lies
in the SE corner of the Cloister, between Chapter House
and Refectory, and was the Monks' Dormitory before the
new dormitory was installed about 1400. That gives a
terminus ante quem for its present form. It was indeed remodelled in 1476. The roof dates from then, and the
panelling with small Flamboyant tracery motifs from
about fifty years later. The Hall rests on a two-aisled Norman basement with tunnel-vaults (see p. 110). But without the new Hall the Prior's Lodging had also been
complete. Its main apartments had been the Camera Inferior and the Camera Superior, that is broadly speaking
the present Drawing Room and the rooms below it. This
part, as also the masonry of the NE part, is mid C14.
Camera Inferior and Camera Superior are connected by a
stone newel staircase in a projecting turret. The Camera
Inferior is now subdivided, and the lower part has four
wooden Tuscan columns of the late C17. The Camera
Superior has Georgian windows of about 1760 and a contemporary ceiling. But its E end was at that time cut off
and here one bay of the original timber roof can still be
admired. Projecting from the E end of this room (the C14
Hall or Solar) and extending to the E is the Prior's Chapel,
the architecturally most valuable part of the Deanery,
though inside subdivided into a suite of rooms. It must
date from about 1220–30 and has nook-shafted lancet
windows (2E, 2N, 2W; the s windows are Georgian and
domestic) and a fine W doorway with one order of colonnettes. The chapel is on the upper floor. The doorway
now leads nowhere. It must originally have had an open
staircase or some timber gallery to the Camera Superior.
The Undercroft of the Chapel is in its pristine state. It

has a simpler single-chamfered doorway and four bays inside with short circular piers with moulded capitals and heavy single-chamfered arches and ribs. N of the Chapel the main NE rooms and the Library, which is (though nothing proves it to the eye now) the C14 Prior's Study. The windows and the bay window are Victorian. The basement below is tunnel-vaulted. N of this is King James I's Room. This has an excellent C15 ceiling with a cornice with a frieze of leafy tendrils and a cresting above (in the Devon chancel screen manner) and ribbed panels and bosses.

THE COLLEGE GREEN. The College Green is extremely pleasant to the eye, smaller and more secluded than a cathedral close, but larger, more lovable, and architecturally more informal than a cloister. None of the buildings around are of special value, but together and with the lawn and the loosely planted trees in the middle they could hardly be improved. The Green is entered from the outside world by the GATEHOUSE on the E which connects it with North Bailey. It is of the early C16, of two bays with star-vaults and bosses. The outer and inner gateways are single, the in-between gateway has a special side opening for pedestrians. Muniment Room above. Between the Gatehouse and the Deanery is the former Exchequer, the best of the houses on the Green. The inner walls are medieval, but the exterior with two projecting wings and all the windows are of about 1720. The S side of the Green is one solid but irregularly grouped and sized terrace of Georgian stone houses. Of earlier remains there are some C14 arches in the basement of the two houses W of the Choir School and a large blocked arcade of three arches on tall circular piers at the W end of the terrace. This is said to be part of the C14 GRANARY. The house used by the CHOIR SCHOOL follows to the W. It lies back and on its own and has a cemented seven-bay front of two and a half storeys with Gothick or Tudor windows of c. 1800 or a little later. But inside is a good late C17 staircase with thick twisted balusters. In front of the W range of buildings a CON-

DUIT HOUSE was placed in 1751, a remarkable effort in the early Gothic Revival, octagonal with little circular windows, a corbel-table with head-corbels and a parapet with the typical blank trefoils in circles of the C18 Gothic style (cf. Bishop Auckland, Gatehouse). Behind this stands the REGISTRY, early C19 Tudor, cemented and castellated. It has a three-aisled undercroft with short circular piers and single-chamfered arches and ribs. Then to the N, after an insignificant one-storeyed house of six bays, the STABLES in the NW corner, close to the Galilee, and in front of them part of the CITY WALL. The N wall of the Stables is Norman. It has in the lofts small windows, and these prove beyond doubt that we have here the remains of the monks' LATRINES. The windows gave light to the individual seats. 23 ft below the Stables, accessible by a newel-stair, still remains the MONKS' PRISON for major offences, a tunnel-vaulted Norman chamber with large blank arcades, obviously not in their original state. The room, rarely entered, remains one of the most moving evocations of the early monastery as known to us from the *Rites of Durham*.

THE CASTLE

St Cuthbert's Shrine reached Durham in 995. The site must 41 (after the Danish experiences) have been fortified in some form at once. It resisted sieges of the Scots about 1006 and 1038. These early structures were no doubt of wood. But a stone castle was begun immediately after the Conquest. In 1075 it was considered strong enough to be of value against a foreseen Danish attack. The Chapel indeed seems to go back to the seventies. Bishop Flambard early in the C12 built the wall between cathedral choir and keep and also new town walls, and Bishop Pudsey in the second half of the C12 did much to enlarge and beautify the castle. At his time the area occupied by buildings was considerable and hardly less than now, though the buildings were no doubt not of the intricacy of those of to-day.

Prior Laurence of Durham, in his C12 description, speaks indeed of the lofty embattled walls, of four gates, the keep, and a string of palatial structures with *porticus*.

The GATEHOUSE is mid C12 (*see* its rich zigzag arch and its rib-vault), though it was altered by Bishop Tunstall about 1530–50 and again beautified and romanticized under Bishop Barrington by *Wyatt* (cf. Bishop Auckland). The heavy doors are early C16. Of the buildings surrounding the Inner Bailey from W to NE the SW block, now occupied by the Kitchens and partly hidden by a lower block built by Cosin, i.e. *c.* 1660–70 (still with hood-moulded mullioned windows with round tops to the individual lights), is Norman. Norman is the main range due N with the former Great Hall and the present Gallery over, and Norman is the chapel E of this. Norman, of course, also was the original keep. Durham Castle is without doubt, although overlaid by much from many periods, one of the most completely preserved and most easily appreciated Norman strongholds in the country. It should teach those who still believe that the whole population of a Norman castle permanently crowded together in one keep, how extensive and solidly constructed and how luxurious the accommodation of a C12 castle could be.

The main contributors to the later building history of the castle were bishops Bek in the early C14, Hatfield in the late C14, Tunstall in the early C16, and Cosin between 1661 and 1672.

The buildings shall now be described topographically from W to E.

The Norman block just mentioned, at the SW end, was perhaps originally the keep. Bishop Fox in 1499 converted it into the KITCHEN and offices for the Great Hall to its N. His is the huge fireplace, his the brickwork (the earliest in Durham), his the louvre roof, and his the fine big wooden hatches. Dishes were passed through them, and servants then carried them into the Hall.

The GREAT HALL was probably built by Bishop Bek on Norman foundations. The undercroft with broad

arches but no piers is still extant. Of Bek's time is the
Doorway, sadly decayed, though protected by a porch and
portal added by Bishop Cosin in 1663. This has coupled
Ionic columns and a big rounded pediment decorated
with large branches. Urns above the columns, a crest
above the pediment. Cosin also added the heavy polygonal buttresses towards the courtyard with their ogee
tops. But before his time Bishop Hatfield, with his master
mason *John Lewyn*, had already made certain alterations
to the Hall. The timber roof is theirs. The windows have
been much tampered with in the C19. Reliable and
evidently of Bek's time are only the two shorter ones on
the w side, of two lights, with geometrical tracery. The
STAINED GLASS in the N window is by *Kempe*, 1882.
The gallery at the s end is also C19, but the two stone balconies above it belong to Fox's time, i.e. *c.* 1510. The Hall
now serves as the Dining Hall of University College,
Durham, and with its nearly 100 by 35 ft need not fear
comparison with the grandest halls of Oxford and Cambridge (Christ Church 115 by 40 ft, Trinity Cambridge
100 by 40 ft).

In the angle between the w or Hall range and the Norman N range, Cosin in 1662 built the BLACK STAIR-57b
CASE, one of the most impressive staircases of its time in
England. It has square stone walls with windows still like
those of the early C16, i.e. pre-classical (hood-moulds,
mullions, and arched lights), and runs up through three
upper storeys around a square open well. The balustrades
have thick pierced foliage carving. The newel posts are
now connected by Tuscan columns, but these are a later
addition. Originally the steps were only bonded into the
wall and otherwise unsupported.

The Norman range along the N side of the courtyard
does not tell its age to the onlooker from the courtyard or
the town. On the ground floor and first floor galleries have
been placed by Tunstall, i.e. in the second third of the
C16, in front of Pudsey's exterior masonry. A broad staircase tower with a newel staircase, wider than those of the
earlier Middle Ages, terminates them to the E. The upper

gallery windows are straightheaded under hood-moulds, of three lights with the lights ending in round arches. The galleries are closed by typical Cosin screens with Gothic and Baroque forms. Inside the galleries the broad flat Norman buttresses appear, and near the E end of the first floor gallery PUDSEY'S DOORWAY. This must have been the ceremonial entrance to his Hall, reached no doubt by an outer staircase from the courtyard. It is the most sumptuous piece of Norman work in the county. It has three orders of columns, the inner doubled, with ornamental scalloped capitals and upright bands of ornament between. The broad arches are decorated with a multitude of geometrical elements. Zigzag, the routine motif of the C12, is used only for minor purposes. The major arches have more complex motifs in thick relief: friezes of octagons, of interlocked squares, and so on. The detail is very different both from that of the Galilee (no doubt an earlier design) and from Pudsey's late, Transitional, work. The most similar piece is the Cloister Doorway in the Cathedral. Pudsey's Hall itself exists no longer. Rooms of minor importance have at various times been built into the space occupied by it.

Among them is the SENATE ROOM with a sumptuous wooden fireplace of c. 1610 still entirely Elizabethan in style. The room was otherwise remodelled in the Georgian style. Two more rooms close to it in the same C18 style. S of this suite, known as the JUDGE'S LODGINGS, lies the SENIOR COMMON ROOM with two big, mid C18, Gothick windows. This gothicizing at Durham Castle was done by *Sanderson Miller*, one of the pioneers of medieval revival in the mid C18.* Again further S and at a different level the BISHOP'S ROOMS with two very fine fireplaces of c. 1750, in style exactly like the contemporary ones at the Bishop's Palace at Auckland. The ceilings are stuccoed in the Palladian taste of the time. The N windows, however, are gothicized.

Above Pudsey's Hall, on the second or third upper floor (for the levels interlock), is the Constable's Hall or

* Information kindly provided by Mr Christopher Lyster.

NORMAN GALLERY, in many ways the most remarkable 44a
room in the castle. It dates from Pudsey's time and has
deep window seats with columns in the corners. Thus,
while from outside one can only see widely spaced
(Gothick) windows, inside a complex rhythm is created of
wall, window-seat, column, window, column, window-
seat, wall. The richness which this created in two as well
as three dimensions is yet increased by the thick zigzag
friezes of the arches. The W side of the Gallery has been
altered, and on the N its width has been considerably re-
duced by the insertion of small rooms.

E of this range follows the CHAPEL RANGE, so called 42
after the two chapels which it still contains. The Norman
Chapel is no doubt only the undercroft of a more sumptuous chapel on the level of Pudsey's Hall. As it is, however, older by nearly a century, it may yet represent the
only chapel provided for the Early Norman castle. It is of
nave and aisles of the same height, with six circular piers,
neither very short nor very long, and capitals with elementary volutes and barbarically decorated with leaves, faces,
beasts (e.g. a stag), chip-carved stars. The style is typical
of c. 1070–80. The vaults are rudely groined. The two
windows to the N are now partly below ground. They are
quite large and only slightly splayed on the outside. The
chapel is the most important piece of Early Norman
architecture in the county.

Whatever Pudsey's chapel was like, Bishop Tunstall
about 1542, i.e. after the Reformation, found it necessary
to build a new one. It remains in its original state, except
that it was lengthened at the E end, probably about 1700.
The E window belongs rather to 1700 than to 1542. Tunstall's windows are of three lights under a depressed
pointed arch, with one transome. – The STALLS come
from the palace of Auckland. They were made for Bishop
Ruthall (1509–23) and are the best of the pre-Reformation
stalls in the county. The ends with coats of arms and
tracery and poppy-heads on top are gorgeous. Among the
original misericords are fables, a muzzled bear, a man
pushing his infuriated wife in a wheel-barrow. One of the

poppy-heads was renewed or replaced under Cosin, and the difference between the original Perp nobbly leaves and the acanthus-like leaves of the C17 is instructive. Cosin also provided the SCREEN, of the same style as the screen in Tunstall's gallery mentioned above. The W WALL PAINTING is dated 1698. The ORGAN is part of Father Smith's magnificent instrument in the cathedral (*see* p. 106) and dates from 1683. The STAINED GLASS in the E window is by *Kempe*.

From the E end of the N range a wall runs up the mound to the KEEP. This remarkably impressive polygonal structure was erected under Bishop Hatfield (1345–81) as a shell keep and converted by *Salvin* in 1840 into sleeping quarters for students. It is octagonal and em-battled, with higher, also embattled, angle buttresses or turrets.

Further E still the large remains of a BASTION, now entirely hidden in the backyards of houses. It stands up to the second upper storey. The Bastion formed part of the fortifications connecting Keep and Castle with the big North Gate in Saddler Street. Of this nothing now sur-vives above ground. The street names North Bailey and South Bailey commemorate the fact, easily forgotten, that Cathedral and College both were entirely within the for-tified area. The Inner Bailey is the present courtyard, the Outer Bailey was divided into a N and S half by Cathedral and College. While from that side it is impossible to evoke the medieval appearance of the castle, the view from the river is still essentially as it was before the restoration. Windows have of course been altered and added, but the multi-form crenellated outline remains with such pro-minent details as the windows of the Great Hall and the Norman twin windows further N of the Constable's Hall. It is advisable to study this outside view only after having gone over the interior of the castle. The N view, from the town, is equally impressive, but not so easily enjoyed. Moatside Lane gives the best vantage points, unless access to the N terraces built under Cosin can be obtained.

THE TOWN

INTRODUCTION

The old town lies embraced by the river on two sides, by the
Castle on the third, and open only beyond the Market
Place to the NE. Bishop Flambard built the earliest walls,
early in the C12. New walls to comprise a larger area, including the Market Place, were built two hundred years
later by Bishop Bek. The first Framwellgate Bridge and
the first Elvet Bridge are recorded for the early and the
late C12. As the town grew, the bridges developed bridge-
heads on the outer banks, and houses began to reach
out along the main roads from Durham. It is the usual
ribbon pattern. In a map of 1754 the main roads have
their continuous bands of houses in all directions. Filling
up between them began only in the Victorian Age. The
growth of the town has never been spectacular. The
Industrial Revolution by-passed it. Population was
7,500 in 1801, 13,200 in 1851, 14,700 in 1901. It is now
(1951) 19,283. The chief addition of the C19 to the life of
the town was not factories and an industrial proletariat,
but the university. This was founded in 1833 and given
the buildings of the Castle. Halls, later called Colleges,
became necessary soon, training colleges followed, schools
needed larger premises, and so nearly all the large new
buildings of the late C19 and the C20 (with the deplorable
exception of the Shire Hall) are collegiate and scholastic.
Thus Durham has preserved to this day a more distinctive, more congenial, and at the same time more alive
character than many of the older cathedral towns. May
one hope that this character will be preserved? *Dr Thomas*

Sharp in his plans for the future of Durham has shown the way. But will his plan be heeded?*

CHURCHES

Of the medieval churches of Durham three are in the old city. Of these one, St Nicholas, is in the market place (rebuilt C19), the other two, St Mary-le-Bow and St Mary the Less, are close to Cathedral and College. The remaining three, St Margaret of Antioch, St Oswald, and St Giles, lie on main roads out of the city, where villages had grown up *ante portas*.

ST CUTHBERT, North Road, 1858, by *E. R. Robson*. Quite large and with a semicircular apse and an extremely odd, typically High Victorian, W front. A NW tower with a saddleback roof stands close to the huge roof of the church starting exaggeratedly low down. The details are E.E. Mr Robson was the official architect of West Hartlepool. He must have learnt from E. B. Lamb.

ST CUTHBERT (R.C.), Court Lane, 1827, by *Bonomi*. W tower, nave, and chancel. The exterior altered since. But the inside with W gallery on quatrefoil cast-iron shafts and altar fitments remains in its original state.

ST GILES, Gilesgate. Almost completely hidden from the street, but in a commanding position. The churchyard would offer a magnificent view of the Cathedral if the S and SW were not blocked by a screen of trees. The N side of the nave an impressive piece of Early Norman building, completely plain with just three widely spaced small windows fairly high up, with deep inner splays (one removed). These belong to the original building consecrated in 1112. The chancel followed at the end of the C12; *see* the remains of the chancel arch (single-chamfered on coupled shafts), the string course with the characteristic motif of a three-dimensional zigzag which runs inside from the springing of the arch towards a surviving round-

* The Sharp plan hinges entirely on the cutting through the old town just N of the Market Place. Perhaps he was not aware of a precedent which shows how successfully this can be done. At Le Mans such a cutting combined with a tunnel exists. It adds to the excitement of the streets and the cathedral on the rock.

headed lancet window and forms a hood-mould around it, and the corresponding window on the s side. Both windows are shafted inside and outside. The inside capitals are of the waterleaf variety. The w tower in its lower parts is early C13, with thick clasping buttresses and an arch towards the nave which is double-chamfered on imposts with a big half-dogtooth frieze. The upper part of the tower with battlements and pinnacles is C15 (indulgence of 1414), the s aisle and N porch C19. – PLATE. Chalice and Paten, 1638; Paten on foot, 1728; Flagon, 1772. – MONUMENT. John Heath (of Kepier) † 1591, 40a wooden recumbent effigy, still entirely in the C15 tradition but in Elizabethan dress (cf. Staindrop). Thin, long, sad, bearded face, the feet against two skulls, with the inscription *Hodie michi*.

ST MARGARET OF ANTIOCH, Crossgate. Very new-looking from outside. w tower without buttresses, but with three set-offs; battlements and small pinnacles. All windows re-done. The interior after this is a surprise. The s arcade is of four Norman arches, slightly single-chamfered on short circular piers, with, in three cases, many-scalloped capitals. Above, one original clerestory window survives. The other clerestory windows are Perp. The chancel arch is also Norman, of a vague depressed shape. The responds are C19. But one Norman chancel window still exists. It now opens into the vestry. The N arcade has slim circular piers and consequently wider arches than the s, double-chamfered but still round. Inside the tower is a rib-vaulted chamber. It opens to the nave in an arch dying into the responds. To the N and s of the chancel two Perp chapels were added. That on the s side opens into the chancel with an uncommonly wide arch. The mouldings (as in the N arch as well) have concave members. As records tell of the rebuilding of the s aisle in 1340, we can assume that the C19 two-light Dec windows, and perhaps in this case also the two-light Perp windows of the chancel chapel, are correct reconstructions. The E window is of 1881. The original E window is now the N aisle w window. – STAINED GLASS. E window by *Burlison & Grylls*. –

PLATE. Chalice and Paten, 1675; Paten given 1753; Coffee Pot, 1747–8.

ST MARY-LE-BOW, North Bailey. The W tower of the little church faces the open space in front of the E end of the Cathedral. The church was rebuilt in 1685, the tower added in 1702. The doorway and niche above in the W wall of the tower are original, all other windows belong to the Victorian restoration of 1875. The importance of the church lies in its WOODWORK: ROOD SCREEN, 1707, still in the Cosin tradition, i.e. with thin Gothic tracery; but there are no canopies, and the pierced acanthus frieze below the cornice has gone wider and richer. Also the main vertical divisions have thick hanging garlands. – CHOIR STALLS. The ends of these also have thick hanging garlands, though they are still topped by poppy-heads. – The FONT COVER probably contemporary. – The COMMUNION RAILS are of 1704, with fat short balusters. – In 1731 the CHOIR PANELLING and probably the REREDOS were added, with Corinthian pilasters and plain round-headed panels, i.e. still in the Wren style. – WEST GALLERY, 1741. – PLATE. Chalice, London-made, 1570–1; two Plates, London, 1688; two Flagons, London, 1696; covered Chalice, 1748.

ST MARY THE LESS, South Bailey. As small as a chapel. Nave, chancel, and bellcote. Built in 1846 by *Pickering*, partly with old materials. There is, however, really very little that is Norman. Just some bits of zigzag and similar ornamental motifs. – PANELLING in the chancel, Cosin-style, with strapwork and Gothic motifs and cherubs' heads. – SCULPTURE. An extremely fine, far too little known stone relief of Christ seated in an almond-shaped glory, surrounded by the four symbols of the Evangelists; *c.* 1215, from St Giles (chancel N wall). – Foliated cross tomb-lid (chancel S wall). – STAINED GLASS. Mostly by *Wailes* (TK). – PLATE. Almsdish, C17; Chalice and Paten, 1702; Flagon, 1711; Paten, 1829.

ST MARY MAGDALEN, Magdalen Lane. Ruin of a hospital chapel of 1449–51. No features of architectural significance remain.

ST NICHOLAS, Market Place, 1857–8, by *Pritchett* of Darlington, called at the time by *The Illustrated London News* 'the most beautiful modern specimen of church architecture in the north of England'. Indeed a proud church, proud to display the only spire of Durham, and one of the best churches Pritchett designed. The tower stands in the same place as its predecessor. The shape of the clerestory windows (spheric triangles) is typically Victorian. – PLATE. Chalice and Paten, London, given in 1665; Chalice and Paten, and two Flagons, London, given in 1686.

ST OSWALD. The exterior reveals nothing of the age of the building. The nave is long (indeed six bays long), and when one enters it one can see at once that the E part is older than the rest. The former has circular piers and double-chamfered still roundheaded arches, i.e. belongs to the late C12. The chancel arch is contemporary, as shown by its waterleaf capitals and the slight chamfering of the (pointed) arch. W parts and tower Perp with diagonal buttresses, battlements and pinnacles. Clerestory Perp; E end rebuilt 1864. All windows renewed. – CHOIR STALLS. Early C15 with blank tracery against backs and fronts, and poppy-heads on the ends. – SEDILIA. A very odd double-seat of heavy timber with crook-like raised corner posts instead of arms. The tracery decoration Flamboyant, also some coarse panelling of linenfold type. The most likely date C15. – STAINED GLASS. The W window with exceedingly fine *Ford Madox Brown* glass, made by *Morris & Co.* in 1864. Six small square panels with stories, the other glass white with shields. No strong colours; all subdued and relatively light. – PLATE. Cup, secular, probably C16; Paten, 1699; Almsdish, 1701; two Collecting Dishes, 1736.

OUR LADY OF MERCY AND ST GODRIC (R.C.), Castle Chare, 1864, by *E. W. Pugin* (GR). In a prominent position, especially when viewed from Framwellgate Bridge. A big church. W tower with big pinnacles. No distinction in height between nave and chancel. Chancel with apse and a steep gable to each side of the apse; a German rather than English effect.

CONGREGATIONAL CHURCH, Claypath. The crudely
Gothic church of 1888 (by *Henry Gradon*) with its (ritual)
NW spire hides the humble original chapel of 1751 (now
school). Brick; arched windows and pediment. – PLATE.
two Cups, London-made, 1647–8.

WESLEYAN CHURCH, Old Elvet; *see* Perambulation (B).

PUBLIC BUILDINGS

TOWN HALL, Market Place, 1851, by *P. C. Hardwick*.
Perp, the idiom not very different from George Gilbert
Scott's. An asymmetrical group. For a Victorian town
hall nicely humble. – STAINED GLASS. In the main hall,
by *Ward & Nixon*, 1851 (TK).

SHIRE HALL, Old Elvet, 1897–8, by *H. Barnes* and *F. E.
Coates*. New wing 1905. A building with monumental in-
tentions and disastrous effects on the surrounding Georgian architecture. Big, symmetrical, with a Wrenian dome
in the style of Aston Webb, and faced with that cursedly
imperishable red Victorian brick, which is such crushing
proof of technical proficiency and aesthetic dumbness.

ASSIZE COURTS, Court Lane, 1809–11, by *Francis Sandys*.
Long, low, symmetrical composition with giant portico of
attached Tuscan columns and a small cupola. From the
front good view of the E end of the Cathedral.

UNIVERSITY OF DURHAM. The University of Durham
was founded in 1833, the oldest of the provincial universities of England, and thanks to certain reasons, aesthetic
as well as otherwise, is the only one which has achieved
the creation of a *milieu* that can compare with Oxford and
Cambridge. Create is perhaps not the right word; for
the milieu was there before the university. By receiving
the Castle of the Prince-Bishops as its first seat it came
at once into possession of a Great Hall, older than Christ
Church or Trinity, and of quarters for the students older
than those of nearly all the old colleges. By spreading
during the C19 exclusively on the narrow peninsula of the
city, its now collegiate halls were surrounded by buildings
of style throughout. Wandering along North and South
Bailey to call on members of the university, one may well

(a) *Scenery:* The high moors, from Cowshill

(b) *Scenery:* Hawthorn dene

(a) *Scenery:* Marsden Rock

(b) *Scenery:* High Force, in Teesdale

Roman: Tomb stone from South Shields

(a) *Anglo-Saxon:* St Cuthbert's Cross,
Durham Cathedral

(b) *Anglo-Saxon:* Jarrow, the dedication plate of 684

Anglo-Saxon: Monkwearmouth, West Front, 675. The
upper storeys of the tower are of the ninth or tenth century

(a) *Anglo-Saxon*: Jarrow, Exterior, late seventh century

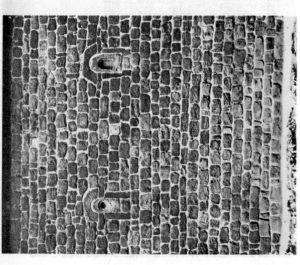

(b) *Anglo-Saxon*: Escomb, Interior, seventh or eighth century

Anglo-Saxon: Escomb, Exterior, seventh or eighth century

(a) *Anglo-Saxon:* St Andrew
Auckland Cross, *c.* 800

(b) *Anglo-Saxon:* St Cuthbert's Maniple,
(detail) Durham Cathedral, *c.* 910–30

8

Durham Cathedral from the Northwest

Durham Cathedral from the Southwest

Norman Churches: Durham Cathedral, the Nave, *c.* 1110–30

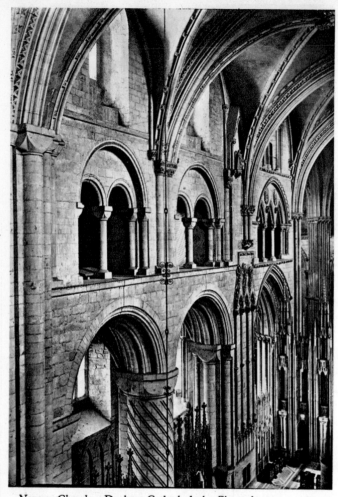

Norman Churches: Durham Cathedral, the Chancel, 1093–*c.* 1104

(a) *Norman Churches*: Durham Cathedral, Rib-vault, in the chancel aisle, *c.* 1095–1100

(b) *Norman Churches*: Pittington, *c.* 1175

13

Norman Churches: Durham Cathedral, the Galilee, *c.* 1170–5

(b) *Norman Sculpture*: Church Kelloe, Cross, *c.* 1200

(a) *Norman Sculpture*: Durham Cathedral, Chapter-House Caryatid, *c.* 1135–40

15

(b) *Early English Church Exteriors:*
West Boldon, the Steeple

(a) *Early English Church Exteriors:* Darlington

16

(a) *Early English Church Exteriors*: Easington, East end, renewed 1852–53

(b) *Early English Church Exteriors*: Gateshead, Holy Trinity, former St Edmund's Chapel

17

Early English Church Interiors: Darlington, Nave, early thirteenth
century

Early English Church Interiors: Hartlepool, St Hilda,
Nave, early thirteenth century

(a) *Thirteenth Century Sculpture:* Finchale Priory,
Capital, *c.* 1250

(b) *Thirteenth Century Sculpture:* Sedgefield, Pier, *c.* 1260

(a) *Thirteenth Century Sculpture:* Durham, St Mary-the-Less,
Christ and the Symbols of the four Evangelists *c.*1215

(b) *Thirteenth Century Sculpture:* Lanchester, Chancel, tympanum,
mid thirteenth century

Thirteenth Century Sculpture: Lanchester, Chancel, head,
mid thirteenth century

Durham Cathedral, Chapel of the Nine Altars, 1242–*c.* 1290

Durham Cathedral, Chapel of the Nine Altars, double tracery
in the north window, *c.* 1280–90

Durham Cathedral, Chancel, caryatid, *c.* 1260–70

Durham Cathedral, Chapel of the Nine Altars, boss in the vault, c. 1280–90

(a) *Church Exteriors*: Durham Cathedral, Windows of the mid fourteenth century

(b) *Church Exteriors*: Houghton-le-Spring, window tracery, early to mid fourteenth century

Church Exteriors: Bishop Auckland, Chapel of the Bishop's Palace, exterior mainly of the 1660s

(b) *Church Exteriors: West Hartlepool,*
Christ Church, by E. B. Lamb, 1854

(a) *Church Exteriors:* Gibside, Chapel (originally Mausoleum),
1760, by James Paine (*Copyright Country Life*)

(b) *Church Interiors: Gibside, Chapel, 1760 and 1809–12 (Copyright Country Life)*

(a) *Church Interiors: Sunderland, Holy Trinity, 1719*

Church Interiors: Roker, by E. S. Prior, 1907

(b) *Church Furnishings*: Jarrow, sixteenth-century bench-end

(a) *Church Furnishings*: Durham Cathedral, door-knocker, early twelfth century

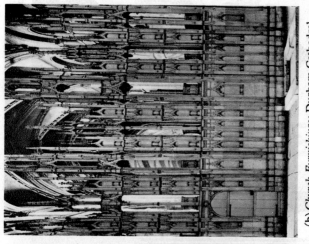

(a) *Church Furnishings*: Durham Cathedral, Bishop's Throne, 1370–80

(b) *Church Furnishings*: Durham Cathedral, Neville Screen, 1372–80

33

(b) *Church Furnishings*: Haughton-le-Skerne, Pulpit, *c.* 1662 or earlier

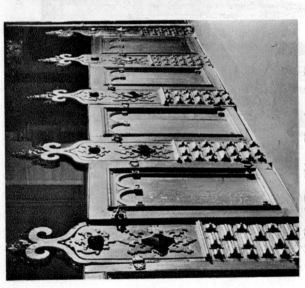

(a) *Church Furnishings*: Haughton-le-Skerne, Benches, *c.* 1662 or earlier

34

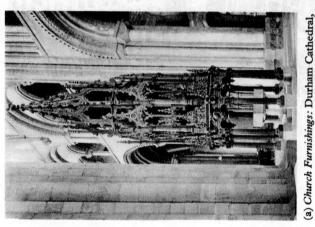

(a) *Church Furnishings*: Durham Cathedral, Font Cover, c. 1663

(b) *Church Furnishings*: Durham Cathedral, Font Cover, c. 1663, detail

35

Church Furnishings: Sedgefield, Screen, *c.* 1670

(a) *Church Furnishings*: Durham Cathedral,
Chancel stalls, detail, 1665

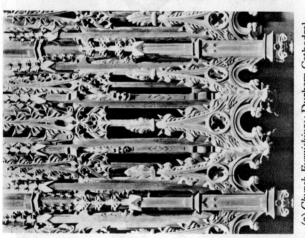

(b) *Church Furnishings*: Stockton-on-Tees,
Pulpit, c. 1715

37

Church Monuments: Norton-on-Tees, early fourteenth century

(a) *Church Monuments:* Durham Cathedral,
John Lord Neville, 1388

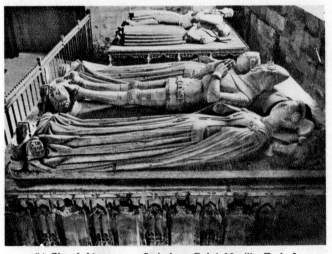

(b) *Church Monuments:* Staindrop, Ralph Neville, Earl of
Westmoreland, 1425

39

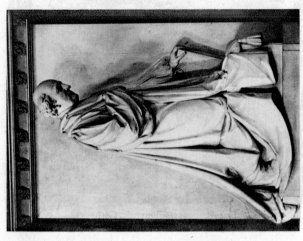

(b) *Church Monuments*: Durham Cathedral, Bishop Barrington, 1833, by Sir F. Chantrey

(a) *Church Monuments*: Durham, St Giles, John Heath, 1591

Castles: Durham Castle, Norman and later; the Keep is mid fourteenth century, re-conditioned in 1840

Castles: Durham Castle, Chapel, *c.* 1075–80
(*Copyright Country Life*)

Castles: Durham Castle, Detail from the Doorway into Bishop
Pudsey's apartments, *c.* 1180

(a) *Castles:* Durham Castle, Bishop Pudsey's Gallery, *c.* 1175

(b) *Castles:* Barnard Castle, Round Tower, early fourteenth century

Castles: Brancepeth, fourteenth century and later

Castles: Raby, 1378 and after (*Copyright Country Life*)

Castles: Lumley Castle, 1389 and later

Castles: Lumley Castle, Gateway to the Great Hall, late fourteenth century (*Copyright Country Life*)

(a) *Castles:* Hylton Castle, early fifteenth century

(b) *Town Walls:* Hartlepool, Sandwell Gate

(a) *Medieval Domestic Architecture:* Bishop Auckland, Bishop Pudsey's Hall, now chapel, begun c. 1190

(b) *Medieval Domestic Architecture:* Durham Cathedral, the Monks' Dormitory, now library and museum, 1398–1404

Medieval Domestic Architecture: Durham Cathedral, the Monks' Kitchen, 1366–70, vault and louvre (*Copyright Country Life*)

Medieval Domestic Architecture: Barnard Castle, Blagroves House, early sixteenth century

(a) *Country Houses:* Walworth Castle, *c.* 1600

(b) *Country Houses:* Gainford Hall, 1603

Country Houses: Horden Hall, c. 1600

Country Houses: Lumley Castle, former Library, by Sir John Vanbrugh,
c. 1725 *(Copyright Country Life)*

(b) *Country Houses*: Bishop Auckland, Bishop's Palace, gateway, 1760

(a) *Country Houses*: Hardwick, the Temple, 1754–7, probably by James Paine

56

(a) *Country Houses:* Croxdale, Staircase ceiling, *c.* 1760
(Copyright Country Life)

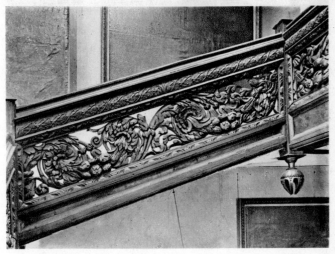

(b) *Town Houses:* Durham Castle, Black Staircase, 1662

Town Houses: Durham, Bishop Cosin's Hall, early eighteenth century

Town Houses: Paradise Row, Stockton-on-Tees, *c.* 1730–40

(a) *Village Street:* Norton, near Stockton-on-Tees

(b) *Town Halls:* Stockton-on-Tees, 1736

(a) *Town Halls:* Barnard Castle, 1747

(b) *The Nineteenth Century:* Penshaw Monument, 1844

The Nineteenth Century: Monkwearmouth Station, 1848, by
John Dobson

(a) *The Twentieth Century:* Blackhall Pithead Bath, 1934, by
F. G. Frizzell

(b) *The Twentieth Century:* Team Valley Trading Estate, Gateshead.
Factory by Yorke, Rosenberg, & Mardell, 1948

The Twentieth Century: West Building, University of Durham, by J. S. Allen, 1951–2

feel transported into the streets of Oxford or Cambridge. Birmingham or Manchester could never even try to achieve that.

UNIVERSITY LIBRARY and UNION BUILDING; *see* Perambulation (A) below.

UNIVERSITY COLLEGE; *see* Castle, above.

HATFIELD COLLEGE. Three main parts now; for the fourth, the former Rectory of St Mary-le-Bow, *see* Perambulation (A). The Tudor stone building is of 1848 by *Salvin*. To its l., attached to it, a big and indifferent brick addition of 1932. To the l. of that the friendly Pace Building of 1946–50 by *Vincent Harris*, stone, with a big hipped roof and front doorways (with Gibbs surrounds) to the various sets. Nice rhythm of the windows towards the river.

ST CHAD'S COLLEGE and ST JOHN'S COLLEGE, South Bailey; *see* Perambulation (A).

ST MARY'S COLLEGE, Potters Bank. To a building of the 1920s a very large new building by *Vincent Harris* is being added: stone, classical detail, big hipped roofs. The most ambitious edifice so far sponsored by the University.

OBSERVATORY, 1841, by *Salvin*. A small Late Classical stone building with observatory dome. The plan a Greek cross with E and W arms elongated. Timber pediments. No embellishments whatsoever. About a mile exactly due N (close to St Cuthbert) an OBELISK was erected at the same time, as a N point for the Observatory. It is of a curious, exaggeratedly tapering outline.

SCIENCE DEPARTMENTS, South Road. Original building 1924; small extension 1930; considerable extension 1939–43 by *Marshall & Tweedy*; further additional building by *Professor J. S. Allen* 1950–1, a first instalment of a twenty-year plan for the Durham Colleges. The new building 64 houses various departments and is therefore grouped loosely. The composition is not monumental, yet the ensemble has unquestionable dignity. Long, single main range, with two wings projecting unevenly in depth, height and character of design. The one houses a large lecture theatre and a library, and the façade, especially on the N

CD.—7

side succeeds in conveying this. The other wing contains smaller rooms and projects only on the N, not on the S side. Pleasing variety of facing materials, including vertical copper sheeting. The whole is a model of what the old universities might do.

NEVILLE'S CROSS COLLEGE, County Training College for Women. Red brick, Neo-Georgian, 1913, etc., by *W. Rushworth*, completed by *F. Willey*.

BEDE COLLEGE. Original buildings 1846–7; additions between then and 1858, and again 1875. Chapel 1938–9 by *Seely & Paget*. Very odd walls with two overhangs inside and a vault of no period precedent.

ST HILD'S COLLEGE, 1858; W wing 1907 by *J. Potts*; Chapel 1912 and E wing 1925 by the same.

DURHAM SCHOOL, Margery Lane. The original buildings of 1844 by *Salvin*. Additions by *Sir Arthur Blomfield*, e.g. Library of 1876 and the wing of 1884 continuing it. Also by *Blomfield* the classrooms of 1887 at the corner opposite the Grove. Many more later additions. Chapel 1924–6 by *Walter H. Brierley*. This has an impressive exterior without tower or turret, and a heavy and sombre interior with square piers and rib-vaults.

JOHNSTON SCHOOL, South Street. In a prominent position above the river. Red brick. Norman Shaw style with Dutch gables; 1899, with an addition of 1906, the latter known to be by *Oliver, Leeson & Wood* of Newcastle. At r. angles to the school the Chapel with a vast Neo-Perp N window.

GIRLS' GRAMMAR SCHOOL, Providence Row. Nice Neo-Georgian by *Rushworth*, 1913, with additions of 1938–9.

GRAMMAR TECHNICAL SCHOOL, Crossgate Moor, 1952, by *D. McIntyre*. One of those large low modern schools stretching out many tentacles. The main group is on the S side, with Hall, Dining Hall, etc.

FRAMWELLGATE BRIDGE. First built by Bishop Flambard early in the C12. A gatehouse stood on the town side. The present bridge is that of Bishop Skirlaw, i.e. of *c.* 1400, widened in 1856. Two elliptical arches, closely ribbed.

OLD ELVET BRIDGE. The first bridge was built by Bishop Pudsey. It had two chapels. Later there were shops and houses on the bridge. Widening by means of semicircular arches in 1805.

PREBENDS' BRIDGE, 1772–7, by *George Nicholson*, architect to the Dean and Chapter. Three fine, high, semicircular arches with rusticated faces.

NEVILLE'S CROSS. Only the base and a stump of the shaft remain of this memorial of the battle between David Bruce and the English. The battle was fought in 1346; the cross probably erected shortly after.

STATUE OF NEPTUNE, 1729, from the former Market Hall in the Market Place. Now in WHARTON PARK, the other side of the Station.

PERAMBULATIONS

(A) The City on the Rock; (B) The town across the River and beyond the Market Place.

(A) *The City on the Rock*. The MARKET PLACE of Durham should be the civic counterpart of Castle and Cathedral; it is not. It has little to recommend it aesthetically, save the C19 church of St Nicholas. The few quoined Georgian houses are indifferent. The best building is *Gibson's* NATIONAL PROVINCIAL BANK of 1876, remarkably dignified and carefully detailed in its two superimposed orders of classical columns. In the middle of the square the EQUESTRIAN STATUE of the third Marquess of Londonderry, in uniform, with shako, by *R. Monti*, 1861. From here the principal way for most visitors of Durham is the way up to the Cathedral, that is along SADDLER STREET and Owengate, both streets, as indeed all streets in the town centre, with pleasantly solid unbroken walls on both sides. The only notable façades are Nos 43 and 50 on the l., the former built as a theatre in 1791, the latter of *c.* 1825 now the Salvation Army. In 1791 the columns of the doorpiece are still Roman Doric, in 1825 they are Greek Doric. Also the handsome segmental arch placed immediately above the Roman Doric columns and continued to the l. and r. into the cornices of shops would not have pleased the severer early C19. In OWENGATE lies on the r. (No. 5) one of the few remaining timber-framed fronts with overhanging upper storeys. The first floor rests on a projected moulded beam, the second on brackets. At the end of Owengate, with BISHOP COSIN'S ALMS-HOUSES of 1838, Tudor, stone, gabled, two-storeyed, PALACE GREEN is reached, the very centre of the rock, with the Cathedral along the whole S end and the Castle in the NW corner. So only the E and W sides concern us here. The E side begins with a Neo-Tudor lavatory and is continued by BISHOP COSIN'S HALL, a seven-bay, three-storeyed brick mansion with a sumptuous early C18 door-piece. It was originally known as Archdeacon's Inn. Fluted Ionic pilasters with a raised segmental, near semicircular pediment and below it rich carvings of branches with leaves. Next to this tall and square house stands the BISHOP'S HOSPITAL of 1666, actually a combination of three buildings. The whole is of six bays, one-storeyed with the two end-bays gabled. On the l. side inscription : Schola pro addiscendis rudimentis literarum ; on the r. Schola pro plano canto et arte scribendi ; in the middle Hospitale . . . pro VIII pauperibus . . . fundatum 1666. Light brown stone with mullioned windows. The next house (Pemberton Buildings) is of 1931, but looks late C19, dark grey stone with mixed Neo-Tudor and late C17 details. With the slightly recessed ABBEY HOUSE, plain C18 five-bay ashlar front, the corner of Duncow Lane is reached and the E end of the Cathedral. On the W side of Palace Green the W end of the Cathedral has opposite the GRAMMAR SCHOOL, founded in 1541. Its W half is a normal two-storeyed five-bay house with a façade of late C17 character. Attached to it is the school proper, built soon after 1661. This has two large mullioned and transomed windows going right up into dormers. Between the two a small four-centred arched doorway. All much renewed in the C19. The UNION BUILDING of the University was built in 1820, one-storeyed and castellated with the centre containing the entrance a little raised. The UNIVERSITY LIBRARY is largely by *Salvin*, 1858, but its N part is Bishop Cosin's Library, founded in 1669. The window shapes are characteristic, though renewed, and, inside, the gallery along all sides. Two book presses remain, their ends similar to Cosin's chancel stalls. The series of portraits of great scholars in groups of three should also be noted. The scholars include both Suarez and Melanchthon. Past the Castle entrance on the N the Green is closed by the MASTER'S HOUSE, with a very tall, plain, L-shaped front.

The best streets of Durham are North and South Bailey, running S from the meeting of Saddler Street and Owengate. Their names mark the confines on the E side of the outer castle bailey. Houses again solidly on both sides, giving the street a pleasant feeling of being interior space. When openings occur they are all the more poignant. In NORTH BAILEY the impression is one of solid C18. No. 5 has a tripartite doorpiece with shell-hood, Nos 41–43 nicely pedimented doors (No. 43 scrolly and open pediment). By St Mary-le-Bow the E end of the Cathedral appears suddenly in its whole width, as if it were a W façade. It makes the parish church look duly homely. In front of the Cathedral the well-designed WAR MEMORIAL (by whom?), a circular pier of a design similar to the piers inside the Cathedral and a Celtic-looking cross on it. To the N of the Cathedral Duncow Lane runs up; to the S of St Mary BOW LANE runs down. It leads to a terrace from which a steep footpath descends to the river. What remains of the CITY WALLS can best be studied from here.

SOUTH BAILEY is the continuation of North Bailey. The joint is where the College Gatehouse gives access to the College Green. In South Bailey the two stateliest houses are now colleges of the University: ST CHAD'S COLLEGE, seven windows wide and three storeys high, of ashlar, and ST JOHN'S COLLEGE of c. 1730, also seven windows wide, but the middle three projected and pedimented. Banded rustication throughout, and a fine broad doorway with a straight hood on big brackets. The staircase is worth looking at, with a handrail on columns of alternating flutings. To the S the street ends with the WATER GATE, a plain archway of 1778. From here the road runs unpaved down to the Prebends' Bridge, where one gets the most famous view of the Cathedral. The CORN MILL and FULLING MILL below on the two banks of the river, facing each other, are ideal to give the picture scale. On the town side of the bridge a lane, a little above the river, turns back and runs parallel with and below South Bailey. It takes one to the surprising sight of a little tetrastyle, prostyle, Greek Doric Temple known as COUNT'S HOUSE. It was originally no doubt a garden house and must date from *c.* 1820–30.

That ends the walk through the town centre, since the street from the Market Place to Framwellgate Bridge, Silver Street, contains nothing of importance. MOAT-SIDE LANE behind it, however, deserves mention, because it affords the best views up to the N walls of the Castle.

(B) *The Town across the River and beyond the Market Place.* This Perambulation will best be done in three parts: along Claypath and Gilesgate and beyond, across the river to the E, and to the W.

In Claypath nothing, but off to the S the sweet little LEAZES PLACE of *c.* 1840 with identical brick cottages l. and r. The doorways of a minimum Grecian style. The street leads to LEAZES HOUSE, *c.* 1848. In GILESGATE No. 167 is the only house of interest. It is Early Georgian, of red brick, tall and broad, and had originally Venetian windows on the top floor on the N, S, and W sides. Visually the important thing about Gilesgate is that coming in from the NE the traveller here receives his first broadside view of the Cathedral, whereas leaving Durham from the NE the traveller, on reaching the upper part of Gilesgate, is suddenly in an entirely different atmosphere. Instead of the steep banks and the groves of Durham he now walks on a plain, along what seems a village green with two generously spaced rows of trees.

From opposite St Giles's Church a footpath leads N to the

KEPIER HOSPITAL. This was founded by Bishop Flambard and re-founded by Pudsey. Nothing of the C12 survives, however. What survives is the GATEHOUSE, as big
as that of the College. It was built by Bishop Bury in
1341. It has buttresses with set-offs, a gateway with a two-
centred, double-chamfered arch and a window above, also
with a two-centred head, and ends in a gable. The gateway is vaulted inside in two bays with cross-ribs of a
typical convex-concave section. To the former courtyard
the elevation is almost the same, but a stair-turret is
added. All the rest of the Hospital has gone. And the
mansion of the Heath family built into, and on the
site of, the Hospital after the Dissolution has not had a
better fate. In the last fifty years it has disappeared completely save for one three-bay open loggia to the S. The
round arches rest on short columns, and to their r. is a
doorway with a four-centred head and a big hood-mould.
The whole site should be made something of by the City
of Durham. The setting by the river is fine and still
entirely rural.

The other side of Elvet Bridge to the E was the West End of
Durham in the C18 and later. OLD ELVET is a fine street,
or was, until in 1895 the Shire Hall began to raise its fiery
red head, and the METHODIST CHURCH put a spiky
spire next to this in 1903. The two buildings have ruined
the unity of this remarkable street, remarkable although it
has no houses of outstanding merit. The nicest to look at
is perhaps the ROYAL COUNTY HOTEL, early C18 with
giant Ionic angle pilasters and pilasters to frame the central three of the seven bays. Later Georgian doorway and
good big 'Egyptian' lettering probably of c. 1820–30.
Inside, a pretty staircase. Inside the DUNELM HOTEL also
a good staircase: thick twisted balusters of the late C17.
Chapel Passage leads to a disused METHODIST CHAPEL
of stone, good, solid Late Georgian work of 1808. The
doorway and the space for the communion table are in the
middle of the long, not the short sides. It is now a bakery
and the galleries look odd in it. Nos 53–55 are early C19,
of nine bays with a three-bay pediment and an arched

ground floor. Further E the crushingly High Victorian, but fortunately small, MASONIC HALL (1868, by *T. C. Eddy*), with short coupled columns of pink Aberdeen granite at the entrance and much heavy Gothic detail. No. 30 has a Grecian balcony of cast iron. The street remains enjoyable to the very end, where Nos 22 and 24 face each other. NEW ELVET is the poor relation of Old Elvet, of the same character, but with more modest houses. Not one requires individual mention. Nos 80–82 are one plain eleven-bay design, red brick, three-storeyed. No. 20 has a good doorway with pediment on corbels. New Elvet is continued by CHURCH STREET half r. and by Hallgarth Street half l. Church Street has plain three-storey houses, the best being the COUNTY PLANNING DEPARTMENT, a recessed five-bay house with a broad late C18 doorway. At the foot of the street small public garden, just right to enjoy an E view of the Cathedral. In HALLGARTH STREET HALL GARTH HOUSE, *c.* 1700, brick with stone dressings, five bays as usual, but of specially long, low proportions. Stone bands run along above the windows. Opposite, up an alley, a remarkable medieval relic, the BARNS, etc., of the Priory. One long stone range (windows new) and, at r. angles, a wing with a stone ground floor and a timber and brick upper floor. The tour beginning at Framwellgate Bridge also ends with a medieval building. Both (as also the Kepier Hospital at the end of the first tour) must be visualized as standing outside the old town. From the W end of the bridge SOUTH STREET turns at once S. No houses of special merit, but from No. 37 one gets a dead-on view of the Cathedral from the W which no one should miss. The Castle spreads out on the l., the College on the r. From the bridge to the W the streets are dominated by the stone RAILWAY VIADUCT of 1857. In Crossgate the WORK-HOUSE of 1837 (much enlarged) and at its back, in ALLER-GATE, the former Infirmary (1792–3). Framwellgate is continued NW in Framwellgate Path, where, rather hidden, the FRAM WELLHEAD, a parallelogram with angle buttresses and a pyramid roof: 1450, but rebuilt 1847.

Finally Framwellgate Waterside turns N by the bridge,
and near its end a little elevated is CROOK HALL, a
precious relic, as its outbuildings on the E are the main
rooms of a medieval manor house, the Hall with single-
light, trefoiled, ogeeheaded windows, the Kitchen with an
enormous fireplace and a most primitive staircase to the
upper floor. The steps are simply beams cut diagonally.
The medieval part is joined to a smaller part built in 1671
(one hood-moulded window on the ground floor), and
that to a three-bay, three-storey Georgian brick house.
The staircase balustrade has alternating fluted colonnettes and colonnettes intermittently blocked.

ALDIN GRANGE *see p.* 43.

ALDIN GRANGE see p. 43.

EASINGTON

ST MARY. Norman W tower, originally without buttresses,
otherwise preserved right up to the corbel-table below
the battlements. Later, probably in the C13, thick
diagonal buttresses were added. W window long and
roundheaded, tower arch towards the nave slightly depressed and roundheaded. Responds and arches with two
slight chamfers. The rest of the church is E.E., long and
relatively low outside, of broad, generous, and stately proportions inside. A S doorway of 1852–3 leads into the
tower. It is in the E.E. style. The aisle W windows are
original E.E., and also (a rarity) the clerestory windows,
four widely spaced small lancets. Curiously, these do not
correspond to the arcades inside which are of five arches.
They rest on alternating circular and octagonal piers,
alternating not only from W to E, but also between N and
S (cf., for example, Darlington). The responds are keeled.
Moulded capitals, one with finely ribbed upright leaves,
still of Norman traditions. Also some little nailhead. The
arches are double-chamfered. The aisle windows are
Perp, renewed, but the inner frames old. The chancel
starts with a double-chamfered arch on corbels and ends
with a group of lancets of 1852–3. The inner division,
however, by tall shafts of Frosterley marble with shaft-
rings seems genuine, and also, to the l. and r. of the

group, a blank niche. So the whole inner E wall is filled by one composition. N chancel chapel with two big late C13 windows; the tracery of the two-light variety which in the case of three and more lights is called intersected. – PEWS. In the Cosin style; still with poppy-heads, but the ends decorated by ribbonwork and bunches of hanging leaves. Can they be the ones called in 1634 'lately made new and erected uniforme'? Hardly; Cosin's son-in-law, Denis Granville, was made Rector of Easington in 1662. – SCREEN. Of the same time, but only little remains that is original (frieze of acanthus foliage). The rest was removed in 1852–3. – STAINED GLASS. E window by *O'Connor*. – PLATE. Set of 1816 and 1817, made in London; Flemish Pewter Flagon, *c.* 1600. – MONUMENTS. Lady wearing a wimple; *c.* 1300, Frosterley marble. – Cross-legged knight with well-preserved shield, perhaps Marmaduke Fitz Galfrid; died late C13?.

RECTORY (now Home for the Aged). The house incorporates fragments of the medieval manor house of Easington; *see* the buttressed part of the front, and in the long building at the back the two pointed first floor windows.

PITHEAD BATH, 1937, by *F. G. Frizzell*. The style is C20, a little *à la* Mendelsohn, with projecting parallel bands running round curved corners (*see* Introduction, p. 41).

PETERLEE *see p.* 191.

EAST BOLDON

BOLDON HOUSE. Mid C18 five-bay two-storey brick house. The doorway with pediment on Tuscan demi-columns, typically bulging-out frieze.

EASTGATE

ALL SAINTS. A handsome Neo-Perp church with a *flèche*. By *Johnson*, 1887.

EAST HARTBURN

(The MHLG calls the main street 'very attractive', with trees and front gardens. Hartburn House, Hartburn Farm House, and No. 15 are referred to as the best buildings.)

EBCHESTER

ST EBBA. Almost entirely modern. Original only the two small Early Norman windows now in the W wall (no outer splays at all). In the tower a Roman altar and built-in Roman fragments. – FONT. An odd Norman stone (capital?) used as font bowl.

ROMAN FORT. The church stands in the SW corner of the fort (*Vindomora*) which was occupied at the same time as Binchester.

EDMONDBYERS

ST EDMUND. Small Norman church, consisting only of nave with bellcote and chancel. Extensively restored. Of the windows only the narrow ones in the chancel S wall and possibly one in the nave N wall are original. The chancel arch in Norman days was single. It was given its present picturesque triple shape in 1858 (?). The vestry doorway is said to be from St Nicholas at Durham. – WOODWORK. Pew Ends at the W end from the chapel of Bishop Auckland Castle, Panelling round the top from the organ case of St Mary Redcliffe, Bristol, Shield from the organ case of Durham Cathedral, Pew End Tops from the chapel of Durham Castle, and Bosses from the Cathedral Cloister.* – PLATE. Cup of 1737–8.

EGGLESCLIFFE

ST MARY. Few churches in the county are remembered as Perp; Egglescliffe probably will be. For its W tower with diagonal buttresses, a broad S stair-turret, battlements, and small pinnacles is C15 and its windows are too. That at the E end is of five lights with panel tracery of a familiar pattern. Others on the N and S sides are of three-stepped, cusped lancet lights under a depressed arch. Attached to the S porch is a two-bay S aisle or S chapel with an octagonal pier into which the arches die. Only the S doorway is considerably older, Norman, with one curious

* Information on the woodwork of the church kindly provided by the Reverend G. Suthrien.

capital with a human head and two elementary volutes above; and the chancel arch is C13, pointed and double-chamfered, with alternating red and white stones. The shafts of the Sedilia belong to the same date. Of great interest are the contributions of the C17 to the furnishing of the church. They are in the Cosin style: the simple panelled roof, the PEWS whose doors have their upper parts open and divided by balusters (cf. Aycliffe, Cockfield, Ryton), the SCREEN with a mixture of Renaissance and Gothic motifs, acanthus foliage, and cherubs' heads, and also round arches on long balusters, a Renaissance motif, but enriched by cusping, a Gothic motif; the CHOIR STALLS whose ends still have poppy-heads, but also hanging-down swags of fruit, and backs with balusters and cusped arches; and the CHOIR PANELLING. – FONT COVER. Steep pyramid shape, probably also of the C17. – PULPIT. Three-decker of the C18; partly renewed recently. – SCULPTURE. In the porch one baluster shaft, interesting evidence of the existence of an Early Anglo-Saxon church here. – Foliated cross tomb-lid. – STAINED GLASS. Two S windows of 1886, evidently by *Kempe*. – PLATE. Chalice of *c.* 1664; Paten of 1687. – MONUMENTS. Two effigies of cross-legged knights, sandstone, the earlier *c.* 1300 (with mail-coif).

Round the church a few Georgian houses. The YARM BRIDGE across the Tees was built *c.* 1400 by Bishop Skirlaw. It consists of five arches, the middle ones pointed, and has since been widened. Close to it a RAILWAY VIADUCT of forty-three brick arches. It was built in 1849.

EGGLESTONE

EGGLESTONE HALL. A restrained square stone mansion of *c.* 1822 (or *c.* 1813?) with a one-storeyed Greek Doric colonnade and a porch on Greek Doric columns.

In the grounds the ruined CHURCH, a small C18 building with a Venetian window at the E end and all other windows heavily arched.

EGGLESTONE BRIDGE. C17, narrow, of two arches with a breakwater between.

ELEMORE HALL

Mid c18 brick mansion of three storeys, rather grim, looking from a distance. Centre of five bays, the three middle ones slightly projecting, and wings of two bays depth ending in Venetian windows on the front side. The doorway with intermittently rusticated pilasters and pediment. The side entrance on the E side with a Gibbs surround. The quoins also treated in a similar way with intermittently flat and raised stones. Inside, two ceilings with pretty Rococo stuccowork and a good original staircase.

ELTON

St John. No more than a chapel by the roadside, 52 ft long and consisting of nave and chancel with bellcote. Built in 1841, but incorporating a Norman s doorway (zigzag arch on plain imposts) and a Norman chancel arch with stylized beakheads, in 1841 picturesquely made into the centre of a three-arch composition. Doubly picturesque now that the tripartite opening is closed by a rood screen of 1907 with Flamboyant tracery and the three figures of the rood. The screen and figures were designed by *Sir Ninian Comper*. Over the vestry door a hood-mould of *c.* 1200, semicircular with nailhead decoration. – PLATE. Chalice of 1570, made at York. – MONUMENT. Effigy of a cross-legged knight, early c14.

ELWICK HALL

Handsome village green (at Elwick) with one row of irregularly placed trees along the middle. The church lies sw of the green.

St Peter. Small, with its churchyard on the N as well as the w, close to a steep dene. Nave of *c.* 1200, chancel originally of the same date, but rebuilt with the old materials in Bishop Cosin's time; tower rebuilt also of old materials in 1813 (top stage 1860). It stands in the place usual for a s porch, and the porch leads indeed through it. Arcades of four bays with short circular piers, moulded

capitals, and double-chamfered arches. The NW and NE
responds have waterleaf capitals unmistakable in their
date, the NW respond a little nailhead embellishment in
addition. Chancel S windows and BENCH-ENDS of 1665.
– SCULPTURE. Two small square panels from a Saxon
cross with Adam and Eve and a cross, built high up into
the nave E wall to the l. and r. of the chancel arch. – Very
decayed relief of the Crucifixion, S aisle E end. – PLATE.
Chalice and Paten, 1667, made at York; Chalice, 1754,
made in London; Paten and Almsdish, 1785, also London-made.

ESCOMB

6b ST JOHN THE EVANGELIST. Escomb church in the des-
7 perately sordid surroundings of its village is one of the
most important and most moving survivals of the architecture of the times of Bede. It is Northumbrian in its tall,
narrow proportions. Long nave and narrower chancel
separated by a chancel arch which with its plain responds
(differing from each other) is yet the only piece of decoration in the church. The masonry is excellent, of large
blocks, probably of Roman origin, from Vinovia. The
jambs of the chancel arch have carefully fitted long-and-
short work. The same typically Anglo-Saxon technique at
the angles of the building. The surviving windows are
extremely small with deep splays inside, especially at the
foot. The two windows on the S side are roundheaded, the
two on the N side straightheaded. The lancet windows are
an insertion of the C13; the three larger windows date
from the early C19. The porch is, of course, not original
either. But two straightheaded original doorways remain
blocked on the N side. Towards the W end a fragment of
the Saxon cobble flooring. Against the N wall fragments
of Saxon CROSSES, above the altar another small Saxon
CROSS. – PLATE. Cup, Plate, Flagon, 1669.

ESH

ST MICHAEL. Nothing seems to remain visible of the
church of 1770. In the church EFFIGY of a lady, badly

preserved, *c.* 1300, sandstone. – PLATE. Chalice and Paten, 1711.

ESH HALL. The magnificent gateposts crowned by thick scrolly openwork finials promise more than the house holds. It is interesting, however, to note the open segmental pediments of the windows and a doorway. They show a change in style against C17 traditions which can here be dated 1687, the year said to have been legible until recently on a sun-dial on the garden front.

FELLING
1¾ m. ESE of Gateshead

CHRIST CHURCH, Carlisle Street, 1866, by *Austin & Johnson*; N aisle, etc., later. E.E., longish, with apse but without tower. In the clerestory N side two windows with STAINED GLASS by *Cottier*, 1874 (cf. Birtley).

ST PATRICK (R.C.), High Street, 1893–5, by *Charles Walker* of Newcastle. A bold, if towerless, building in the E.E. style on the hillside. The W doorway reached by a double outer stairway. Roomy, but uninteresting inside. The transept subdivided by a tall shaft towards the nave as at Fountains Abbey.

CROW HALL, Crow Hall Lane. C18, five bays, three storeys, with parapet.

FINCHALE PRIORY

By far the most important monastic remains in County Durham, comparable to, though by no means as spacious and grand as, Fountains and Rievaulx further S, in Yorkshire. The situation is lovely. The river Wear forms a loop and plays its part in pictures of the ruins from three sides. The far bank is thickly wooded so that, on approaching the priory from the W or standing in the church and looking E, the background is always a wall of lush trees.

St Godric first settled here about 1110. He had been a pedlar and then a ship-owner, had travelled to Spain, lived for a time at Santiago de Compostela, one of Europe's most famous shrines, and knew St Gilles in Provence as well as Rome. His sanctity attracted visitors and a small stone church was built, the foundations of which are enclosed by the chancel of the priory church. In this first stone church St Godric was buried when, at the ripe age of 105, he died in 1170. Shortly after, Bishop Pudsey's son wished to found a Benedictine monastery near Durham. There were quarrels with the Prior and Chapter of Durham over the siting of it, until about 1196 building was begun at Finchale. What precisely was begun we cannot say. Of the church three altars were consecrated in 1239. The church can, however, hardly have been complete then. In style it is rather mid than early C13.

It consisted of aisled nave, transepts, crossing with crossing tower, aisled chancel, and square aisleless E end. The evidence of this plan is obscured by the fact that in 1364–5 the aisles were pulled down and the arcades blocked and provided with three-light windows. These are important in the architectural history of County Durham, because their tracery is still of the reticulated variety, that is entirely pre-Perp, though thirty years later than the beginnings of Perp tracery at Gloucester. The E end had double-shafted lancet windows with shaft-rings. On the N side a shafted single lancet is still recognizable with a roll-moulding up the jambs and along the arch. Opposite is the Double Piscina with crocket capitals and the Sedilia. The arcades, before they were blocked, had circular piers with very fine stiff-leaf capitals with fir cones (specially well preserved, because only recently exposed) and many-moulded arches. The crossing tower, still standing in the C17, rests on fat big attached circular piers. The N transept has on the E a blocked opening to the former Chapel of St Godric and on the W two immensely long lancet windows. On the N was a high and wider window. The S transept never had such a window. Here on the S side the Dormitory was built against the church, and an open stone staircase led up to the door into it. On the E side is the blocked opening into the chancel aisle and next to it a

20a

very big window originally of five cusped lancet lights under one two-centred arch, that is of *c.* 1300. On the w side a later door led into the cloisters. The nave had arcades of four bays with alternating circular and octagonal piers. The w end has a doorway of moderate size with three orders of colonnettes and, above, three well-spaced lancet windows. To the sw of the façade a tower was erected in the C14 (cf., for example, Fountains Abbey). The later Middle Ages were fond everywhere of such isolated big towers.

Now for the monastic buildings. The CLOISTERS are in the usual position s of the church in the angle between nave and transept. They were rebuilt in the C14. Bases of shafts of the original C13 cloisters can still be seen in the s walk. The N walk was simply the s aisle of the church re-used. One respond of a transverse arch from wall to nave still stands. The E side of the cloisters had, as usual, the DOR-MITORY on the upper floor, a long room (subdivided only by timber partitions) of which only one lancet window (to the E) remains, and the CHAPTER HOUSE and some minor rooms on the groundfloor. The Chapter House at Finchale is small (the priory never had many monks : fifteen in 1278) and rectangular. The entrance wall sur-vives with a doorway with one order of colonnettes and simply single-chamfered windows to the l. and r. At the s end of the Dormitory the RERE-DORTER projected to the E, with the garderobes. The s range of the cloister buildings was, again as usual, the REFECTORY. It stands on a vaulted undercroft with octagonal piers and heavy ribs dying into them. This may well be a C14 re-arrange-ment of the original arrangement, indicated by the keeled responds and moulded capitals. At the w end a fine door-way with two orders of colonnettes led up to the Refec-tory itself. This has four widely spaced lancet windows towards the cloisters and five more narrowly spaced outer windows. The w part of the range was divided off and three-storeyed, that is with two storeys to the one of the refectory. The arrangement corresponds to that of par-lour and solar in the secular manor house. On the w side of the cloisters it was customary to have cellars, guest-rooms, or the abbot's lodgings. At Finchale there is a plain wall here, and the PRIOR'S HOUSE is s of the chancel, projecting beyond its E end.

Finchale Priory in the C14 and C15 was apparently used as a holiday hostel for the Durham Cathedral monks. The permanent staff was only a prior and four monks, but groups of four came out to Finchale every three weeks. They seem to have dined at the Prior's Table. The Prior's House is also arranged just like the standard manor house. The Hall was on the upper floor at the W end of a long straight range s of the chancel. It had its entrance from that side. To its W the Kitchens (*see* the oven and hatch) lay in the usual position and connected the house with the monastic buildings. To its E, also usual, was the Solar, that is the Prior's Camera. This has a fine tall two-light E window towards the river. Its tracery is geometrical, that is of the late C13 (Sir Charles Peers: C15). To its immediate N is a projecting spiral staircase. To the s of the E part of the Camera was the Prior's Chapel with a three-light, straightheaded C15 E window, to the N of the E part of the Camera the Prior's Study with an oriel window facing N. Below the Study is a tunnel-vaulted room. This whole part seems to be the Douglas Tower mentioned in the 1460s. A curious piece of rude folklore was connected with the oriel window, containing apparently a seat. Grose reports that this was 'said to have the virtue of removing sterility and procuring issue for any woman who having performed certain ceremonies sat down thereon. . . . It may perhaps be needless to observe', adds Grose, 'that since the removal of the monks it has entirely lost its efficacy.'

Finally the buildings indicated by the low walls E of the Prior's Lodgings and E of the church must be accounted for. The former are explained as bakehouse and brew-house, the latter (a very interesting survival) as the temporary structures put up, while the monastery was being built.

FRIARSIDE *see* LINTZFORD

FROSTERLEY

St Michael, 1869, by *G. E. Street*, but nothing special, except perhaps for the pretty arrangement of the Sedilia niche with the windows in it, and for the sympathetic use of stone. The w tower has a broached spire, not at all a local motif.

At Frosterley the so-called marble of that name is quarried, a black limestone very rich in fossils. It was used in the county during the Middle Ages as a substitute for the fine Purbeck marble of the South. Shafts were made of it in the c13, and many fonts.

GAINFORD

St Mary. A beautiful church, of mellow grey stone, in a beautiful position close to and above the river Tees. The church is sizable and almost entirely of the early c13. The only evidence of the Norman period is one scalloped capital built into the N porch. The c13 work consists of nave and aisles, originally also clerestory, chancel, and w tower. The tower is unbuttressed and not high. The w stair-turret was added in 1786. The aisles project as far w as the w side of the tower. The upper aisle windows, small with ogee tops, must be c14 if they are at all original. The chancel has lancet windows and a fine group of three stepped lancets in the E with a vesica window above. In the interior the three lancets are separated by shafts with shaft-rings, decorated by a tiny nailhead frieze. The s aisle has at its E end one lancet and also a vesica window above. – The nave is divided from the aisles by tall and slim circular piers. The abaci are round except for one octagonal one. One of the round abaci has nailhead decoration. The capital of the NE respond is distinguished by sparse upright leaves, flatter than the more usual crockets and perhaps an earlier stage of development. The arches are double-chamfered. So is the chancel arch, on later corbels. The tower arch and the arches from tower to aisles have broad demi-shafts in the responds. – FONT COVER. Steep pyramidal, of Jacobean style. – Fragments of a Saxon CROSS SHAFT against the W wall. – Fragments of tomb-lid with FOLIATED CROSS in the N porch. – Also in the N porch fragment of an INCISED EFFIGY of a priest, either early C13 or much later rustic work. – MONUMENT. John Middleton † 1709, epitaph with putti and handsome decoration. – PLATE. Chalice, 1606; Paten, 1642; two Plates, 1779 (?).

53b GAINFORD HALL. A tall, compact, impressive stone house of 1603, in shape a parallelogram, nearly a square. Three storeys in height. In the centre of each side a rectangular projection. This has on the main front a profusely but flatly decorated doorway. It led into the Hall, distinguished by a broad, though low, six-light mullioned and transomed window. On the opposite side the projection is four-storeyed. The projections are all gabled, and on the E and W side the recessed parts have also gables. Above the middle of the house rises a row of eleven chimneys. The house was in a ruinous condition in the C19, but has been well restored. Inside, some minor plasterwork and panelling. Nearby a big circular stone DOVECOTE, and in the gardens, in line with the W tower of the church, a tall Tuscan column as a MEMORIAL to the Peace of Aachen of 1748. It stood originally at Stanwick Hall.

The VILLAGE GREEN has no particularly interesting houses, but is visually exceptionally successful thanks to its irregular shape, asymmetrical planting of trees, and a change of level between the N side and the rest. Dr Thomas Sharp has drawn attention to the way in which, in spite of its position along a main thoroughfare, all views are closed.

GATESHEAD

Gateshead with (1951) 115,000 inhabitants is the second largest town of County Durham, yet, in appearance, it can hardly be called a town at all, so much is it overshadowed by its bigger neighbour Newcastle, across the river. No one would choose to investigate the sights of Gateshead for fun, nor are there any to be reckoned amongst the really enjoyable ones of the county. However, a few things have to be noted and may be followed with profit.

ST MARY. S doorway of *c*. 1200 with hood-mould decorated by that Durham favourite, the nutmeg motif. The rest C14, remodelled in the C18 and restored in 1875. All windows new, except one small C12 window on the N side of the chancel. Five-bay C14 arcades with octagonal piers and double-chamfered arches dying into them. N and S transepts. Double-chamfered chancel arch on corbels. C15 nave roof, nearly flat. W tower of 1740, the upper parts altered *c*. 1773. Attached to the church on the N side an ancient ANCHORAGE, rebuilt apparently in the C18. – PEWS with their ends decorated by strapwork and foliage and with poppy-heads; made in 1634. – CHANCEL STALLS. Of the same type, but 1695. The wealth of old seating is quite out of the ordinary. – SCULPTURE. Foliated cross tomb-lids in the porch. – STAINED GLASS. A C13 panel of French style with Pilate washing his hands; bought at Tours in 1937 (S aisle). – PLATE. Chalice and Paten, 1660; two Flagons given 1672; Paten given 1732; Almsdish given 1780; Chalice and Paten and two Almsdishes of London make given in 1785.

The church lies in an ample churchyard without many large trees. To the E a square MAUSOLEUM (Green Family, but said to have been built by *R. Trollop*, the architect of the Exchange at Newcastle, for his own use; i.e. late C17) with an obelisk on skulls at the top. The churchyard is placed close to, but well above, the river. Until a hundred years ago there were crowded houses between; now the river can be fully seen. To the W another surprise; the high bridge over to Newcastle which makes the church and the old parts of Gateshead look very humble.

For Gateshead up to *c*. 1800 was no more than a few streets by the church and a ribbon development along the Gates Head, or bridgehead S from the old bridge. Of that time hardly anything survives, except a few houses in OAK-WELLGATE, especially the Bush Inn, a stately seven-bay three-storey stone house with a carriage-way in and a central pediment. It was all but derelict at the time of writing. Opposite two five-bay, two-storeyed brick houses.

Up the High Street, on the E side, the only other piece of

antiquarian interest: HOLY TRINITY whose S aisle is
the C13 ST EDMUND'S CHAPEL. It has a fine C13 front
and a three-order doorway flanked by two tiers of pointed
trefoiled blank arches with a splendid group of seven
stepped lancet arches of which three contain windows.
The S side has shafted lancet windows. The chapel became later part of a hospital founded in the C14. This in
its turn was made into a private house at the Dissolution,
and from that comes the Elizabethan GATEWAY to the
SW of the church front. In 1837 *John Dobson* enlarged the
chapel into a new parish church for Gateshead by making
it the S aisle of a new nave in the E.E. style. *Dobson's*
church was altered by *S. Piper* in 1897.

To follow the development of Gateshead from 1800 to about
1840 one must walk along West Street, High West Street,
and Bensham Road. The dates of the houses can easily be
recognized from their styles. WATERLOO TERRACE in
High West Street, three-storeyed, is dated 1815. A map
of 1830 has more terraces along the same side of High
West Street.

HALL TERRACE off Bensham Road and WALKER TER-
RACE in Bensham Road must have come immediately
after that. Walker Terrace South is remarkable for being
composed of five-bay houses. Their doorways have
Tuscan pilasters. REGENT TERRACE and then a little
further out to the S such streets as Albert Street, Leopold
Street, Coburg Street, and Prince Consort Road date
themselves. Along BENSHAM ROAD a few larger detached houses, notably Holly House on the N side (C17,
refaced C18) and the Rectory of 1825 (five-bay ashlar
front).

The commercial and administrative centre at the N end of
West Street was developed at the same time; *see* No. 22
(three bays, plain but quite distinguished classical) and
No. 44 of 1848.* At the corner of Nelson Street the former DISPENSARY, four by three bays, brick, with the
typical Gateshead (and Newcastle) doorway with Tuscan

* Opposite this lived and died Thomas Bewick. The site is now
occupied by the Post Office.

pilasters. The date must be *c.* 1830. Lower down is
GATESHEAD WEST STATION, 1868, by *Thomas Prosser*.

A confirmation of the dates of development is the church of
ST EDMUND in Brunswick Street of 1810, the former
Presbyterian Church of 1836, and Bethesda Chapel, also
of 1836; the former is in ELLISON STREET WEST, the
latter in MELBOURNE STREET.

Of C19 churches there is little of interest. ST CUTHBERT,
Bensham Road, 1848, by *Dobson* (with aisle of 1875 : GR),
in a Neo-Norman style with E.E. tower at the SW end;
ST JOSEPH (R.C.), Bensham Road and High West Street,
elaborately and proudly Dec, 1859, by *A. H. Dunn* (GR);
and ST GEORGE, Durham Road, 1895, by *Stephen Piper*,
large and rockfaced E.E.

Finally, in the outer districts, a few houses which once stood
on their own and did not form part of Gateshead. To
these belonged PARK HOUSE, now within the works of
Messrs Clarke, Chapman & Co., and deprived of all its
dignity. It is a seven-bay, three-storey brick house and
had once a staircase of uncommonly high quality.* Still
outside the town NORTH LEAM, Leam Lane, by *Dobson*,
c. 1840, a stately stone house with one front of six bays
adorned by giant pilasters, the other with a broad doorway with Tuscan pilasters.

The most recent development of Gateshead is the TEAM 63b
VALLEY TRADING ESTATE, originated in 1936 to help
against the unemployment and distress of Tyneside. It is
a remarkable example of planned architecture (by *W.
Holford*), very C20 in appearance, and not picturesque at
all. Long straight avenues and low, red brick factories,
mostly smokeless, along them. The centre is a main block,
curved in shape and symmetrical, with post office, banks,
etc. The style is C20 throughout, though very much varying

* Park House was built before 1714, 'gutted' and extensively altered
between 1714 and 1718 and again in 1730. The alterations of 1730 were
done to the designs of *James Gibbs* for Henry Ellison, nephew of Col.
Liddell of Ravensworth and uncle of Ralph Carr of St Helen Auk-
land. The information comes from Mr E. Hughes's *North Country
Life*, 1953. It is particularly interesting in this book to follow the
relationships between patrons of architecture.

in quality. The best individual building is the factory
for SIGMUND PUMPS, by *F. R. S. Yorke, Rosenberg, &
Mardell*, 1948. It has a two-storeyed administrative block
to the W and a canteen block in the NW corner with a
garden. The buildings are of brick, with much glass, two
screen walls of random rubble, and porches with upward-
curving roofs, that is all the motifs of 1945–50; but they
are all handled with much refinement. Amongst the other
factories the following may be mentioned: Durham China
Company by *Newrick & Blackwell*, completed 1951;
Armstrong Cork Company by *D. McIntyre*, completed
1948; Anglo-Scottish Tool Company by *J. Gibson Cowe*,
completed 1950.

GIBSIDE

That the buildings of the Gibside Estate have been allowed
to fall into ruin is a great loss to the county.

The HALL, 1603–20 and 1805, has a three-storeyed symmetrical E front with four mullioned and transomed bay
windows and a central porch with columns on tall
pedestals. The big top parapet with its broad battlements
belongs to the remodelling of 1805, as does the whole
long, completely plain W front, beautifully overlooking
the Derwent, and the N wing.

The buildings which adorn the grounds are by *Paine*,
c. 1750–60. To the S of the Hall is the ORANGERY with
seven arched windows and vases on the parapet. To the
NE of the Hall the plain STABLES and further NE, on the
top of the steep hill, the BANQUETING HOUSE, a gem
of early Gothic Revival. Angle turrets and between them
one Gothick window on each side and a bow window
between. This is crowned by three crocketed steep sham-
Dec gables. The building must be urgently recommended
for preservation as a picturesque ruin. The grounds were
landscaped by *Capability Brown, c*. 1760–70.

The best building architecturally on the Gibside Estate
(for the Banqueting House is not much more than a
whim), fortunately, stands complete and is still in use, the
29a   CHURCH, by *Paine*, begun in 1760 as a mausoleum for

the Bowes family, converted into a church in 1809 and consecrated in 1812. It is a perfect example of a Georgian church in the most select classical style. A Greek cross with three apses, outside square-ended. The returns of the arms are filled in by small squares. Above the crossing a raised dome on a low drum decorated with swags, on the four small corner rooms smaller domes – that is essentially a plan of Byzantine origin, Venetian tradition, and taken up by Wren (St Anne and St Agnes). On the ritual w (actually NE) side a portico with stairs up and giant unfluted Ionic columns. The detail inside and out of the finest, the tooling of the stones, for instance, most delicate. The furnishing wonderfully complete: holy table in the centre surrounded by rails, three-decker pulpit to its E, still partly under the crossing, with the staircases leading up to the preacher's place; oval sounding board supported by one Ionic column, box pews in the side apses and the corner rooms; all the joinery of the best cherrywood. 30b

A long avenue stretches out NE from the portico towards a COLUMN erected by George Bowes in 1750–7. It carries a statue of British Liberty 12 ft high and originally gilt, a splendid symbol of Whiggery. *Christopher Richardson* was the carver. The column is of the Tuscan variety and so tall that it might well stand in the most ambitious of London squares. In fact its 140 ft make it just a little higher than the Nelson column. The grounds are the best example of a Georgian landscape in Durham.

GREAT BURDON

Nice village green with brick houses.

GREATHAM

ST JOHN THE BAPTIST. The records read: Rebuilt 1792, enlarged 1855, w tower new in 1909. In the rebuilding the nave arcades of four bays were left standing. They belong to the Transitional style. Piers octagonal and circular (sw corbel oddly fluted), capitals simply moulded,

arches pointed and slightly double-chamfered except for
two on the N side which are enriched by zigzag. – SCULP-
TURE. At the E end of the N aisle minor bits of Saxon
crosses. – PLATE. London-made Chalice and Paten, 1571;
Chalice, London-made, 1839.

HOSPITAL OF GOD, ST MARY AND ST CUTHBERT.
Founded 1272, re-founded 1610. The present buildings
of 1788 (Chapel) and 1803–4 (Hospital). The Chapel
stands just W of the church. It is a plain rectangle with a
modest W tower with pyramid roof. The furnishings were
renewed in 1899.* The Hospital is by *Jeffry Wyatt*
(*Wyatville*). Yet it is undeniably mean in size and finish.
One-storeyed, with widely spaced two-light windows and
the Hall in the centre emphasized by a loggia of three
pointed arches and a starved bell turret. The little building is stuccoed.‡ The Master's House is so much statelier
and more solid than the rest that it tends to shock the C20
traveller. Five-bay front, two-and-a-half-storeyed, of solid
stone, built (inscription) in 1725.

A group of nice houses at the S end of the village green. To
the SE the large salt-works (Greatham salt-pans were
operating as early as the C11) and a RAILWAY VIADUCT
of thirty-four brick arches, built in 1840.

GREAT STAINTON

ALL SAINTS, 1876, by *Pritchett* (GR). With broach-spire on
a tower whose angle buttresses have many set-offs. –
PLATE. Fine secular Cup of 1569; Paten with inscription
of 1705.

GREENCROFT HALL *see* LANCHESTER

GRINDON

ST THOMAS BECKET. In ruins. The chancel of rubble
masonry was the oldest part, it is said. No details now

---

* PLATE. Chalice and Paten, 1670.
‡ PLATE. Chalice, Cover, and Paten, made in London, 1670; German Flagon, *c.* 1600.

remain to confirm it. The nave is ashlar-built. The s doorway and the w, s, and n single lancets date it as *c.* 1200 or a little earlier.

HAMSTERLEY

St James. An E.E. church without tower, quite on its own to the w of the village. Only the s doorway is older (Norman, completely plain); the w window and the very pretty twin bellcote (c17?) and the s windows (c19) are younger. The E.E. windows are lancets (much renewed) except for the n transept n window which is of the type of *c.* 1300 with three stepped and cusped lancets under one pointed arch (cf. Stanhope nearby). – A foliated cross tomb-lid with the c13 Effigy of a priest against the n transept e wall and half hidden by it. – Plate. Paten of 1519–20, London-made, with relief of the Vernicle.

The Castles. Remains of a fortified camp; native work after the departure of the Romans.

Hoppyland Hall *see p.* 169.

HAMSTERLEY HALL
3¾ m. NE of Shotley Bridge

The house is of medium size, Gothick of *c.* 1770, with crenellations and ogee-headed windows, but it incorporates mullioned and transomed windows and a mullioned and transomed two-storey bay window and a sentry-box-like pavilion from Beaudesert, all *c.* 1610. The main doorway is of *c.* 1700, beautifully carved woodwork with a generous shell hood. In the centre of the front lawn stands, like a conduit, a pinnacle from the Early Victorian Houses of Parliament, brought here, when it was replaced at a restoration. The interior has several pretty Gothick rooms, especially the Dining Room and the Drawing Room. In the Dining Room a simple late c15 fireplace from Crosby Hall, Bishopsgate, London. In one of the bedrooms the magnificent state bed from Stoke Edith in Herefordshire which was built in 1697–9. Hamsterley Hall was the house of Surtees, the author of *Jorrocks*.

HAGG HOUSE, ½ m. NW. C17 and C18, stone. Two three-light mullioned windows, the other C18. MHLG.)

(DERWENT COTE, I m. WNW. Disused steel furnace. Long, low, plain building with conical furnace. Said to be the earliest surviving steel furnace in England. Is it true? MHLG.)

HARDWICK HALL
I m. NW of Sedgefield

The house is plain, and spacious, with an ingenious secret chamber in an attic chimney breast. It does not in the least prepare one for the fun Mr John Burdon, its owner from 1748, has had in his grounds. Unfortunately, of the buildings which *James Paine* put up for him there, two have vanished completely, the Bathing House by the pool just below the house on the W, and the Library, and the remaining three are in a ruinous state. One might say that at least in one case that does not matter much: in the case of the GATEHOUSE which was erected as a sham ruin. Except for the typically Gothick circular tower by the side of the gateway it looks surprisingly convincing. No wonder, as it incorporates genuine fragments from Guisborough Priory (*see*, for example, the vaulting). As to the BANQUETING HOUSE which was an exceedingly fine structure of *c.* 1760, the devastation is most regrettable. The façade is as good as that of Gibside chapel, three bays, at the angles coupled Corinthian pilasters, between the bays single ones. In the outer bays windows with broken pediments and Ionic columns intermittently blocked. In the centre bay a doorway with Venetian surround again with Ionic columns. The cornice crowning the building is exemplarily detailed. The plasterwork inside is in the last stages of disintegration. Outside the present estate to the W the TEMPLE, a domed octagonal building of 1754–7, surrounded by a square one-storey colonnade, six columns on each side.

56a

HARPERLEY

HARPERLEY OLD HALL, Low Harperley. C16 house with a few of the original windows preserved. They are of three lights, straightheaded under hood-moulds, with depressed arches for each light. The centre of the house was the Hall, which has still its large fireplace. One doorway to the offices or Kitchen also remains. The front of the house has slightly projecting wings to the l. and r. of the Hall.

HART

St Mary Magdalene. A pleasantly unrestored looking church, with architectural contributions from divers periods. Long and low, against a screen of trees to the N, and with a view from the E over the sea. The historically most remarkable features are in the nave, clear evidence of an Anglo-Saxon church without aisles, but with a chancel. They are externally the traces of long-and-short work at all four angles, most clearly visible in the SE, and internally the fragment of the chancel arch just above the present arch, and the triangular-headed window above (cf. Norton and places in other counties, e.g. Hexham, Deerhurst, etc.). The corbel-heads above the N arcade, however, are not Saxon, but Norman. Also Norman the short, broad, square W tower, without buttresses and battlements; see the arch towards the nave on responds with angle shafts. The arch mouldings correspond to the responds. The upper part of the tower has small pointed lancets, that is dates from a somewhat later phase, say c. 1200. Of the same the s aisle W window (lancet with nail-head decoration in the hood-mould). The round chancel arch and the N arcade of two bays with octagonal pier and round arches are C15. The S arcade and S porch are dated by the Victoria County History c. 1600. No C14 windows, some Perp windows (renewed); most of the windows, however, C17 or C18 replacements, round-arched with one or two plain mullions. Chancel rebuilt 1806 and restored 1898. – FONTS. One font is Norman, big and square with angle shafts with block capitals, a form uncommon in Durham and perhaps the work of the mason of the tower arch; the other ornate late C15, octagonal, with heads carved at the foot, standing figures under ogee arches on the stem, angels on the underside of the bowl, and more figures on the bowl, all richly but badly carved, the figures with broad, mannered coiffures, still in a C14 tradition. – SCULPTURE. Early Anglo-Saxon shafts as at Monkwearmouth and Jarrow; several interlace, etc., fragments from Anglo-Saxon crosses; corbel-heads in the s porch; panel of *c.* 1500 with St George in the outer s wall of the church. – PLATE. Chalice, 1571; Paten of London make, 1784.

THE HARTLEPOOLS

Although Hartlepool and West Hartlepool are administratively distinct boroughs, there is visually no distinction between them, and as this book is concerned with visual affairs, the two must be described as one. The history of Hartlepool goes back to the mid C7, when a monastery was founded here which became famous through its late C7 abbess Hilda. Hartlepool as a town certainly existed by the middle of the C12. In 1200 it received a charter from King John. Of Saxon remains the most important was a cemetery discovered in 1833. Finds were distributed between the British Museum, Durham, and Newcastle. Of remains of about 1200 there is more, and it is still visible much in its pristine pride: the parish church of St Hilda. The history of West Hartlepool, on the other hand, is of American brevity. It begins with the formation in 1831 of a company to get a railway to Hartlepool and build a dock. The Old Harbour was opened in 1835 which had until then for centuries been just a creek. The railway to Stockton was opened in 1841. In 1840 the first cargo of timber arrived, and the import of timber and export of coal have remained the staple trades of West Hartlepool. The Victoria Dock was opened in 1840, the New Harbour in 1847, the Jackson Dock in 1852, the Swansea Dock in 1850, and so on. In 1854 the West Hartlepool Town Improvement Company was established. No building worth noting seems older than 1835. The population was 4,700 in 1851. It grew to 21,000 in 1871 and 63,000 in 1901. It is now 73,000 (plus Hartlepool 17,000).

CHURCHES

St Hilda, Hartlepool. One of the most important parish churches in the county, situated close to the tip of the peninsula on which Hartlepool grew, and soon outgrew its mother church at Hart of which it was only a chapelry (Hart-le-Pool). The church is the product of about fifty years or less, with the exception of the s portal which is Norman and decorated by several zigzags in the voussoirs, and of the chancel, rebuilt by *Pritchett* in 1870. The nave 19 of six bays, the chancel arch, and the remaining original w bay of the chancel are all in the earliest E.E., of *c*. 1200. The s arcade is a little earlier in style than the N arcade, as a comparison of the piers and arches will show. On the s side there are alternatingly square piers with four keeled demi-shafts and octagonal piers with eight attached shafts; on the N side the piers have four main keeled shafts and four minor attached shafts. The capitals are all simply moulded, the abaci all circular. The arches on the N are more finely moulded than those on the s. The s hood-moulds are enriched by nutmeg ornament. On both sides vaulting-shafts rise on corbels right above the capitals, and the clerestory windows are single lancets with nook-shafts inside, but outside made into handsome groups of three by blank arches to the l. and r. The aisles have now renewed Perp windows except for lancets (also renewed, but fairly correctly) on the s side of the chancel aisle. Transverse arches connect the arcade piers with the aisle walls. They rest on interestingly decorated corbels, with the exception of one (s side, last bay before chancel) where there is a proper respond, keeled, with a shaft-ring. The chancel elevation is different in most of its details from the nave, though not in its character. The piers have four main shafts with fillets and four slim shafts in the diagonals. There are no vaulting-shafts, and the clerestory has a tripartite division inside as well as outside. The chancel arch rests on complex responds with capitals similar to waterleaf. But the most interesting part is the w tower. It is decorated outside by tall blank arcading

with shaft-rings and has lancet windows. The top is later,
with big battlements and simple pinnacles. Cyclopic buttresses project at r. angles from the angles to N, S, and W.
They are preposterously heavy for their purpose, and as
inside blocked arches are visible to the N and S and a much
taller, richly shafted, quite obviously blocked arch to the
W identical with that towards the nave on the E, and as,
moreover, a finely detailed E.E. portal with three orders
of colonnettes and a cusped arch leads from the S into the
present low chapel W of the W tower, there can be no
question that originally the church was meant to have a W
extension and lower N and S extensions as well, that is a
cruciform plan at the W instead of the E end. That sounds
hardly credible, but there is at least one parallel in Britain:
the W end of Kelso, datable late C12. The type is German,
not French. – FONT. Of baluster shape, 1728. – PLATE.
Set given in 1813 and 1818. – MONUMENT. Brass to Jane
Bell † 1593, N wall.

29b CHRIST CHURCH, West Hartlepool. The parish church of
the new town, built in 1854, in the middle of Church
Square, close to the other important buildings to come.
What made the promoters of West Hartlepool choose *E.
B. Lamb*, the naughtiest of mid-Victorian architects, we
do not know. He provided a low wide building with an excessively high W tower. The E.E. style of the rest of the
exterior does not apply to the tower which is without
historical precedent. It is unbuttressed but rises with two
mighty set-backs, and it ends in an oversized parapet above
which there is a second, pierced, parapet, and the stair-
turret rises yet higher and has a roguish obelisk roof.
The interior is not high and seems exaggeratedly low because of the extremely low springing of the big heavy
timber arches of the roof. The chancel is apsed and there
are transepts. At the crossing is the weeniest cupola, sky-
lit, and supported on the same cyclopic timber arches as
the roof, only thrown across diagonally. To support these
various arches the crossing piers are of a shape which
defeats description.

ST MARY (R.C.), Brougham Street, H. 1850–1, by *J. A.*

Hansom, with its E.E. façade facing the street between ordinary houses.

ST PAUL, Grange Road, W.H. 1885–6, by *C. Hodgson Fowler*, and one of his most expensive and most successful efforts in the county. Red brick, with very tall, slim, NW tower with angle turrets and pyramidal roof. Lancet windows (E end with group of five stepped lancets).

HOLY TRINITY, Vane Street, H. 1850–1, by *John Middleton*. Towerless and rather mean, though the windows are in the Dec style.

METHODIST CHURCH, Victoria Road, W.H. 1871–3. Large, of brick, with arched windows and a proud stone façade in a good position. The Corinthian giant portico is the most monumental element of ecclesiastical architecture of West Hartlepool.

METHODIST CHURCH, Grange Road, W.H. 1905, by *Henry Barnes*. In a pretty, free, mixed Neo-Gothic style. Front with angle turrets, but steep pediments over the twin W entrances and a large window above in which Perp tracery has gone completely straight. The result is a grid of mullions and transomes under a depressed arch.

METHODIST CHURCH, Brougham Street, H. 1851, the usual arched front with big pediment. Stuccoed.

INDEPENDENT CHAPEL, Brougham Street, H. 1843, with pedimented four-pilaster front.

For other Nonconformist places of worship, *see* Perambulations.

PUBLIC BUILDINGS

TOWN HALL, Middlegate, H., 1866, by *C. J. Adams*. Red brick, on a modest scale, but with a very Victorian, vaguely Continental, Baronial tower.

TOWN HALL, Lauder Road, W.H., 1893, by *H. A. Cheers*. Red brick, Neo-Perp with Neo-Georgian turret or louvre. Very Nonconformist in looks.

MUNICIPAL BUILDINGS, Clarence Street, W.H. The front towards the parish church 1889, in the George & Peto style, that is between Franco-Flemish Flamboyant and Neo-Dutch. The back, next to the Library, in the meekly debased Latest Classical of the 50s.

CD.—8

PUBLIC LIBRARY, Clarence Road, W.H. 1895, by *J. W. Brown* with additions of 1914.

JACKSON DOCK. Adjoining this is a stately Latest Neo-Classical warehouse with pediments. It was built in 1858.

PERAMBULATION

(A) HARTLEPOOL. St Hilda has still its churchyard, though not in a very well-kept state. It is surrounded by mean houses on all sides. Nothing survives to testify to the prosperity of the town and its harbour in the Middle Ages. And prosperity in the late C17 and C18 is indicated only by the CONSERVATIVE CLUB in Church Walk, which consists of a stone core and amongst additions a fine ballroom.* To the SW of the church some fragments of the
49b   medieval TOWN WALL remain, especially SANDWELL GATE with its breakwater-like turrets and its pointed arch between. Above, in the street called Town Wall, a few wealthy Georgian houses, notably the SANDSIDE CAFÉ (door with Gibbs surround). Since the Second World War the slums and the Georgian remains have become mixed up with suburban semi-detached housing, an untidy sight altogether. The streets to the SE of the church, such as ALBION TERRACE, SOUTH CRESCENT, etc., have minor Early Victorian or just pre-Victorian terraces. Such street names as REGENT STREET, DUKE STREET, SUSSEX STREET tell the same story. FRIAR TERRACE N of the church deserves a look too.

(B) WEST HARTLEPOOL. Considering the existence of the Town Improvement Company and the great affluence of the new town in the fifties and sixties, one imagines something very much more splendid or at least dignified than what West Hartlepool is. The raised wand of the church steeple has roused nothing around. The earlier buildings are low and no more spectacular than, say, the medievalizing CHURCH SQUARE SCHOOL of 1857 (by *W. Young*) or the classical MASONIC LODGE of 1864 (by *Tilman* of Sunderland, a mason himself). To get something bigger

* The MHLG lists suggest (very rightly) restoration and conversion into an institute or museum.

one must walk on to the W to the GRAND HOTEL of 1899 (by *J. Garry*), red brick with yellow terra-cotta, or the CO-OPERATIVE STORE of 1913–5 by *Lionel G. Ekins* (of the Co-operative Wholesale Society) in Stockton Street. Its giant columns and its Neo-Wren cupola are the most prominent piece of architecture in the town. The only early building of some self-respect is the ATHE-NAEUM in Church Street (1851–2 by *R. H. Robson*, the Land Agent to the Dock Company) with its stone front and giant Tuscan pilasters. Tuscan pilasters or fluted demi-columns on a small scale also frame the doorways of the earliest terraces in such streets as YORK ROAD, BRUNSWICK STREET, etc. The rich men of the High Victorian era built their villas out to the W, towards the Ward Jackson Park, at the top of Church, Park, and Grange Roads.

HAUGHTON-LE-SKERNE

ST ANDREW. Norman except for the transepts, vestry, and S porch, which were added in 1895. Broad W tower in two stages, unbuttressed. W doorway in axis with the nave, not with the tower, with one order of colonnettes, an un-usually big lintel, and an unsculptured tympanum. Broad rectangular SE stair-turret, the upper parts polygonal. The turret is flush with the nave S wall. This has a doorway like the one in the tower, but with a hood-mould decorated by a billet frieze. The chancel has on the S and N sides round-headed windows; and at the E end, inside and outside, a group of three tall Norman windows can still be detected. They had nook-shafts in the interior with scalloped capitals. The chancel arch is also Norman, low and one-stepped on the plainest responds. On the N side of the nave close to the W end a tall blocked C13 lancet window. – Most of the FURNISHINGS are of the Cosin period, bought it is said, from a parish rate ordered in 1662. The style is, however, so similar to that of the woodwork at Gateshead that a date in the 1630's seems more likely. The church gives a very complete picture of that date. The

nave has BOX PEWS with their ends rusticated below,
34a decorated with strapwork higher up, and crowned by
poppy-heads, the walls of the nave and the chancel are
panelled (as are also those of the transepts). To the l. and
34b r. of the chancel arch are PULPIT and READER'S DESK,
in identical position and of similar design, still with
strapwork decoration. Of the same type of decoration a
broad canopy above the s door. The FONT COVER is the
only piece which may well be of *c.* 1662. The modern
TOWER SCREEN incorporates canopies of the same type,
probably from chancel stalls. – ANGLO-SAXON FRAG-
MENTS, collected against the N wall of the nave. –
Fragments of tomb-lids with FOLIATED CROSSES, etc.,
in the porch. – ROYAL ARMS. 1737. – PLATE. Paten,
London, 1684; Flagon, London, 1754.
NE of the church the RECTORY, brick, C18. Further E the
long, pretty village green.

HAVERTON HILL
2 m. E of Billingham

ST JOHN THE EVANGELIST, 1865. – PLATE. Chalice, 1664,
and Paten inscribed 1687, both from Egglescliffe.

HAWTHORN

HAWTHORN TOWER. Down a wooded dene, close to the
sea. Castellated and cemented, with three- and four-light
mullioned and hood-moulded windows. Dugdale writes
(*c.* 1815) that the house was built 'some years ago as a
summer retreat named Sailors' Hall'. The railway has
spoilt its position.

HEADLAM HALL

A perfect example of a medium-sized manor house of stone,
Jacobean on one side, of the early C18 on two others. The
Jacobean front is symmetrical, of three storeys, with
three-light and four-light windows, mullioned, and mul-

lioned and transomed; the C18 fronts are of two and a half storeys, quoined.

HEBBURN

HEBBURN HALL (Ellison Hall Infirmary). A big C17 house, refaced in 1790. Nine bays by five bays. The main front with a three-bay pedimented projection, the other with a doorway with columns set inside the jambs. The principal windows on both fronts emphasized by pediments. The W part of the house is supposed to incorporate masonry from the C14 Hebburn peel tower.

The stables were converted in 1887 (by *M. T. Wilson*) into the church of St JOHN. Complicated seven-light imitation Early Dec chancel window.

St ANDREW PRESBYTERIAN CHURCH. E.E. with excessively tall NW spire 1872; by *Johnson* of Newcastle.

The HEBBURN COLLIERY began to work in 1656 at the latest, and the earliest shafts still in operation were sunk in 8794.

HEIGHINGTON

St MICHAEL. A Norman church, except for the S aisle and its arcade which is C13, the N aisle and arcade which is C19, and the C15 tower top. The tower is unbuttressed, in three stages, without set-backs, has small arched windows, large twin bell-openings with block capitals and a one-stepped arch moulding, and a S doorway with one order of colonnettes and a more finely moulded arch. A joint in the W wall of the S aisle shows that there was no aisle originally. The doorway to the S aisle was (as happens so often) removed later to its present position. It has also an order of colonnettes, and in the arch a broad, flat zigzag and a roll moulding. The hood-mould shows a billet-frieze. The E windows of the aisle area group of small stepped lancets. The other windows must have been replaced later. They are straightheaded, of three lights, with ogee tops to the lights. The E end of the church is of a very rare type: square presbytery and then slightly narrower and lower square apse (if thus it can be called). In the Sanctuary one

Norman N window and one blocked C13 lancet on the S
side. The chief Norman feature inside is the chancel arch.
Its responds are broad demi-piers with singularly heavy,
massive two-scallop capitals. The arch has a demi-roll
moulding and concave quarter-circle mouldings. The
same moulding in the tower arch. That perhaps dates
these parts, as it is exactly as in the earliest ribs of Durham, c. 1095. The S arcade of three bays has octagonal
piers and double-chamfered arches. – PULPIT. Early C16,
wood, polygonal, with panels with Flamboyant tracery in
the tops and an inscription below the rim: 'Orate pro
animabus Alexandri Flettcher et Agnetis uxoris sue'. –
CHANCEL STALLS. Probably about same date; a few
poppy-heads. – PLATE. Paten, 1744; Cup and Flagon,
1818. – MONUMENTS. Foliated cross tomb-lid in
chancel. – Two female effigies under the tower, badly
preserved, C13 or early C14. – George Crosyer † 1662,
brass inscription plate with coarse stone surround (chancel).

The VILLAGE GREEN is very large, and the church and
churchyard are placed into the middle of its N side, dividing it to the eye into two greens. E and S of the churchyard
some houses have intruded, and that also helps to give
variety. The main road runs S–N on the E side of the W
part of the green, and a secondary road meets it which
comes along the N side. The arrangement and altogether
the spaciousness and composition of the green must be
seen to be appreciated. Dr Sharp rightly illustrates it in
his *The Anatomy of the Village*.

LEGS CROSS, 2½ m. W. Base and Shaft, with (says J. E.
Hodgkin) traces of Anglo-Saxon interlace.

HELMINGTON HALL
½ m. N of Hunwick

Most of the house has been pulled down. The remaining
part shows the same windows as had the rest, with scrolled
open segmental pediments. In connexion with this motif
and its position in the history of domestic architecture in

County Durham it is worth noting that the house possessed an inscription with the date 1686.

HESLEDON see MONK HESLEDON

HETTON-LE-HOLE

St Nicholas, 1898–1901, by *S. Piper*. A good picturesque w front with, on the ground floor, a Baptistery with three parallel gables, and above it a group of five lancets under a gable. Gabled buttresses; bellcote. The interior with tall, square, slightly chamfered piers and arches high up dying into them.

Fairies' Cradle. Off Houghton Road. Supposed to be a cairn. Confirmation required.

HEWORTH
2½ m. ese of Gateshead

St Mary, 1822, by the rector, *John Hodgson*. The plans said to have been made for him by *John Stokoe* (GR). w tower unbuttressed and narrower than the nave. Nave, transepts, and chancel. Flat roof, tall transomed two-light lancets with a little Dec tracery, typical of the date of the church. – STAINED GLASS by *Ballantyne* (MHLG). – PLATE. Pre-Reformation Chalice and Paten; Paten, 1772. – In the churchyard MONUMENT to the Haddon children, 1717. They lie in bed in a stone four-poster with four alternatingly rusticated pillows, well tucked in under a patterned blanket.

Heworth Hall (Conservative Club). To the e of the church; an uncommonly good house of *c.* 1700 with a late C18 back. The front, unfortunately immediately above the railway, is of five bays and two storeys with a doorpiece with fluted Ionic pilasters and a big segmental pediment. The back has an Adamish four-column porch and a broken pediment over the middle three bays.

HIGH CONISCLIFFE see CONISCLIFFE

HILTON CASTLE see HYLTON CASTLE

HOLLINSIDE
1½ m. SW of Whickham

Ruins of a fortified manor house beautifully placed right above the river Derwent. The Hall was a long oblong with, at its S end, high up (i.e. originally on the upper floor) a two-light, C13 window with a pierced circle in the spandrel. To the E an entrance tower with a hugely high open arch, 20 ft high by 9 ft wide (cf. Lumley). To its N a barrel-vaulted room. Towards the river, at the S end, seems to have been a smaller tower. The wall of the house stands fairly high up here, in good sheer masonry.

Off the lane to Hollinside from the Whickham–Barnopfield road, on the r. the odd MONUMENT to John English, 1854, a bust on a tall column, to commemorate a stone mason who was famous as a strong man.

HOLMSIDE
2½ m. NE of Lanchester

HOLMSIDE HALL. The medieval buildings, according to H. R. Leighton, once ranged round a courtyard. Now there are only very few features of interest left of them, chiefly an oddly shaped three-light window in the W gable of a long barn and two doorways in the same barn. The window seems to consist of two ogee-arched lights and a narrower two-centred arched light between them, the whole under a straight head with a hood-mould. The mullions are broken out, and in their stead a rudely carved figure has been put in, playing the bagpipes (?). The style of the figure is not easily datable; it may just be rustic C17 or C18 work.

HOLMSIDE NEW HALL. Originally called Little Holmside according to the inscription above the door. This inscription also dates the spacious foursquare house. The date is 1668. It refers to the S wing, two-and-a-half-storeyed, of five bays, and symmetrical. The ground floor has (or had) four-light windows at the l. and r. ends, and in the middle two two-light windows close to the doorway. The first floor again had four-light, two-light, two-light, four-light windows. Above these all windows are of two lights. They are all still hood-moulded. The r. end of the front was altered early in the C18, when a new E front was put on. This is of five bays and two storeys and has a central doorway with curly open pediment above an eared door frame.

HOPPYLAND HALL
1½ m. NW of Hamsterley

A remarkably impressive house of convincing medieval castle character, thanks to its bold crenellations and projecting towers. Built, it is said, in imitation of Witton Castle, after a fire which took place in 1793.

HORDEN HALL

Well preserved small manor house of *c.* 1600 (Conyers family). Symmetrical N front with central porch. Two-storeyed with a third in the gables on the E and W and at the S end of the wing extending S behind the house. The front porch with coupled Tuscan columns and above a seven-light window. The porch doorway is roundheaded. To the l. and the r. of the porch two three-light mullioned windows under hood-moulds on each floor. Three fireplaces inside; but a wooden overmantel and the staircase taken to Castle Eden (*see* p. 64).

HOUGHALL
1½ m. SSE of Durham

Farmhouse incorporating a square Jacobean staircase with sturdy balusters. It leads round an open wall in three flights to the first floor and in another three to the second. Front with one remaining three-light mullioned and transomed window and a door with a four-centred head. A secret chamber in the main chimney may have been contrived by Father Richard Holtby.

HOUGHTON-LE-SPRING

St Michael and All Angels. A big, prominent
church, with transepts and crossing tower. The existence
of a Norman church is proved by one window in the N
wall of the chancel and, next to it, the door to the vestry
with a small and rather dainty tympanum with two fight-
ing intertwined animals and leaf scrolls. The rest of the
chancel, the transepts, and a good deal of the rest of the
church is C13. In the chancel the finest feature is the S
wall with eight lancet windows, closely set, and on the
inside all shafted (cf. Darlington). Their inner arch
mouldings are oddly depressed (with nailhead decoration). One such window also on the N side of the chancel.
They have all on the outside plain hood-moulds. The E
end is strengthened by big diagonal buttresses. The transept E windows are of the same type as the chancel windows. But on the W side of the transept the style is more
advanced. An early stage of tracery can here be observed:
coupled lancets and above them a quatrefoil; an odd-
shaped hood-mould runs round the whole. The crossing
tower rests on arches with C13 responds, and externally
the lower stage has small lancet windows. The upper
stage is of 1824–36. The nave arcades of four bays rest
on piers with four keeled major and four minor shafts.
Moulded capitals and double-chamfered arches, all still
C13, though the whitewashing throughout (and the roof)
give the interior a curious early C19 appearance.* But perhaps the most remarkable thing about the church is the
big W, E, and S windows, all early C14 and in the Dec
style, which is so rare in the county. The W window is
of five lights with reticulated tracery, the E (five-light)
and the N and S (four-light) windows have tracery of
flowing forms more familiar in East Anglia and South
Yorkshire. Later still the interesting addition of a small
detached two-storeyed, embattled Chapel of the Guild of

---

* *Philip Hardwick* made plans for the new roof in 1831. He probably also heightened the tower, and he inserted the richly Dec N
transept N window.

the Holy Trinity. This belongs to the late C15 (funds left in 1480), *see* the Perp two- and three-light windows with straight heads or depressed pointed arches. It is connected with the church only by a passage. The aisle windows belong to the restoration of 1857–8. – PLATE. Salver, perhaps French, mentioned 1712. – MONUMENTS. Cross-legged Knight with cylindrical helmet covering his face entirely, and shield held very high up (cf. Pittington); late C13. The effigy lies in a shafted C13 recess in the S transept. – Cross-legged Knight with mail-coif, sandstone, *c.* 1300. – Brass to Margery Belassis † 1587, small plaque with group of kneeling figures (S transept). – Bernard Gilpin, the Apostle of the North, Rector of Houghton-le-Spring, † 1583; no effigy; just an uncommonly big tomb--chest whose sides are decorated by large panels with squares and circles.

Houghton is clearly a town, not a village, even in that narrowest centre, where all its worth while buildings stand. In all directions from the church there is something to be examined and enjoyed, although admittedly nothing of prime architectural value. The E end of the churchyard, away from the main road which runs below the church on the W side from S to N, has the DAVENPORT ALMSHOUSES of 1668, a small, pantiled, one-storey building with projecting wings, mullioned windows, and hood-moulds over windows and central doorway; and the former KEPIER GRAMMAR SCHOOL. This is a rambling, very attractive group whose N end comes forward with a gable and blocked mullioned windows. This part belongs to the foundation building of 1574. The five-bay part to its S is probably of 1724, and the S end has a date tablet of 1779. But the S doorway with a pretty, small hood on corbels looks again more like 1724. Up the S side of the churchyard runs CHURCH STREET, continued into NESHAM PLACE. Here, especially at the Nesham Place end, stand the well-to-do Georgian houses of Houghton. But at the corner of Hall Lane is first HOUGHTON HALL (now a Social Club), the manor house of the original village, a tall, square, forbidding building of *c.* 1600, two-

and-a-half-storeyed, with a later parapet and no gables. The façade has four bays, with four-light mullioned windows. The entrance unfortunately is covered up by a recent wooden porch and a brick structure marked 'Gents'. The back is also four windows wide, but they are of three lights. The staircase windows break the symmetry. They are on a level different from the others. Some panelling inside.

w of the churchyard, across the main street, the RECTORY (Council Offices). The core of the house is medieval, but it has been much pulled about. Licence to embattle was given before 1483. £300 was spent on it about 1560–70. About 1670 all was rebuilt, except the original tower-like structure. The E and W wings date from the late C18. Evidence on the spot should once more be compared with these recorded dates. The main street leads to the N up between church and rectory to the WHITE LION, early C19, quoined, with Tuscan porch. Here the street forks. Sunderland Street curves up the hill to the NE past houses of no individual interest but of generally fitting scale and character and reaches the top of the hill where it is cut deep into the limestone rock.

At COPT HILL is the earliest barrow in the county.

HUNSTANWORTH

The scattered village on the wooded hillside with church, vicarage, school, etc. (e.g. High Garden House, outside the village, on the W side), was built at one go in 1863 by the then owner, the Rev. D. Capper of Lyston Court, Herefordshire. The architect he chose was *Teulon* (GR), one of the most ruthless of the High Victorians, insensitive, ham-fisted, and self-assertive. Here, where he cannot play with multi-coloured bricks as in the South, he devises at least patterns of light or dark slates in the roofs, and plays (it must be admitted, wholly successfully) with three colours of local stone, a smooth pale biscuit for dressings, and a darker, rougher buff and rust-brown irregularly arranged for the walls. There are, of course, also plenty of gables and a number of odd little Gothic windows, but on the whole Teulon lets us off lightly.

ST JAMES. Nave and N aisle, apsed chancel, tower with pyramidal roof at the E end of the aisle. Typically Teulonian crude plate tracery. – STAINED GLASS in the nave by *Kempe*, 1879 and 1881. – PLATE. Elizabethan Chalice; Chalice of London make, 1733.

HUNWICK

ST PAUL, 1844, by *W. Thompson*, enlarged 1887 by *Pritchett* (GR).

HUNWICK OLD HALL. Now a farmhouse, but one of the most important surviving examples in the county of a small medieval manor house. The chapel is now a barn. Its large E window remains complete, with Perp tracery, curiously conservative in its use of the geometrical style motif of the cusped circle at the top of the tracery. The house itself retains a one-storeyed bay window, of the unusual shape of a half-hexagon (cf. Bishop Auckland), with cusped four-centred windows and buttresses between them. A sumptuous Jacobean fireplace was removed from the house *c.* 1900. Of the same date a window with an odd two-stepped hood-mould.

HELMINGTON HALL *see* p. 166.

HURWORTH-ON-TEES

ALL SAINTS. C15 W tower, the rest rebuilt 1831–2, but the whole so thoroughly restored in 1870 (by *Pritchett*; GR) that it all appears now Victorian. The arcade piers alternatingly round and octagonal. – MONUMENTS. Unknown Knight, with crossed legs, of Frosterley marble, much mutilated, with cylindrical helmet, completely hiding the face, *c.* 1310. – Unknown Knight, perhaps Robert Fitz William † 1316, also cross-legged, also badly preserved (from Neasham Abbey).

Handsome long GREEN. The only noteworthy house MANOR HOUSE, dated 1728 on a rainwater-head.

At the E end of the Green SCURFIELD MEMORIAL, 1911,
like a sumptuous Georgian gatepost. Who may the designer be?

HYLTON CASTLE
2½ m. NW of Sunderland

49a First mentioned in 1448, but in all probability built about
1400 (cf. Lumley and Raby Castles). Called the Tower
of Hylton in 1461. So what we see to-day is not the
gatehouse of a vanished castle but a complete castle of
the tower-house type. Parallelogram with square angle
turrets and broader square turrets flanking the former
entrance. At the back corbelled-out circular angle turrets
and the centrepiece broad and higher. Sculptured men-
in-arms placed on the turrets (cf. Raby). No record survives of outbuildings, except for the mysterious chapel
(*see* below). The late C17 built a domestic wing to one side,
and in the C18 another was built on the other side. These
were demolished in the C19. The windows are all restored,
though their form (one- and two-light with cusped lights)
is convincing. The back obviously altered in the C19.

The CHAPEL is also C15 and seems always to have been a
a detached structure. It is not in axis with the main building. It has a Perp five-light window, and a similar one
with a transome at the W end. The latter, however, was
interfered with, when in the mid C18 a blank arch was
built on the W front and a doorway with a Gibbs surround
was inserted. The chapel may well have served after the
Dissolution as a Hall or Summer House; for it was provided with wide transeptal canted bay windows on the N
and S. These are in two tiers as if there had been two
storeys inside. They have nine lights on each tier altogether, each light with a depressed arched top. The
date may be *c.* 1560 or even later. The building is mentioned as a chapel in 1558.

JARROW

The least likely spot that could be imagined for one of the
most venerable churches in the kingdom. The church is

close to the docks of Tyneside and surrounded by the waste-land of years of industrial distress. To its s is a rapidly developing Trading Estate of sleek brick factories. To its N, entirely on its own, JARROW HALL, a bow-fronted and pedimented brick villa of *c.* 1800.

ST PAUL. Yet not only the chancel and the tower of the church, but even portions of the walls of the monastery still stand which was founded in 684 by Benedict Biscop (*see* Monkwearmouth). Its first abbot was Ceolfrid and the dedication inscription is still in existence. It reads: DEDICATIO BASILICAE SCI PAULI VIII KL MAI ANNO XV ECFRIDI REG CEOLFRIDI ABB EIUSDEMQ Q ECCL DO AUCTORE CONDITORIS ANNO IIII. Of his time is the chancel which originally was the nave. It is 41½ by 16 ft, that is very tall and narrow, and had a narrower chancel to the E. The walls are of large squared blocks of rubble, a remarkably fine job of masonry for the date and probably due to the masons Benedict Biscop had brought from France because they could build 'juxta Romanorum quem semper amabat morem' (as Bede says). There are small original roundheaded windows and doorways on the N and S sides. In the late C13 and early C14 a three-light intersected and a three-light Dec window were inserted, and later still a three-light straightheaded window with rather conservative tracery. At the W end of the Saxon nave stands a tower which now appears as a crossing tower. This probably dates from the restoration of Prior Aldwin *c.* 1075, a necessary undertaking, it seems, as the monastery apparently had never recovered from the ravages of the Vikings. The tower is of four stages with twin openings on the two upper ones. W of the tower stood a Norman nave which was destroyed in 1786. It is now replaced by one with a N aisle which was built in 1866 by *Sir G. G. Scott*. This has no special merit. – SCULPTURE. Several turned balusters, just as at Monkwearmouth. How they were used remains unknown. – Two pieces of cross shafts, one with interlace, the other, earlier, with birds and a man in a foliage scroll. – STAINED GLASS. E window, 'expressionistic', by *L. C. Evetts*, 1950. – STALLS with good carving. – BADGE of Prior Castel (1494–1519). –

32b CHAIR. Very plain medieval woodwork, with high back of horizontal planks and diagonally trimmed planks as arms. Called Bede's Chair, but probably C14. – PLATE. Chalice, London-made, 1571 (cf. Monkwearmouth, Lanchester); Flagon, 1746.

Of the MONASTERY two walls are the chief remaining fragments. One runs N–S starting just S of the W parts of the nave wall, the other at r. angles towards E. The first is *c.* 75 ft long, the second *c.* 80. S of its E end it was irregularly continued to the S. The excellent masonry of the walls is ascribed to the late C11, and one doorway with one order of heavy columns with block capitals goes indeed well with such a date. But another doorway has a triangular head, and so the wall may well be Saxon. At its head the sills of windows can still be seen.

KELLOE *see* CHURCH KELLOE

KIRK MERRINGTON

ST JOHN THE EVANGELIST. The present church of 1850 is a copy of its predecessor, which was one of the most interesting Norman churches in the county. It is of the tripartite type with aisleless nave, central crossing tower with twin bell-openings, and aisleless chancel of the same length as the nave. In 1850 a further chancel was added. The crossing tower rests on arches with pier-responds. There is a three-order S portal into the nave. Inside the church the most interesting thing is the SCREEN, of typical Cosin forms, *c.* 1660–70. The sections above the dado are divided by balusters and have cusped ogee tracery. Above them runs a broad acanthus frieze, and on this is a curly open pediment. Of the same date and style the CHANCEL STALLS with poppy-heads and the COMMUNION RAIL. – PLATE. Chalice, 1617; Paten given in 1709.

LAMBTON CASTLE

There can be no two views about the picturesqueness of Lambton Castle in the variety of its embattled towers and turrets, its buttressed hall, and its curtain walls, as they appear above the river Wear across the sweeping lawns and the groves of the extensive grounds. Nothing of the building is in fact genuine, except the solid, beautifully biscuit-coloured stone. The old castle was dismantled by William Henry Lambton, father of the first Earl of Durham, in 1797, and replaced by a house called Lambton Hall. This was 'in the modern style' (J. Dugdale) and designed by the elder *Bonomi* (Sykes). About 1833 it was 'greatly enlarged ... and castellated' and thereafter re-named Lambton Castle (Mackenzie and Ross). In 1854 the castle is said to have been 'almost wrecked by sub-sidence' (J. Jamieson) and alterations are recorded for 1875, though it does not seem to be known what they were. The interiors are not of great interest and have recently been much modified, owing to the conversion of the castle into an educational establishment.

LAMESLEY

ST ANDREW. Nothing visible of the church of 1758. What is visible seems to belong to the remodelling of 1821 : w tower arcade with tall quatrefoil piers, N and S galleries, and tall traceried windows. – PLATE. Chalice inscribed 1696; Paten of London make, 1735; Flagon, 1784. – MONUMENT to Frances Jane Liddell (of Ravensworth Castle) † 1823, quite an ambitious standing wall monu-ment, with all-round figures of a mourning woman bent over an altar and a little putto the other side of the altar. Unsigned.

LANCHESTER

ALL SAINTS. One of the most rewarding parish churches in the county. Essentially Norman and E.E., and very fine in both styles. Norman the spectacular chancel arch on responds with three attached columns and heavy one-scallop capitals. The voussoirs closely beset with zigzag. The arch stands on an odd plain substructure (perhaps because the chancel was originally raised by some steps).

In its present form the substructure is certainly renewed.
Norman remains also in the S doorway, the outer doorway of the S porch (not *in situ*, it seems; the arch is treble-
chamfered and pointed), in a blocked opening in the
chancel S wall, and in a S aisle recess. The zigzag arch
here is obviously re-used. The nave and the arcades to
the S and N aisles (four bays) are Transitional, with circular piers, (these have monolithic shafts looted from the
Roman stations) elementarily moulded capitals, round
arches with one keeled moulding and one chamfer, and
nutmeg ornament in the hood-moulds. Then, about the
middle of the C13, the chancel was rebuilt, with tall lancet
windows (at the E end three stepped lancets), their jambs
trefoiled to the inside. The great surprise of the chancel is

21b   its sculpture, a delightful, though somewhat defaced tympanum in the twice-cusped pointed vestry door, with the
small figures of a seated Christ and two angels (typical
style of the mid C13), and in the intrados of the arch below the tympanum a beast, a bird, a naturalistic sprig,
and one unidentifiable subject. Also in the chancel in odd

22   places head-corbels, one especially of *c.* 1250–70, very
fine with the slanting eyes which the Westminster angels
took over from Reims, and Lincoln from Westminster.
The nearest parallels are in the Nine Altars at Durham.
The corbels were used as candle-brackets.* In 1283 the
church was made collegiate by Bishop Bek. To put in stalls
for the prebendaries a chancel chapel was added on the N
side with a depressed four-chamfered arch and, facing it
on the S side, a niche was hollowed out of the wall, also under a four-chamfered arch supported by the most curious
squinches. The old lancet here was replaced by a wide,
airy, three-light window with three stepped but cusped
lancet lights under one arch (the centre light uncusped).
To its W a similar two-light window was inserted, and at
the E end of the S aisle a broad-arched three-light window with different tracery (a quatrefoil in a circle is the
chief motif). The S and W windows are lancet with ogee-

* In the vestry E wall the head of a contemporary window and in the
vestry N wall a reset pointed quatrefoil window.

cusping in the top. Early Perp the N aisle windows and the
whole w tower, which is tall and unbuttressed, has a handsome eight-ribbed vault on the ground floor, and battlements and miniature pinnacles. Later Perp the s aisle s
windows, and the clerestory (including the nearly flat
nave roof). The whole church except for the chancel is
also embattled. – CHANCEL STALLS with traceried backs
and insignificant foliage misericords. – COMMUNION
RAIL. Jacobean with sparsely set balusters. – SCULPTURE.
A fine Roman altar to the goddess Garmangabis in the
porch. – Also in the porch two plain foliated cross tomb-
lids. – STAINED GLASS. Three exceptionally fine pieces of
the early C13: Flight into Egypt, Annunciation to the
Shepherds, Adoration of the Magi (very probably French
and from a cathedral). – PLATE. A Roman silver-gilt
Paten, found in 1575; Chalice of London make, 1570;
Paten of London make, 1710; two Plates inscribed 1762;
Flagon of London make, 1763. – MONUMENTS. Effigy of
a Priest holding a chalice, early C14.

ROMAN FORT. The Roman fort of Lanchester (*Longo-
vicium*) lies ½ mile sw of the village, on the Wolsingham
road. It measures 560 by 485 ft over its stone walls, first
built about A.D. 122. Occupation is attested during the
last quarter of C2, followed by destruction in A.D. 197.
Restoration took place only about A.D. 240, when two inscriptions now in the Chapter Library, Durham, records
a headquarters with armouries and a bath with a hall.
The fort remained in use until the end of C4.

GREENCROFT HALL, 2 m. NW. Seven-bay front plus
slightly projecting one-bay wings. Tuscan porch with
pediment. Said to have been built in 1670.

LANGLEY HALL
1¾ m. NW of Witton Gilbert

Built early in the C16 by Henry Lord Scrope. Now in ruins
and not easily comprehended, as it is all much overgrown.
The remaining fragments still stand up high. They are
parts of the E and W ranges of a building which once had a

square courtyard. Windows of two lights, straightheaded under hood-moulds, with depressed arches to the individual lights. Boyle locates the Great Hall in the E wing, with fireplace at the S end, and the Kitchen at the N end of the same wing. This also still has a fireplace. The W wing was three-storeyed and has two fireplaces and a huge oven adjoining.

LEGS CROSS see HEIGHINGTON

LINTZFORD
1½ m. WNW of Burnopfield, but just off the A 694 road

A pretty group: one-span C18 bridge; Lintzford House, handsome five-bay, two-storey, Georgian stone front; and buildings of a former paper mill.
(A little to the E FRIARSIDE CHAPEL, a C14 chapel, roofless, but could be restored. MHLG.)

LONG NEWTON

ST MARY, 1856–7, by *Teulon* (GR), but of no interest. To the N of the chancel the vaulted Vane Mausoleum. In its centre stood the monument to the third Marquess of Londonderry, now at Wynyard Park. In the mausoleum MONUMENT to Sir Henry Vane Tempest † 1813, by *Westmacott*, epitaph with kneeling allegorical figure. – PLATE. Chalice, London made, 1371.

LOW BUTTERBY see BUTTERBY

LOW DINSDALE

ST JOHN THE BAPTIST, *c.* 1196, restored 1875. Red sandstone, nave and S aisle of two bays with low octagonal pier and single-chamfered arch with chamfered hood-mould. The window tracery renewed. If the S aisle E windows are representative of the original form, this chapel must be late C13: three-light intersected tracery with a vesica window above. Of the same period or a little later the W tower with diagonal buttresses – SCULPTURE. Anglo-

Saxon fragments in the porch and also part of a hogback gravestone in the nave. – STAINED GLASS. S aisle E, by *O'Connor & Taylor*, 1876; undisciplined and not at all imitation-medieval. – PLATE. Chalice and Cover, 1571; Paten, 1726 (?); Flagon of London make, 1751.

S of the church the pretty, irregular MANOR HOUSE of brick, in appearance mostly Georgian.

LOW HARPERLEY see HARPERLEY

LOW MIDDLETON see MIDDLETON-ONE-ROW

LUDWORTH

LUDWORTH TOWER. Licence to crenellate granted by Cardinal Langley in 1422. Few fragments remain now. The E and W walls collapsed in 1890. S of the road walls of several rooms; N of the road a tunnel-vaulted ground floor room and above it a three-storeyed wall, obviously later, with window openings and remains of a fireplace.

LUMLEY CASTLE

Lumley belongs to the most impressive type of castle of its period, the type with ranges of buildings on the four sides of a quadrangular courtyard and bold massive angle projections in the four corners. At Lumley all four have big diagonal buttresses and bold crenellations. Where the towers have square turrets the crenellations are set diagonally so as to obtain openings below them for throwing down missiles. Licences to crenellate were granted to Sir Ralph Lumley in 1389 by the Bishop, and in 1392 by the King. The castle is essentially still as it was built then. The only important alterations were made about 1580, etc., by John Lord Lumley, and shortly after 1721 by the second Earl of Scarborough. His architect was *Sir John Vanbrugh*. Vanbrugh's hand is unmistakable in one room only, but he was no doubt also at least partly responsible for the refenestration of the S and W fronts, the enlargement of the Great Hall by the elimination of the medieval pantry and buttery, and the insertion of the broad corridor and principal staircase on the courtyard side of the s range. The castle is now a residential hostel of the University of Durham.

Entry is through a GATEHOUSE in the middle of the E front. It has angle turrets, a depressed arch over the gateway, and high up between the turrets another depressed and richly cusped arch projecting in front of the wall so as to serve the purpose of machicolation. The outer wall of the gatehouse is decorated by shields. On entering the COURTYARD one has (as usual) the Hall opposite. This is on the first floor; but it has its own entry from the courtyard into the basement, a doorway between polygonal turrets. The display of eighteen shields up the wall above the doorway is the work of John Lord Lumley, an ardent medievalist (*see* the consciously medievalizing family tombs at Chester-le-Street). The shields can be dated after 1577.

The COURTYARD has mostly Tudor windows, but two of the transomed two-light Perp windows of the Hall (of *c*. 1400) survive. One of them is blocked. The s side has Early Georgian windows (two of the Venetian type) and the staircase projection (also with a Venetian window). Until *Vanbrugh* added this staircase, communication had been entirely by means of the four narrow newel staircases in the four corners of the courtyard.

The OUTER FRONTS look powerful from a distance, but have little of detail interest. On the w front after 1721 an outer stairway was built to reach the Hall. The doorway is simple, but marked by a cupola on the roof. The Hall windows are tall and plain with oval windows above. The s front also has Early Georgian windows. The building here is three-storeyed, but the angle towers or angle blocks are four-storeyed. A few original windows remain in the NE angle block.

Of the INTERIORS the most important is the Hall standing on an UNDERCROFT at courtyard level with original
48 tunnel-vaulting. The HALL had originally more transomed pointed windows than now. But Lord Lumley

about 1580 closed some to put a big fireplace with Roman
Doric columns and some plaited decoration. At the s end
of the room is a handsome Washing Fountain with a
pelican. The part of the Hall N of the gate towers (*see*
above) was originally the pantry and buttery. Beyond it
lies the very large original KITCHEN. S of the Hall in the
angle block is the BALLROOM with a plaster ceiling and
plaster-decorated walls (medallions of Roman Emperors)
of *c.* 1730. There follow along the s front the STATE
ROOMS, not very spectacular in their sizes or furnishing.
Architecturally the most interesting feature is the fact
that the very centre is not a room but a short broad corridor in axis with the (surprisingly plain) main Georgian
staircase. Below the Ballroom lies the most remarkable
room of the house, the only one which must be designed
entirely by *Vanbrugh*. It is known as the LIBRARY and is [55]
divided into three aisles by pillars with crazy, oversized,
diamond-cut rustication.

MAINSFORTH HALL

The house where Robert Surtees, the Durham historian,
lived. Five bays by four bays, two and a half storeys,
cemented, with the window frames and door frames
typical of *c.* 1725.

MARSDEN

SOUTER POINT LIGHTHOUSE. A handsome nautical composition of 1871. The lighthouse is attached by a passage
to an axially placed symmetrical building. This has projecting wings to the back, later connected by a range
across. It all looks still early C19, that is before historicism in architecture confounded all the issues.

MEDOMSLEY

ST MARY MAGDALEN, 1878, except for the excellent E.E.
chancel. This has an E end with three isolated stepped
lancets, shafted inside (with shaft-rings) and the keeled
arch mouldings slightly trefoiled; outside a plain hood-
moulding over all three windows. On the s side three

small lancets and a trefoiled piscina. Against the walls
four human heads, for the purpose of supporting candles,
as at Lanchester. They are no doubt by the same workmen (*see* the slanting eyes and other details). The date
must be *c.* 1260–70; and this determines the age of the
whole chancel; a late date, considering the fact that
tracery is entirely absent.

MERRINGTON *see* KIRK MERRINGTON

MIDDLETON-IN-TEESDALE

St Mary, 1886, by *Hodgson Fowler*, except for one Dec
window in the vestry. – A late C13 three-light window re-
erected in the garden of the former Vicarage, N of the
church. – In the N wall of the new church a number of
foliated cross tomb-lids. – To the N of the church stands
the former BELFRY, quite a distance away. It was built
c. 1557 and looks like a summerhouse. – PLATE. Two
Chalices, *c.* 1690; two Patens, London-made, 1694.

In the village the BAINBRIDGE MEMORIAL FOUNTAIN,
1877, a florid cast-iron canopy with the figure of a child,
still much in the 1851 taste.

At the NW end of the village the WORKMEN'S CLUB, Early
Georgian, with handsome Ionic doorway, the BAPTIST
CHAPEL of 1827, and MIDDLETON HOUSE, early C19,
in a fine elevated position.

About 2 m. WNW, the Tees, 200 years ago, was crossed by
the earliest of all European suspension bridges, the
WINCH BRIDGE. It was built *c.* 1741. Its length was 70
ft, its width no more than 2. It had iron chains and a
handrail only on one side. Hutchinson says that it was
used principally by miners, 'a restless gangway to which
few strangers dare trust themselves'.

STOTLEY HALL *see* p. 224.

MIDDLETON-ONE-ROW

St George. Nave (widened on the N side in the C18) and
chancel. Chancel arch probably C13, on two head-corbels.
The W tower was added in 1883.

St Laurence, 1871, by *Pritchett* (GR), with a funny polygonal turret at the SE end of the nave. In the porch tomb-
lid with FOLIATED CROSS.

Lower Middleton Hall. The garden front of ten bays
and two and a half storeys, brick, absolutely plain, was
built in 1721. Other parts added in C19 Neo-Gothic.

MIDDLETON ST GEORGE
see MIDDLETON-ONE-ROW

MIDDRIDGE GRANGE
1 m. N of Redworth Hall

Gabled farmhouse with some mullion-and-transome-cross
windows and a handsome early C18 doorway with eared
door frame, two big foliated corbels not supporting anything, and a flat open triangular pediment. Of the same
date some panelling inside.

MONK HESLEDEN

St John with St Mary. The church presents the curious
case of one character, very complete in itself, overlaying
another which becomes apparent only to the student. The
former is that of *c.* 1800 when the pyramid-roofed bell-
turret was placed above the W wall, the windows were remodelled and given their Gothick glazing bars and the
interior was refurnished (cheaply) with box pews, a
squire's pew, and a primitive form of three-decker pulpit.
The FONT also belongs to that date (oval basin on baluster
stem). But the S doorway is Norman, on the S side of the
nave is a blocked late C13 window of three lancet lights,
on the N side of the nave a blocked C13 doorway, and on
the N side of the chancel two blocked large arches, once,
no doubt, opening into a chantry chapel. – PLATE.
Chalice of 1724.

MONKTON

The village is an oasis in the Gateshead-Jarrow-South-
Shields industrial desert. It has still something like a
Green and a few worth while houses along it, though the

s side is rapidly deteriorating. On the N side MONKTON
FARMHOUSE and BEDE HOUSE, a pair, the former C18
ashlar-faced, of five bays and two storeys with a doorway
with Tuscan pilasters, the latter lower, C17, small, with
mullioned windows. MONKTON HALL, further W, is of
1735 (rainwater head), five bays, three storeys, with a
door frame with flat rustication.

MONKWEARMOUTH

ST PETER WITH ST CUTHBERT. Benedict Biscop was a
man of noble Anglian birth: 'nobile quidem stirpe gentis
Anglorum', writes Bede, 'sed non minori nobilitate
mentis'. He became a monk at Lérins in the South of
France, returned to England with St Theodore of Tarsus
in 669, and was for two years in charge of St Peter and
St Paul at Canterbury. Then the King granted him land
close to the mouth of the river Wear, and here in 675 he
founded his monastery. The whole building was completed in one year. Later Jarrow was built by Benedict, and the two sister houses flourished so vigorously
that at Bede's time they had nearly 600 monks. Bede
was, he tells us, when he was seven years old 'delivered
by the hands of my friends and kinsfolk, to be brought
up by the most reverend Abbot Benet, and after Ceolfrid'. 'From which time', Bede continues, 'I spent all
the days of my life in the mansion of the same monastery'
(which, of course, refers to Jarrow). What is left of the
monastic establishment at Monkwearmouth is only part
of the church, but even so it remains a precious relic, too
precious for its sordid setting.

The church consisted of a nave and a chancel (replaced
in the C14; four-centred chancel arch, renewed five-light
E window), N and S 'porticus', that is neither aisles nor
transepts but separate chambers, and a two-storeyed W
porch. Above the porch rises a tower of the C9 or C10.
The nave is of rubble with squared stones at the angles. It
is uncommonly tall for its length and width (31 ft height
to 65 by 19 ft), a Northumbrian peculiarity (cf. Escomb,

also Corbridge, Northumberland). The w wall has a door from the upper storey of the porch and two roundheaded windows yet higher up, under the extremely steep w gable. The porch is the most interesting feature of the church. It is tunnel-vaulted (the earliest vault in England). Its doorway has pairs of turned stone balusters in the responds starting on plinths with carved intertwined animals. Above the doorway is a window and above this, where originally the gable of the porch was, the faint traces of a large standing figure in relief: the earliest piece of major architectural sculpture in the county.

A N aisle was added in 1874. – SCULPTURE. In cases more baluster shafts. They were evidently a favourite decorative motif (cf. Jarrow, Hart, Egglescliffe). Also remains of a carved animal frieze from the tower, two stones with lions in relief which formed part of an Abbot's Throne, and a sepulchral CROSS of the shape which is known from the illustrations of the Lindisfarne Gospels. – PLATE. Chalice of 1571–2 (cf. Jarrow and Lanchester). – MONUMENTS. Defaced effigy of a Priest, C14; defaced effigy of a Knight.

ALL SAINTS, 1846–9, by *Dobson* of Newcastle. E.E., with small polygonal SW turret.

RAILWAY STATION. If one does not mind a railway 62 station looking exactly like a Literary and Scientific Institution or a provincial Athenaeum, then Monkwearmouth is one of the most handsome early stations in existence. It is by *Dobson* and was built in 1848. It is of purest Neo-Greek, with tetrastyle unfluted Ionic giant portico and pediment, coupled pilasters at the outer angles, then quadrant curves with Doric columns *in antis*, and then recessed outer wings with arched windows separated by pilasters.

Of the same date no doubt also the houses N of the station (Democratic Working Men's Club) and opposite it in Barclay Street (Greek Doric porches).

MORTON HOUSE 2 m. w of Houghton-le-Spring (Excellent stone house dates 1709. Doorway with broken pediment on rich brackets).

MUGGLESWICK

Muggleswick lies high up with the bracken-clad hills on one side and wide views down on the other. In this isolated spot the Priors of Durham had a Grange or *refugium*, built by Prior Hugh of Darlington (1258–72). The remains are impressive; a tall gable flanked by two square projecting turrets with machicolations below the top. In the gable the top of a large blocked three-light window with cusped intersected tracery, rather later in style than Prior Hugh's time. On the inner side of the window, curiously enough, is a fireplace lower down. In another part an undercroft with one circular pier with moulded capital.

CHURCH, 1869. – PLATE. Flagon of London make, 1679 (?); Paten of London make, 1754; Chalice inscribed 1829.

MURTON

2 m. SW of Seaham Harbour

PITHEAD BATH, 1939, of especially pleasant design.

NEWFIELD

1¼ m. SE of Willington

MANOR HOUSE. Half derelict. With three- and four-light mullioned windows.

NEWHOUSE see ST JOHN'S CHAPEL

NEWTON AYCLIFFE see AYCLIFFE

NORTH LEAM see GATESHEAD

NORTON

60a Although there is now no longer any break between Norton and the Norton Road at Stockton, the village has kept its individuality to perfection and is still the finest in the county, at least in the eyes of those who like their villages wealthy and not inhabited by farmers. Norton must already in the C18 have been the place of residence of the well-to-do of Stockton or at least the well-to-do connected with Stockton.

St MARY. The church lies at the NW end of the village. It is one of the most rewarding of the village churches in County Durham, owing specially to the almost complete survival of its Anglo-Saxon crossing tower. Inside, of the four tower arches two are still essentially Saxon, although much of the detail is obliterated. The arches are surprisingly generous in width. The tower itself has its lowest tier of windows triangular-headed (cf. Hart, and in other counties, e.g. Hexham and Deerhurst). The exceedingly steep Saxon roof line (cf. Monkwearmouth) appears above one of these windows, on the N side. L. and r. of this small arched Saxon windows. The top of the tower is Perp, with battlements. It is on three sides very prettily (though to the all-out archeologist irritatingly) covered with ivy. The church itself is also embattled. In order of history the Saxon remains which probably date from the early C11 and are the only evidence in the county of a cruciform Saxon church, are followed by a faint indication of vanished Norman building activity (stones with zigzag decoration in the S porch) and then by much more in the Transitional style. To this belong the nave arcades of three bays: circular piers, capitals moulded or with some waterleaf embellishment, pointed arches with complex mouldings incorporating keeled roll mouldings. Also Transitional and also with keeled roll mouldings the E and W arches of the crossing tower. As to windows, to this phase belong the round-arched ones of the clerestory on the N and partly on the S, and of the S and N transepts, on their E sides (that on the N blocked). Fully E.E. the remains of the shafted E windows of the chancel (with shaft-rings) and the Sedile (with dogtooth and hood-mould on leaf stops). Originally there were apparently Sedilia instead, but the evidence is confusing. The E window and two S windows Perp, datable 1496, with simple panel tracery. Of the same time the nave roof. The W end and the S transept S window C19, the low aisle windows C20. – STAINED GLASS. N transept N by *Kempe*, 1896; chancel S by his successor *Tower*, 1916, still entirely in the C19 style. – PLATE. Set of 1807–8. – MONUMENTS. Foliated

cross tomb-lid in the s porch. – Also in the s porch very
38 damaged but originally fine effigy of a Lady, c14. – Effigy
of a Knight, early c14, the arms altered in the c16 to those
of the Blakiston family, originally no doubt a Fulthorpe.
It is the best effigy of its date in the county. Bare head,
long curls, crossed legs in chain-mail. Above the head a
cusped arch ending in a slight ogee. Below the feet
animals and a little seated bedes-man reading his prayers.
Over the rim of the shield reaches another little figure,
humorously carved.

ST MICHAEL, 1912–3, by *Temple Moore* (GR). Nice interior with N aisle (S aisle planned) and timber-boarded
tunnel-vaults. The outside with W tower and Neo-Perp
windows unfortunately in rather cheap-looking brickwork.

The HIGH STREET leading N from Stockton to the Green
and the church has an uncommon number of worth
while houses, worth while, at least, as houses in County
Durham go. In the Home Counties one would ask for
more to pay special attention. The numbers to watch for
are 71 and opposite 78, both with two bow windows, 80,
then Thorpe House enriched about 1860 with thoroughly
debased High Victorian detail, 90 which seems early c18,
altered later, 100 with bay windows and a doorway with
posts half-classical, half-Gothick, 104, and finally 108 of
c. 1700 (specially good). The High Street has two rows of
trees all the way up. At its end lies the Green. This has a
complicated shape which happens to be visually very attractive. It opens first to the W, and then to the E. Between the two parts is an island, as in many Durham
Greens. The houses around the Green are a nice background but no more, with the exception of the VICAR-
AGE, a stately house essentially of 1762. Immediately to
its NW the church.

PELTON

HOLY TRINITY, 1842, by *John Green* (GR). E.E., with
polygonal bellcote and angle pinnacles; in the details still
pre-archaeological.

PENSHAW

MONUMENT. Dedicated by the citizens of Newcastle to the 61b
first Earl of Durham, the great liberal politician and first
High Commissioner for Canada. Erected in 1844. A
Greek Doric temple (but the columns are unfluted) of
seven by four columns with entablatures and pediments,
but no roof and no walls. The columns stand on a stylo-
bate but there are no steps. There is no inscription either.
From a distance, especially the E, the monument appears
as an apparition of the Acropolis under hyperborean skies.
Standing by the monument the landscape is no longer
Grecian: collieries in the near distance everywhere.

PETERLEE

One of the New Towns under the bold planning programme
of the years immediately after the Second World War.
The planning consultant was *B. Lubetkin* and the plan one
of the best. So little, however, has as yet been carried out,
and what has been carried out is so much at variance
either with the plan or with the kind of architecture foreseen in it, that no details need here be given.

PIERCEBRIDGE

The village lies largely within a 10¾-acre Roman fort,
erected soon after A.D. 297 to the W of the Roman bridge
taking the Watling Street across the river Tees. The NW
angle, with ancient sewerage, is open for inspection. The
present bridge further E is a stately three-arch structure,
essentially of 1789. Between it and the Church lies the
spacious GREEN a remarkably attractive composition,
although its visual qualities are no doubt partly due to
accident. The Green is rectangular and reached obliquely
from the Bridge. No island breaks its continuity, but the
NW carries the special accent of a group of big
trees.

ST MARY, 1873, by *Cory & Fergusson* (GR).

PITTINGTON

13b ST LAWRENCE. The N arcade is one of the most exciting
pieces of architecture in the county, work of Bishop
Pudsey's men, though not as elegant as the Durham
Galilee. But the high spirits and over-abundance of the
Castle portal can perhaps be recognized at Pittington. The
arcade is of six bays. The two to the E are restoration of
1846. They were originally like those of the S arcade. At
the W end of these two remains of the former nave E wall
show that Pudsey's nave was shorter than the present
nave. It can in point of fact be called Pudsey's nave only
to a limited degree. The small windows above the arcades
are clearly Saxon (cf. Jarrow, Escomb, Seaham). So there
had been an aisleless Saxon church to which Pudsey gave
a N aisle. The simple windows of the aisle are preserved.
His arcade alternates between octagonal and circular piers,
the octagonal ones with alternately square and round
reeding, the circular ones with a snaky spiral moulding
wound round. The motifs come clearly from the Durham
piers; but while there they are incised and thus kept under
strict discipline, their thick relief here makes them appear
much livelier and even wilder.* The arches with their zigzag (and an inner chamfer) are in accordance with the
mood of the piers. – The W tower may have been contemporary with the N arcade (see the door opening into
the original nave roof), but the tower arch and the upper
stages are E.E. At the same time probably the heavy and
irregular buttresses were added and the W stair-turret.
Also from that time dates the provision of a S arcade. This
has circular piers, moulded capitals, double-chamfered
pointed arches, and hood-moulds with head-stops. The
responds are keeled, as are those of the tower arch. The
chancel arch and the whole chancel are of 1846 (altered
1905). Also 1846 the rebuilding of the N and S walls of
the aisles. But out of the original chancel chapel opened a
chantry, and the beautiful crocket capitals of the arch
remain (at the E end of the N aisle). Of later date are the

* The same design at Orford in Suffolk.

clerestory windows. – FONT COVER. Handsome scrolly late C17 work. – WALL PAINTINGS. Important C12 wall paintings in the jambs of the westernmost of the Saxon N windows, not easily recognizable. On one side the Consecration of St Cuthbert by Archbishop Theodore, on the other St Cuthbert's Vision at the table of the Abbess of Whitby. – PLATE. Chalice of 1570. – MONUMENTS. A tiny twin stone for two boys of noble birth, no more than 12 in. long, each with a toy sword carved on; early C13. Cross-legged Knight with square helmet hiding the face entirely; the shield held high up; Frosterley marble, c. 1280. – Tombstone to a man called Christian, with inscription referring to him as 'abens nomen Christi'. In 1183 a 'Christian' was Bisop Pudsey's master mason.

PONTOP HALL

3½ m. ENE of Shotley Bridge

The front c. 1700, ashlared, of four bays, with dormers. The staircase and panelling of the same period. In the roof a former Roman Catholic Chapel. The house served for a short time (1794–5) as a R.C. Seminary, before Crook Hall, which came before Ushaw.

RABY CASTLE

The largest medieval castle in the county, and one of the most impressive in the N of England. Raby is an example of how complex and free from rigid planning conventions military and domestic architecture had become in the C14. For the C14 is the great century of Raby (the licence to crenellate is of 1378), although there are older parts dating back to the late C12, and the late C18 and the C19 have done much altering, though little adding. The castle was in the hands of the Neville family from the C13 to 1569 and came to the Vanes c. 1624. They were made Lords Barnard in 1698. In the C18 and C19 they were Earls of Darlington and Dukes of Cleveland. The castle stands in large grounds, landscaped and provided with two lakes in the later C18. The GARDEN GATE in the S wall is of the early C18 and comes from Shipbourne Church, Kent, close to Fairlawn, the property of the Vanes.

The castle is approached from the N through the C14 GATE-HOUSE which formed part of the outer curtain wall. The two towers to its l. and r. are late C18 ('in a spruced up taste', said Lord Torrington in 1792). The gateway has still the original grooves for a portcullis and one strong oak door (to the Porter's Room). On the battlements are stone figures of late C14 date. These stood originally above the central E entrance, that is the Chapel Tower. Such figures are characteristic of N country fortresses (cf. Alnwick, Bothal, Hylton). The entrance to the inner courtyard of the castle is by the NEVILLE GATEWAY with two obliquely placed square outer angle towers. The long gateway itself consists of two parts, the outer covered by a lierne-vault, the inner by a tunnel-vault with heavy transverse arches of segmental shape. They indicate a later lengthening to the W, and this is confirmed by a similar addition on the W side of the SW angle tower called JOAN'S TOWER. This stands to the S of the Gateway separated from it by a piece of the original curtain wall lying somewhat back. To the N of the Gateway is another specially well preserved part of the curtain wall. Both stretches are machicolated. Carrying on to the N there follows the wall of the Servants Hall and then the far projecting NW or CLIFFORD'S TOWER. Of the C14 windows only three survive (one high up W, the others NE). E of Clifford's Tower again machicolated curtain wall and then the KITCHEN TOWER with its high stone louvre; also a piece of later C14 architecture. The rounded NE corner which connects the Kitchen with Mount Reskelf is of c. 1760. MOUNT RESKELF is connected by some curtain wall to the CHAPEL TOWER, the centre of the E side. This has been considerably altered. The chapel is on the first floor (see below) but its window dates only from 1901. The ground floor had originally a postern gate strengthened by a barbican. This was removed when in the later C18 a carriage drive was opened through this front into the Inner Courtyard.

The SE corner is formed by BULMER'S TOWER, which dates back to the C12 but was heightened in the C14. Originally it stood entirely free. It is of an interesting plan characteristic of its original date: a square with a triangular spur to the N (cf. the similar spur of Château Gaillard). The whole S front was remodelled by *William Burn* in the 1840s. At its W end Joan's Tower is reached and the circuit is complete.

Inside the INNER COURTYARD some of the best preserved parts are on the N, especially the KEEP. It forms the N side of the NE angle. Its E side is the Great Hall. This lies on the first floor and underneath it is a LOWER HALL with two rows of octagonal piers. It was built *c.* 1325 but much interfered with for the sake of the carriageway from the E leading right through it into the courtyard. The UPPER HALL was added on top of the older hall *c.* 1370. It was lengthened by *Burn* to the S. Originally it was 80 ft long (by 36 ft in width). The stone Minstrels' Gallery is genuine. So are the five transomed W windows. Their tracery is Perp. The MAIN STAIRCASE N of the Hall dates only from 1864. It leads to the KITCHEN, the most remarkable C14 room in the castle, with a rib vault on the pattern of the Durham Kitchen and a tall stone louvre. The S extension of the Hall stands on the OCTAGON DRAWING ROOM. This is part of the suite of rooms provided by *Burn* in the 1840s. To the E of the Drawing Room is the Dining Room; to the W the Library.

The only other rooms of importance are the SERVANTS' HALL S of Clifford's Tower, 57 by 20 ft, with a stone vault, and the CHAPEL extending E of the Upper Hall. Its floor was raised in 1848, and its windows are all renewed. But the W arcading is original work, and so is the quadripartite stone vaulting. They look, in fact, rather earlier than 1378, the date of the licence.

RAVENSWORTH CASTLE

Ravensworth Castle was the most splendid and the most picturesque monument of the romantic medieval revival in the county. In spite of that it is under demolition (at

the time of writing). The Castle was built for a member
of the Liddell family (who had accumulated great riches
in the coal trade during the C17) by *John Nash*. It was
begun in 1808 and enlarged about 1822 (John Summer-
son). But in 1834 the N side is still called unfinished, and
more was added in the 40s. The *Illustrated London News*
shows the completed building in 1846 and says that the
principal front was designed by the *Hon. H. T. Liddell*,
eldest son of Lord Ravensworth. The mansion, as completed, displayed numerous embattled towers and turrets,
including, as part of the stableyard to the E, two medieval
towers, lower and humbler than the others. Originally
these seem to have formed part of a square walled enclosure with four angle towers (*see* Buck's engraving,
1728). *Nash's* Great Hall was a tremendous apartment
with the grand staircase at its W end and nine windows,
tall and transomed *à la* Penshurst, high up. It was one of
the nearest approaches to the thrills of Fonthill which one
could still experience anywhere. A little to the N stands
the so-called BUTLER CROSS, a tall medieval cross on a
long polygonal shaft. Its date is controversial.

REDMARSHALL

ST CUTHBERT. From the main road the church, hidden in
trees, shuts off the tiny village to its s. Unbuttressed w
tower, nave, s chapel, and chancel. The w tower is Norman, with unmoulded inner tower arch on the plainest
imposts and Perp battlements. The nave walls, chancel
arch, and the re-used s porch doorway also are Norman,
but heavily over-restored. The chancel was rebuilt and a
chapel added in the C13 with a broad single-chamfered
arch on two head-corbels. The Sedilia are Perp, an unusual style for this piece of church furnishing. The shape
is one frequent for C15 three-light windows. Of about the
same time the Easter Sepulchre recess opposite. The windows are all C19. – FONT. Circular, *c*. 1200; the cover
probably C17 Gothic rather than Early Victorian (V. C.
H.: 1845). – PEWS. *c*. 1630 with the upper halves of the

doors pierced and provided with little balusters, just as at Egglescliffe not far away. – Of the same period the COM-MUNION RAIL with heavy balusters. – MONUMENT. Recumbent alabaster effigies of Thomas de Langton † 1440 and his wife. He is in armour, she wears a horned headdress. The figures are not well preserved.

REDWORTH HALL

Elizabethan mansion with the centre part added in 1744 and further large additions of 1899. The old part is plain-gabled and has mullioned and transomed bay windows.

ROKER

ST ANDREW, 1906–7, by *E. S. Prior*. One of the architec-turally most interesting and successful churches of its date in England. The essentials and all the details can still be called Neo-Gothic, that is the church still adheres to the historicism of the C19, but not one motif is to be found that is not treated originally. Grey, rough Marsden stone with a big tower and a wide aisleless nave and tran-septs. The tower is placed above the chancel at the E end of the church, and the E end of the chancel projects very slightly beyond the tower so that a gable is visible. The nave is articulated inside by wide and broad stone arches across, starting nearly from the ground. They are in fact carried on very short double shafts, polygonal and with-out capitals, and behind these is just enough space left, not for an aisle, but for a passage to reach the pews. Again the transepts are in the usual position, but their arches to-wards the nave are struck diagonally from the narrower chancel arch towards the wider nave walls. Finally, the windows are mostly of Gothic shapes, but the tracery is of unheard-of varieties. Arches are everywhere in it replaced by straight lines and the mullions are unmoulded poly-gonal shafts. The building is a model of how personality can be combined with just enough adherence to tradition to make it acceptable for a church. – All the FURNISH-INGS are worth examining too. The reredos is a *Burne-Jones* tapestry woven by *Morris & Co.*, the chancel carpet is a *Morris* design, the altar cross and the processional cross are exquisite works of *Ernest Gimson* who also designed the Lectern, wood with ebony and metal inlay. The Dedication Plates are early works of *Eric Gill*. The Stone Font is carved by *Randall Wells*, the Stained Glass in the E window designed and coloured by *H. A. Payne* of Birmingham. No wonder that so much care was lavished on the furnishings. Prior himself twenty years before had been closely connected with the developing Arts and Crafts movement.

RYHOPE

ST PAUL, 1870, by *T. C. Ebdy* (GR). A big ambitious church with a deliberately original S tower with stair-turret and pyramid roof. The porch is in the tower. The doorway has the grossest mouldings, also deliberately original. Chancel and N aisle of 1920.

On the S side of the GREEN to the SE of the church some nice Late Georgian houses.

PITHEAD BATH, 1936. The style is Dutch-1920s, a little mannered (*see* Introduction, p. 41).

RYTON

The prettiest village on Tyneside in the county, tucked away between the A-road and the river and sufficiently high on the wooded bank to give a handsome setting to the church spire.

HOLY CROSS. E.E., with W tower, nave, aisles reaching as far W as the W face of the tower, and chancel. The W tower is broad and unbuttressed, open in wide double-chamfered arches on corbels to the E, N, and S. It has on the W side an outsized lancet window and a smaller one above. The spire starts low, is as high as the tower, broached and lead-covered. The nave is uncommonly wide. The aisle arcades of three bays have corbels instead of responds, and first a pair of circular, then a pair of octagonal piers. The capitals are moulded, the arches double-chamfered; the hood-moulds rest on head-corbels. The chancel arch is also on corbels. The chancel has no N windows, but on the s a group of three lancets, then a buttress, then a group of two, then another buttress, and then one twin window with a quatrefoil in the spandrel. The buttresses are chamfered, and the chamfers end in heads. The s priest's door also has some (decayed) sculptural decoration. The E end is renewed (1844). The aisles have one original lancet each at the E and W ends. The s porch outer and inner doorways are also original. The s aisle s wall must have possessed lancet windows too (*see* the nook-shaft on the inside close to the E end). – SCREEN AND STALLS. Put in by a rector of 1617–59, in the Cosin style. The Screen has its divisions marked by balusters, but the heads of the divisions decorated by Flamboyant tracery. The stalls have poppy-heads. – PANELLING in the aisle, perhaps made up of Jacobean pew-backs (cf. Aycliffe and Cockfield). – SPIRAL STAIR to the tower inside the nave, 1886, extremely successful and original design, not at all imitation-Gothic except for the most discreet ogee arches; essentially a scaffolding of long, close-set uprights with occasional cross-bars and the treads to stress the horizontals, an example how courageous new work can improve even a venerable building of the C13. – SCULPTURE. Two seated Apostles, on the Communion Rail. They look as if they might be from the Lower Rhine, *c.* 1500–10. – PLATE. Chalice and Cover, 1664; two Flagons, 1727; Font, 1732; Paten, 1750. – EFFIGY. Deacon with book, late C13, of Stanhope marble.

ST HILDA, Hedgefield, 1889, by *Oliver & Leeson* (GR). Good work. The W tower very broad and squat with diagonal buttresses with many set-offs.

THE VILLAGE. 'Flourishing (and) containing many handsome buildings inhabited by opulent families' (*The Beauties of England and Wales*, 1803). In the GREEN the base of a Cross dated 1795. To its NW towards the church in its own grounds the RECTORY, in its masonry probable Elizabethan but georgianized in 1709. Nine bays, two on each side project a little. Doorway central and with scrolly broken pediment. (On the W side a window of *c.*

1500, with the names of the then rector Wynham carved in the tracery, has recently been built in. Inside, two good staircases, one *c.* 1709, the other older; MHLG.) At the SW end of the Green RYTON HALL (Conservative Club), brick, late C18. On the N side along the Green a group of earlier, whitewashed cottages; on the S side a three-bay cottage with Venetian windows. N of Ryton Hall in VILLAGE WEST some nice late C18 brick cottages.

Further to the E with its grounds overlooking the river RYTON GROVE, dated 1742 on rainwater-heads, more ambitious than Ryton Hall; with ample stone dressings and a central bay window with the pedimented entrance in it. The river front is also in its original state, but the bow windows are an addition of 1919. Fine Hall and Staircase inside. The S Gate Lodge also original, brick with much stone. Good Iron Gates.

DENT'S HALL, Ryton Woodside. Symmetrical three-bay house of the C17 with hood-moulded mullioned windows and a four-centred doorhead.

BRADLEY HALL *see* p. 58.

SACRISTON

SACRISTON HEUGH. On a site seriously menaced at the time of writing by mining subsidence, stands a farmhouse divided into three tenements which incorporates some remarkable fragments of the country manor of the Sacrist of Durham Cathedral. They are chiefly in the N half of the house. Facing W a tiny two-light trefoiled pointed window cut out of one stone slab, behind it inside the house a square-headed moulded timber door frame, and next to this a pointed stone doorway leading to a stone newel staircase. Beyond this a little lower down a tunnel-vaulted chamber.

SADBERGE

ST ANDREW, 1831. – PLATE. Chalice and Paten, London-made, 1823.

ST ANDREW AUCKLAND

St Andrew. The ancient parish church for Bishop Auckland as well. Happily placed in a large churchyard, between old trees, and a little above the adjoining roads. A dark, mellow building, large as County Durham churches go, the size being explained by its collegiate nature. The church belongs almost entirely to the late C13. It consists of w tower, aisled nave, and aisleless transepts and chancel. The chancel has lancet windows on the sides alternatingly, in a curious rhythm of taller and less tall and of one light and two lights (the pattern is the typical late C13 one where the two lights are taken together by one superordinate lancet arch and the spandrel is left open, the two-light version of what in three-light windows is called intersected tracery). The E end is renewed, but the group of five stepped lancet lights under one superordinate two-centred arch may well represent the original state.* The chancel has a low-pitched embattled roof. The same types of windows as in the chancel also in the transepts and aisles.‡ Only the nave clerestory is different (clearly Perp). The stately two-storeyed s porch is E.E. too, with a two-bay vault inside, contemporary outer and inner doorways, and in the upper floor a s window with a trefoil in the tracery, again typically late C13. Finally the w tower belongs to the same period too (*see* the w lancets). Only the top parts, with battlements but no pinnacles, are later. The interior is as impressive as the exterior: a large, long, remarkably wide nave, with five-bay arcades on piers alternating between octagonal and a typical late C13 shape with four major and four minor shafts. The major shafts of most of these piers have fillets. Moulded capitals; complexly moulded arches. Tower arch treble-chamfered. Chancel arch of 1864. – Several PISCINAE, late C13. – SEDILIA. Two go with the architecture of the church, the third, with a slightly double-cusped pointed arch, looks a

---

* *See*, for example, the illustration in Billings, 1846.
‡ The s transept was rebuilt correctly in the C19.

little later. – CHANCEL STALLS. C15, presented by Cardinal Langley, with misericords with foliage designs and two shields of arms. – SCULPTURE. The St Andrew Auckland Cross, though only fragmentarily preserved, is one of the most important in the country. It is to be dated *c.* 800. The sides have the leaf scrolls with birds and animals familiar from Early Christian sculpture and from the Ruthwell and Bewcastle Crosses. The scroll on the one side starts at the foot with an archer shooting at the birds. The style is considerably harder than it had been about 700. The front and the back have figures in compartments, also of a 'hard, violent barbarism' (Sir T. D. Kendrick) with evident oriental, probably Syrian affinities. The motif of Christ bound to the Cross by ropes, for example, is a Syrian motif. Other representations are a beardless Christ with two disciples (on the base) and a bearded Christ between two angels. – Slab with a cross and interlace decoration, Later Saxon. – Several foliated cross tomb-lids. – PLATE. Set given in 1720 by Bishop Lord Crewe; Paten, 1715; small Chalice, 1723. – MONUMENTS. Effigy of a cross-legged Knight, *c.* 1340, of oak gone black with age. – Stone effigy of a Lady, late C14. – Large brass to a Priest, late C14.

EAST DEANERY, SW of the church, now a farm. A very interesting group of medieval buildings, originally the prebends of the collegiate church. The site was given for their erection by Bishop Bek in 1291. The centre part of the W range may partly go back to the end of the C13. Ground floor room with tunnel-vault. Straightheaded two-light windows with trefoil heads to the lights and pierced spandrels. Spiral staircase. Other windows inserted in the Late Perp style. Cambered beams and joists in the main room to the S of the one with the vault.

ST HELEN AUCKLAND

The village is a happy surprise. Along a main road with modern factories one suddenly comes up against this queer oasis of C13, C17, and C18 buildings, forming a delightfully picturesque group.

ST HELEN. Entirely of the late C12 to early C13. No tower, nave (W window a group of three stepped lancets under one pointed hood-mould) with clerestory (first window on the S side Norman), aisles (W windows small lancets, lancets also one N window and the S aisle E window), chancel with chancel chapels. One of the chancel chapels is probably the one founded as a chantry by Robert Forester *c.* 1233. E window with three stepped lancet lights. The remaining windows Earlier and Later (clerestory) Perp. S porch two-storeyed (cf. St Andrew Auckland). The interior has arcades of three bays, the first being separated from the others by a piece of solid wall. The N arcade an impressive example of the Transitional style, that is with circular pier with a variety of enriched waterleaf capital and round, slightly double-chamfered arches. The N chancel chapel has single-chamfered pointed arches in two bays with an octagonal pier, but a capital still of the same stage of development as that of the nave. The S aisle arcade and S chancel chapel arcade are later, plainer piers, plain capitals, and in the nave a hood-mould with the 'nutmeg' motif of the late C12 (*see* Introduction, p. 21). It is likely that the date 1233 refers to the S chapel. The responds of the aisle arcades at their E ends have keeled demi-columns. The chancel arch goes with them. Perp roofs. The former staircase to the upper floor of the porch projects into the S aisle, with the individual steps sticking out, as if they were to take you over a wall in a field. – CHANCEL STALLS with C17 backs, of early Cosin type, with sparse balusters, some cusped and ogee motifs at the head of each division between the balusters, and little bits of cresting above. – BRASS. In chancel, unimportant. – PLATE. Patens, 1737 and 1790; Chalice undated.

ST HELEN HALL. The group consists of many parts, the oldest being a range along the road, built after 1622. This has a centre of three bays, with three-light hood-moulded windows and gabled dormers reaching up into the roof. Panelling in two rooms. At r. angles to it a startlingly grand C18 addition built by Ralph Carr of Newcastle, a merchant and Member of Parliament. It is of five bays, with a high hipped roof, and of the chastest Palladianism. Ground floor with vermiculated rustication. Upper floor with tall French windows with blank baluster railings and straight hoods. The building may well be by *Paine*. Inside, a truly splendid SALOON with a plaster ceiling with a cupid in the centre and motifs of birds, snakes, etc.; typical Italian workmanship of the mid C18. Fine fireplaces of the same date. Behind this main group is a second group in a style a little earlier, that is rather Vanbrughian than Palladian. To this style belongs the remodelling of one gable of the Hall with two semi-circular windows and between them one large arched (blocked) window, a six bay house with arched windows on the ground floor, and the coach-house with large arched and rusticated entrances and rusticated windows above. *Vanbrugh* was at Lumley in 1721. Might he have looked in at St Helen's on the way to or from the South?

ST JOHN'S CHAPEL

ST JOHN, 1752, with a quoined W tower with pyramid roof. Nave and aisles separated rather grandly by two giant Tuscan columns on each side, and narrower chancel. The square between the columns is covered by a slightly dormed roof. – PLATE. Paten of London make, 1713; Chalice, 1724; small Paten, 1725; two Flagons.

The TOWN HALL of 1868 (recently burnt out) turns a classical little façade towards the square in front of the church; a pretty composition with the surrounding houses.

NEWHOUSE. A long, later C17 mansion with the windows still hood-moulded but no longer low and mullioned. Instead they have now the stone mullion-and-transome-crosses which Inigo Jones popularized in England. Two square projections at the back.

SANDS HALL *see* SEDGEFIELD

SEAHAM

ST MARY. The church lies close to the cliffs above the sea, but in a dell hiding it, and near it are only the Hall and the former Vicarage. It is one of the most worth while of the small churches in the county. Long nave, long chancel, and low embattled W tower. The nave in its masonry is Late Saxon or Earliest Norman; in favour of the former is the size, position, and shape of the small windows (cf. Jarrow and Escomb); in favour of the latter the herringbone masonry on the N side. A window, also still round-headed but large, cuts into the herringbone work. One of the small windows has a treble rope moulding in the arch, a most unusual piece of adornment. The roof was very steep-pitched (*see* the roof line against the tower arch and cf. with Jarrow).* Then, in the C13, the chancel and W tower were added. The tower arch is renewed, the chancel arch rests on head-corbels. The chancel has lancet windows; at the E end two with one hood-mould over, going down and running horizontal between them. Pointed Double Piscina with a little nailhead. At the back of the r. arch later carving of a hand raised in blessing or to confirm the swearing of an oath; very curious and unexplained. The tower is unbuttressed and has on the W side a long lancet and a smaller above it, both pointed. In the C14 (?) the S windows were enlarged (*see* the original arch mouldings inside). The S porch has a pitched stone roof supported by broad transverse ribs and small square-headed W and E windows. – FONT. Circular shaft, and bowl with a band of leafy scrolls along the top rim (cf. Dalton-le-Dale); probably Late Norman or early C13. – PULPIT. Elizabethan, polygonal, decorated with the usual low short blank arcades. – PLATE. Chalice, Paten, and Flagon of London make, 1783.

SEAHAM HALL. Probably Late Georgian; with large additions. Entrance porch with four Tuscan columns. Lord Byron's wedding was celebrated at Seaham Hall. The pretty chimneypiece in the drawing room dates back to that time.

* Professor Richmond kindly drew my attention to a difference in the early masonry between small blocks, some burnt, from a Roman building, perhaps an adjacent signal station, and larger blocks, used a little later. These are also Roman, were brought from South Shields, as their nature and tooling shows, and appear in the larger round-headed windows.

SEAHAM HARBOUR

The town was founded as a harbour for his collieries by the third Marquess of Londonderry in 1828. The layout is due to *John Dobson* of Newcastle. But development proved disappointing. The only building of note is the LONDONDERRY INSTITUTE in Tempest Place, a fine Grecian design with giant tetrastyle Greek Doric portico, no doubt of *c.* 1830. To its l. and r. two Methodist churches, the one of 1871 still Late Classical, the other E.E. At the corner of Tempest Place and the sea front the former INFIRMARY (now Urban District Council) in the Tudor taste. The seafront terraces have remained extremely modest. Yet nearer the sea, in the centre of the little urban composition, the LONDONDERRY OFFICES, debased Classical with French motifs, two wings of four bays each, and a middle tower. The architect is unknown ; the date must lie between 1857 and 1861.

The parish church of Seaham Harbour, ST JOHN THE EVANGELIST, 1835, by *Prosser* (GR), is quite big, Perp in style, and with a w tower.

SEATON CAREW

HOLY TRINITY, 1831, by *Thomas Pickersgill*. Chancel 1842 by *Jackson* (GR). Chancel altered 1891. W tower with tall obelisk pinnacles and thin angle buttresses. Nave with tall lancets in style and proportion of the type known as Commissioners' Churches. Aisleless ; flat ceiling.

THE GREEN. A handsome turfed square open to the sea. The houses mostly early C19. The Seaton Hall Hotel on the W side the most prominent, the Northview Cafe (No. 19) the most attractive (with Gothic doorhead and Gothic bay windows). Sylvern House on the N side abandons the Georgian code of honour and turns resolutely Victorian, with two steep bargeboarded gables. The date is 1864.

THE FRONT, S of the Green. Quite a number of nice homely Late Georgian houses. None of special merit. Whitewash or creamwash with quoins, window frames, etc., picked out in brown, green, purple, or darker cream. The Seaton Hotel is mentioned as 'lately built' in 1803.

SEDGEFIELD

St Edmund. A dominating W tower, a nave of some splendour, and most elaborate and intricate woodwork. The woodwork is Bishop Cosin's, the nave is ripe E.E., the tower Perp throughout, which is rare in the county. It has diagonal buttresses, large two-light bell-openings with depressed arches, battlements and fully developed pinnacles, almost turrets, with little battlements of their own on the polygonal lower parts and spirelets. Most of the windows of the church are later insertions. Those at the E end (five lights) and at the N end of the N transept and the S end of the S transept are Dec with flowing tracery, again something exceptional in County Durham. Simpler Dec windows also on the E sides of the transepts and in the S aisle. Then one late C13 window of two lights with geometrical tracery (a cinquefoil in a circle) in the N aisle (W end). Only one window in the whole church (S aisle, W of the porch) betrays the date E.E. of the most important work at Sedgefield, work commissioned probably from some mason who had worked on the Chapel of the Nine Altars at Durham. His nave is of generous width, and the arches of the arcades are also widely spaced. There are three arches on each side, with quatre-foil piers with shaft- 20b rings (as at Bishop Auckland) and stiff-leaf capitals of the most sumptuous. Heads and monsters between the foliage of some. Arches with several keeled roll-mouldings. Head-stops to the hood-moulds. The aisles open with E arches into the transepts. The responds are of the same date, the arches are double-chamfered. The transept arches and the chancel arch are of a slightly later date, c. 1290 (see their rather finely moulded capitals). The WOOD-WORK in Sedgefield church is matched only by Cosin's work at Brancepeth, and of course at Durham and Bishop Auckland. – The ROOD SCREEN is the most bewildering 36 mixture of styles, self-consciously antiquarian without any doubt. That is proved by the polygonal shafts l. and r. of its entrance. They are decorated by incised lozenges, almost literally taken over from the Norman piers of the Cathedral. The side sections are subdivided by tall balusters, two deep, the loft by extremely rich Neo-Dec pinnacles, with plenty of ogee arches. It is chiefly the flatness of the treatment of the individual members which betrays the real date. – CHOIR STALLS with strapwork on the stall-ends and balusters and depressed cusped arches on the backs. – PANELLING with ogee arches on the one hand, cherubs' heads, thick acanthus foliage, and thick garlands on the other. The date of the woodwork is not known. Two facts may point to it. A letter of 1638 refers to *Robert Barker*, the joiner, busy then at Brancepeth, having gone to Sedgefield about the new seating. On the other hand Cosin's son-in-law, Dennis Granville, was rector from 1667 to 1691. 1670 seems to me a more likely date than 1640. The ORGAN is yet later. It was given by a vicar in 1708 and has abandoned all sympathies with the Gothic style. – FONT. Presented by the same vicar. Of grey marble, octagonal, with concave foot, concave stem, and beautifully fluted bowl decorated by escutcheons in cartouches. – PLATE. Chalice and Paten, 1681–2; another late C17 Chalice; Chalice inscribed 1716; Paten presented 1732. – MONUMENTS. Two recumbent effigies in low recesses in the S wall of the S transept. The lady wears a wimple, the man is now almost completely unrecognizable. The date is no doubt that of the transept, that is *c.* 1290 or a little later, and the effigies represent donors. – Brasses of *c.* 1630 without inscription, showing the skeletons of husband and wife bundled up in shrouds.

Sedgefield, a great home of fox hunting, is a town, not a village. A market was granted in 1312. The church tower eloquently expresses town status. N of the church the COOPER ALMSHOUSES of 1703. The entrance was remodelled in 1868, but the pretty brick gable on the W side is original. The ornamental use of bricks of different shapes and positions (radial, slightly projecting, etc.) should be noted. S of the church the big RECTORY built after a fire of 1792. Garden front with two one-storey bow windows and a three-bay central pediment. w of the church the Green, with an island of houses as a kind of hiatus, as is so often found in the county. Behind this, that is at the w end, the MANOR HOUSE (now Urban District Offices), a stately brick building of five bays and two and a half storeys with a segmental pediment raised above the door, an inserted Palladian window in the garden front, and some fine internal features (staircase with twisted balusters and overmantel). A sun dial on the outside is dated 1707.

SANDS HALL, 1 m. w, 1738. Brick with stone trim, seg- mentheaded windows, five bays with lower two-bay wings, parallel with the main block.

SCOTS HOUSE see WEST BOLDON

SHERBURN HOSPITAL

Founded by Pudsey in 1181 as a lazar-house. Of the original buildings no more exists now than the s wall of the CHAPEL with three roundheaded lancet windows with a roll-moulding on the outside up the jambs and along the arch (cf. the Durham Galilee). The buttresses between the windows are flat. The chancel and the tower were built next. The buttresses of the chancel have set-offs, and there are inside the remains of a Double Piscina with short shafts and thick foliage capitals (badly damaged). The w tower has on the first upper stage pointed lancet windows, in blank arcades on the N and S, and on the second smaller trefoil-pointed arcades. The upper parts of the w towers of the Cathedral were no doubt the pattern. The tower is much renewed, the rest of the church was entirely rebuilt in 1868 (by *Austin & Johnson*). – PLATE. Chalice, London-made, 1564–5; Paten and Flagon, 1712.

Medieval also the GATEHOUSE with a pointed tunnel-vault inside the gateway crossed by heavy transverse ribs, like certain church porches. The gateway has a double-cham- fered entrance arch dying into the jambs.

New quarters for the inmates were built about 1760. They are on the W side, partly one-, partly two-storeyed. They appear very humble compared with the stately, though absolutely plain MASTER'S HOUSE of 1832.

The present main building dates from 1868. It is institutional Gothic, large and symmetrical. The architects were *Austin & Johnson*.

SHOTLEY BRIDGE

Pleasantly situated, though devoid of buildings of special architectural merit. The BRIDGE is of *c.* 1838 (MHLG) and of one arch. In WOOD STREET the remains of a terrace of two-storey cottages built for the sword-cutlers from Solingen in Germany who were brought over in 1691. 1691 is on the inscription on No. 23 which also reads

> Des Herren Segen machet reich
> Ohn alle Sorg, wan du zugleich
> In deinem Stand trew und fleissig bist
> Und duest was dir befohlen ist.

The inscription on No. 24 has disappeared. It said something about Deutschland and Vatterland. One of the families were the Oleys. In 1787 they built up on the hill at Bonfieldside a house for themselves called CUTLER'S HALL. It has a six-bay front with a two-bay wing. Also at Bonfieldside the parish church, ST CUTHBERT, 1850, by *John Dobson* of Newcastle, completed 1881–6 by *J. W. Johnson* (GR). Buff stone, E.E., with NW tower, through which the entrance, and broach spire. Nave and aisles and chancel chapels, no clerestory. Two windows by *Wailes* in the S aisle, 1885 (TK).

PONTOP HALL *see* p. 193.

SHOTTON

SHOTTON HALL, *c.* 1780. Six bays wide with pedimented doorway. At the entrance to the grounds, on the opposite side of the road, another C18 house, with a nice open pediment on Tuscan pilasters with triglyph frieze.

SLEDWICK HALL
1 m. W of Whorlton

Although seemingly all of a piece and Elizabethan in character (a plaster ceiling of 1584 used to be in a room on the
upper floor), the house is supposed to represent quite a
long building history, with ground floor masonry in the W
wing of the C13, the main range, including the S front, of
the later Middle Ages, and extensive Elizabethan restorations. Well restored again in the last forty years.

SOCKBURN

ALL SAINTS. The ruins of the church lie in the grounds of,
and close to, the Hall. They are of red sandstone and consist of the E end with a group of stepped C13 lancets (cf.,
for example, Gainford), the C13 two-bay arcade between
nave and S aisle with a slim, tall, circular pier, the W wall
and the C15 Conyers Chapel, now enclosed as a museum
of remains preserved from various parts of the church.
They consist of many ANGLO-SAXON FRAGMENTS,
cross-shafts as well as hogback gravestones, and also other
carved pieces, e.g. one with two figures of men among
beasts and monsters. – PLATE. Chalice, 1742. – MONU-
MENT. Slender figure of cross-legged knight with chain
coif; sandstone. It can certainly not represent Sir John
Conyers † 1395, as Leland says. The date probably c.
1310–20.

SOUTER POINT LIGHTHOUSE see MARSDEN

SOUTH CHURCH see ST ANDREW AUCKLAND

SOUTH SHIELDS

The architectural history of South Shields goes back far.
Now that the Roman Fort (Arbeia) is being excavated we
can here, by exposed foundations, get an admirably clear
idea of Roman military architecture in Britain. Of the
nunnery founded in the C7, on the other hand, no remains

have been found. In 1743, the *Universal Magazine* described the town as 'a large village in which are two hundred pans for boiling seawater into salt'. The development which one can follow in buildings begins shortly after that.

ST HILDA. Tower *c.* 1768, the rest 1810–11. Wide nave, still with its galleries on three sides. The galleries are painted white, their supports are cast-iron columns. – FONT. Baluster type; by *Robert Trollop*, the designer of the Exchange at Newcastle, 1675. – CHANDELIER. Gilt, early C19. – PLATE. Chalice inscribed 1718; small Chalice, 1727; Flagon, 1757; Staff inscribed 1778.

HOLY TRINITY, Laygate, 1833, by *Salvin*, a native of the county; an early work of his. E.E. with W tower without battlements. The windows E.E., the aisle arcades (of six bays) with circular piers. The transepts later.

ST STEPHEN, Mile End Road, 1846, also by *Salvin*, also E.E., with a NW bellcote. Rockfaced. Not of special interest.

OLD TOWN HALL. In the Market Place, facing St Hilda's Church. A square little building of 1768 with, in the centre of its open ground floor, an older central pillar, a kind of market cross. On it rest the twelve radiating ribs of the ceiling of the room. To the Market Place it opens with three arcades on Tuscan columns, on the opposite side a two-armed outer staircase leads up to the first floor. Here on both sides the centre is a Venetian window. Hipped roof and overlong cupola with stone dome.

With the erection of the church and the Town Hall, the development of South Shields as a town began. For quite a while little followed. To the NE and SW struggling growth along the ribbon of the main street of the village remained in contrast to the small plots set out around the Market Place. Very indifferent early C19 terraces of cottages in BARING STREET, SAVILLE STREET, and GREEN TERRACE (1835). The wealthier citizens went to build further E along what is now BEECH ROAD (formerly Wellington Street), although the terraces there are not ambitious either (Ogle Terrace, Wellington Terrace), or, if they were more affluent, they moved to Westoe Village (*see* p. 239). Modern South Shields boasts a different scale, and the Old Town Hall has been replaced by the new MUNICIPAL BUILDINGS, designed 1903 by *E. E. Fetch* of London, who no doubt had studied his Brydon and Rickards and Mountford. The body of the building is symmetrical, in a loose, Baroque, somewhat Frenchy style, with as its centre a giant arch on coupled columns supporting a broken pediment. The symmetry is boldly upset by the tall tower at the NW corner. Its octagonal top sports gigantic figures and detached columns. The building is the most convincing expression in the county of Edwardian prosperity.

ROMAN FORT, Baring Street. The visible remains of the Roman fort comprise a length of its W wall, one tower of its W gate and most of its principal buildings. These are chiefly long buttressed storehouses, seven displayed almost completely and two in part, which represent stockpiling at the northernmost port in Roman Britain for the Caledonian campaigns of Severus and Caracalla in A.D. 209–11. Imperial lead seals, from consignments accumulated during previous years, are seen in the Museum attached to the site. In Britain only the Claudio-Neronian store-base at Richborough (Kent) in any way resembles this depot.

The principal building other than a storehouse is the administrative headquarters of the unit (the Fifth Cohort of Gauls) in charge of the base. As normally in such buildings, there is a front courtyard, bordered by a colonnade – a fallen column has been re-erected – and by stores or offices; beyond this, a judgement-hall for courts-martial extends right across the building; and behind the hall comes, centrally placed, the shrine of the regimental standards, with two offices on each side, one pair for pay, savings, and regimental funds, the other for administrative records. Steps lead below the shrine to an underground strongroom, for the monies just mentioned, solidly built in massive blocks with dovetail cramp-holes, and still exhibiting the sill of a barred window opening into the judgement-hall. The offices are heated by underground flues (the Roman hypocaust) added in c4. In the courtyard will be observed foundations of successive shrines and offices belonging to two earlier headquarters, each facing N. The judgement-hall of the second was adapted for the c3 building, with the result that a *tribunal* or judge's dais, always on the right of anyone entering the hall, appears at each end, one earlier and the other later. No trace of the early courtyard N of the building now remains, but its water-well was kept in commission and is seen just outside the NW corner of the c3 strong-room.

The early headquarters are matched by long barracks and workshops, whose foundations appear below the row of six granaries. The successive buildings were erected in different stone: the first in magnesium limestone, enduring but hard to cut: the second in pink micaceous sandstone from the local Dean quarries: the third in harder yellow sandstone from Gateshead Fell. The choices indicate a widening appreciation of local resources. The two early periods have been dated by associated finds to Hadrian and to the later c2, probably to the governor Calpurnius Agricola in A.D. 162–3. To this second period belong also the settling-tanks and supply-tank served by an underground pipe-line which fed the fort with water. The improvements of c4 noted in the headquarters connote a wholesale conversion of the stores-base to new needs. The granaries exhibit traces, particularly visible in nos. VI to VII, of a division into numerous three-roomed suites for junior officers. This goes with the arrival of a new force, the *Barcarii Tigrisienses*, or Tigris Lightermen, concerned with transport of stores up river to the Wall, rather than with stock-piling. Another new activity is represented by the conversion of Granary I into a tile-shed with kilns, illustrated by plans and photographs in the Museum.

The Museum contains many interesting exhibits from the site. The inscribed and sculptured stones include a magnificent inscription of A.D. 222 recording the construction of an aqueduct for the Fifth Cohort of Gauls: also two of the finest tombstones in Roman Britain. The first commemorating the Moorish freedman of an auxiliary trooper, showing him dining in splendour. The second is of a British freedwoman, from the district of St Alban's (Verulamium), whose master, a Palmyrene, had married her; wearing her best clothes and jewels, she sits in a fine arm-chair, with jewel-box and sewing-basket at her feet, and her Latin epitaph is followed by a lament written in the Aramaic script of Palmyra. An altar vowed by a Briton to Brigantia, the tutelary goddess of Northern Britain, adds a local touch to the cosmopolitan scene. The same mixture of exotic and native elements occurs in the small objects, such as the fine enamelled belt-fasteners from Gallia Belgica and the hunting trophy consisting of a real boar's head.

SOUTHWICK

Holy Trinity, 1842, by *George L. Jackson* (GR). E.E., with w tower with obelisk pinnacles. Aisleless.

E of the church towards the Green some Georgian houses are left as a reminder of the village existence of what is now a suburb of Sunderland.

STAINDROP

St Mary. One of the most interesting parish churches in the county. The nave walls above the arcades are evidence of the existence of a small Saxon church (*see* the blocked fragments of upper windows). Next a w tower was added, in Norman times, as the one blocked w window proves. The tower is unbuttressed. Aisles followed. They are Transitional of *c.* 1170–80, three bays with circular piers and double-chamfered round arches. The capitals have a few broad upright leaves. One of them comes close to the later crocket type. The arches have hood-moulds, on the s side with the favourite nutmeg motif, on the N side plain, on head-stops. The chancel arch is similar. In the mid C13 the N transept was added with its fine N wall with three separate lancet windows of equal height (trefoiled pointed rear-arches inside),* the two-storeyed vestry (the upper floor probably a priest's dwelling), and the E parts of the chancel (*see* the excellent, remarkably unrestored trefoiled, pointed Sedilia with stiff-leaf capitals and a head-corbel). At the same time the W tower received a small W doorway and a lancet window. Also the bay connecting it with the Saxon nave was given filleted responds. The same responds occur in the pointed arches connecting the tower with nave and both aisles. For the aisles were now carried W as far as the W front of the tower. The tower is unbuttressed and completely preserved to the corbel-table. It has a big rectangular stair-turret on the W side. The tower top is of the early C15. At that time also the clerestory, the nearly flat nave roof, and the (now renewed) chancel windows with their pretty fleuron friezes above were added,‡ and a little earlier the outer walls and windows of the aisles and the S porch. The date given for S aisle and porch is 1343, for the N aisle *c.* 1370. The S aisle has some excellent gargoyles, the porch has a pointed tunnel-vault with transverse ribs, the windows of the S aisle are segmentheaded and decorated by ogee reticulation. – FONT. Of Teesdale marble. Late Perp, octagonal with plain shields. – SCREEN. The only screen in the county of a date before the Reformation. Very plain, with straightheaded four-light divisions with cusped depressed ogee tops to each light. – STALLS. With Perp tracery of backs and ends and poppy-heads on the ends. The provision of the stalls is connected with the establishment *c.* 1410 of a college at the church of Staindrop. – ALTAR TABLE. C17. – STAINED GLASS. Some fragments in the vestry and the S aisle E window. The rest by *Clayton & Bell, c.* 1865. – CHEST. Heavily iron-bound, in N aisle. – PLATE. Two Chalices, London-made, 1629; two Patens, London-made, 1647; two Flagons, 1740 and 1742. – MONUMENTS at the W end. Effigy of a lady, C13. –

39a Ralph Neville, Earl of Westmorland, † 1425, and his two

* Remains of the same type of windows on the W and E sides.
‡ The chancel windows are renewed, but, except for the E window, apparently correctly.

wives, an important alabaster monument with the tomb-chest decorated by alternating flat canopied recesses, no doubt originally painted, perhaps with figures of saints and mourners, and tracery panels between them; good effigies. – Henry Neville, fifth Earl of Westmorland, † 1564, still entirely in the medieval tradition. Of oak, now quite black. Made by *John Tarbotons*. – John Lee † 1792, by *Nollekens*, with bust; epitaph above the s door. – Henry, second Earl of Darlington, † 1792, semi-reclining on sarcophagus with a relief of Raby Castle so relentlessly beautified by him. – Margaret Countess of Darlington † 1800, with allegorical figure under Gothick arch. – Katharine Margaret Countess of Darlington † 1807, on a couch; an angel holds her hand; against the typical obelisk. The last three by *R. Cooke* of London. – William Henry first Duke of Cleveland † 1842, white marble tomb-chest with relief medallions and recumbent effigy on it; by *Westmacott*. – Sophia Duchess of Cleveland † 1859, lying on a tomb-chest; an angel above conducts the soul to heaven. – In the s aisle: Effigy of a Lady, C13. – Effigy of a Boy, small. – Euphemia de Clavering, mid C14, under a big crocketed gable with large tracery motifs. – In the churchyard the Neo-Gothic Mausoleum of the dukes of Cleveland.

The VILLAGE has one of the very long Greens frequent in the county. It narrows towards the church, and here, on the s side, is STAINDROP HOUSE, showing a forbidding face to the street. Jacobean windows irregularly placed. Too little is known about it.

STAINTON-LE-STREET see GREAT STAINTON

STANHOPE

ST THOMAS. The base of the broad, rather short, w tower, with characteristic windows on the ground floor and first floor is Norman. Above, the bell-openings are pointed twins with an E.E. shaft. The battlements probably still later. The tower arch is pointed and double-chamfered.

One should never forget the overlap in date between round and pointed arches. The rather narrow four-bay arcades between nave and N and S aisles have still round arches, one-stepped and single-chamfered, but circular piers with moulded capitals unlikely before the end of the C12. The mouldings of the arch of the S doorway with one order go with such a date. So does the roundheaded S aisle E window. The chancel and N chancel chapel are c. 1300 (see the renewed E and S windows and the original vestry E window). They are of the type with three or five stepped and cusped lancet lights under one pointed arch. The chancel arch is double-chamfered and rests on two head-corbels. – STALL ENDS. Of the Cosin style, that is with Baroque decoration of the ends, but still with poppy-heads. The date is 1663. – PAINTING. Christ bearing the Cross; Flemish, late C16. – SCULPTURE. Two oval wood panels with Adam and Eve and Christ and St Peter; Baroque, and probably Flemish. – PLATE. Two Chalices, 1703; two Patens of London make, 1709; Paten, 1713; Almsdish of London make, 1835.

RECTORY. Built 'anno pacis evangelii Ryswicii', 1697; rebuilt 1821, but apparently as it had been: seven-bay front, with the first and last two slightly projecting; quoined, and with hipped roof.

STANHOPE CASTLE. Large, asymmetrically grouped, and rather plainly detailed mansion of 1798. Castellated throughout. The Castle stands on the W side of the square of the little town, the church on the N side, the Rectory on the E. A few nice C18 houses close to the Castle.

STANHOPE HALL. A large, tall, and interesting house, now subdivided. Its W range seems medieval (see the SW buttress and the corbels on which originally an oriel window may have been placed), though the old windows it still possesses are mullioned and mullioned and transomed, and must have been inserted when the main part of the house was built or remodelled, that is in Elizabethan or Jacobean times. The main front is recessed, of three bays with symmetrically arranged mullion-and-transome-cross windows. Similar windows at the back. Here also the centre is recessed (between two staircase projections). **One** of the staircases survives.

UNTHANK HALL, across the river Wear. Handsome group of buildings, with a central porch on one side and several surviving mullioned windows.

HEATHERY BURN CAVE. In this limestone cave, 500 ft long, 2–30 ft wide, and nowhere more than 10 ft high, were discovered the tools and products of a family of Late Bronze Age metal-workers. The remarkable hoard of objects included tongs, a mould and bone spatulae. Two swords, seven spearheads, seventeen socketed axes, a bronze bucket and gold ornaments were also present. Antler cheek-pieces from horse-bits represent the earliest evidence of chariotry in Great Britain. A series of broken human skulls may suggest that bloodthirsty rites were employed in connection with the metallurgical activities of the occupants.*

STANLEY

ST THOMAS APOSTLE AND MARTYR, Beamish, 1876, by *J. G. Holl* of Manchester (GR). The church is **not** interesting inside, but has a curious W window with geometricized, straightened, reticulated tracery and an E tower over the chancel, broad and squat, with, on each side, three long and squareheaded bell-openings and decorated battlements. This dates from 1931.

STELLA

ST MARY AND ST THOMAS AQUINAS (R.C.), 1831, by *Green*. E.E., with the chancel to the N, and to the S the presbytery attached to the church, gabled and with castellated angle turrets, of good ashlar stone. In the church STAINED GLASS by *Pugin*, 1849 (Mrs Stanton).

STELLA HALL. Large, irregular building, essentially Elizabethan, but the S front partly remodelled in the C18. The Elizabethan parts have mullioned and transomed windows, string courses, crenellation, and gables. They are unchanged, especially to the NW. The C18 put in two

* Information supplied by Mr Jon Manchip White

Venetian windows into the s front on the ground floor, altered the windows, and gave the door and some principal windows pediments. The alterations are said to be by *Paine*. Later alterations by *Dobson* (what are they?). Inside, the Hall, Drawing Room, and Library belong to Paine's time. At the N end of the N wing, directly connected with the outside by a spiral staircase, lies a room which has been identified as a Roman Catholic chapel. A strange setting for the entertainment of Garibaldi and Kossuth who visited Stella Hall.

STOCKTON-ON-TEES

Stockton seems to have become a borough some time in the C13. Its port is first mentioned in 1228; a market was granted in 1310. Yet it was not constituted a separate parish until 1713. Until then it was subordinate to Norton. Its chief medieval building was the castle of the Bishops of Durham of which nothing remains. The character of the town is now principally of the C18 and early C19, at which time it was still the centre of an agricultural district. The change-over to industry is indicated by the opening of the Stockton–Darlington Railway in 1825. Population, which had been 3,700 in 1801, grew to 7,800 in 1831, to 13,000 in 1861, 51,000 in 1901. It is now *c.* 74,000.

CHURCHES

St Thomas, 1710–12. Until then Stockton had been only a chapelry of Norton. Red brick. Quoined, sturdy w tower with short thin pinnacles and an early C19 spire by *John* and *Benjamin Green*. Nave of six bays. Fine large arched tripartite windows. Interior with arches on square piers. Flat ceiling. The galleries were removed in 1946. Chancel rebuilt in 1906 to the design of *R. J. Johnson*. This is much more Baroque than the rest, with a broken E pediment and a big cartouche carved above the E window. On the N and s only circular windows high up. A s chapel was added to the s aisle in 1925 by *W. D. Caroë*. As for the original building, recently found documents prove that *Sir Christopher Wren* had something to do with it, though no more was probably done than to ask the Surveyor-General for advice. He, it seems, disapproved of the tower and wanted stone used instead of brick. But all the same the defaced memorandum reads: 'We owe a very ... kinsman, Christopher Wrene, who is a very fam. ....' It also explicitly says that the rector was 'advised by Mr Wrenne' (*Northeastern Weekly News*, June 1950). – FONT. Baluster shape; probably *c.* 1712. – PULPIT. A fine piece on square rusticated pillars and with a staircase of slender balusters; made up out of the original three-decker pulpit. – PLATE. Chalice and Paten, 1688; Patens of 1702 and 1711, London-made; Flagons of 1728 and 1730; Plates and Almsdish of 1743, London-made; small Chalice and Paten, London-made, 1824. – In the churchyard the WAR MEMORIAL, 1923, by *Lanchester*.

ST JAMES, Portrack Lane, 1867–8, by *Pritchett*. Stone with tall SW spire.

ST JOHN, Alma Street, 1873–4, by *William White*, his only church in the county, and architecturally insignificant. Red and pale brick, with only a bellcote. E apse and apsed transept.

ST MARY (R.C.), Norton Road, 1841–2, by *Pugin*; illustrated in his *Present State*. Also by him STAINED GLASS. E.E. front with two-order portal and grouped lancet windows above. Vesica window in the gable. E.E. also the tall NW tower meant to be crowned by a spire. Lancet windows in the aisles, and clerestory windows in dormers in the roof. Quatrefoil piers inside and apsed E end. The interior finishes distressingly cheap. Additions by *Hadfield* (aisles, *c.* 1866, *c.* 1870).

ST PETER, 1880, by *E. E. Clephan*, with addition of 1906 (GR). Red brick, with big tower. In the E.E. or lancet style.

HOLY TRINITY, 1857, by *J.* and *B. Green*. Chancel 1906–9 (GR). The second oldest parish after St Thomas, and a church exhibiting much more assertiveness than the homely C18 church. Bit W tower with an octagonal upper part supported by flying buttresses and ending in a proud spire. Interior still with three galleries on cast-iron columns, that is before the victory of antiquarianism and ritualism. Tall two-light lancet windows with geometrical tracery. Large leafy churchyard and plenty of space around the building.

CONGREGATIONAL CHURCH, Norton Road, 1845. Three bays with broad pediment. Giant Tuscan pilasters and windows in two tiers between.

FRIENDS MEETING HOUSE, Dovecot Street, 1816. Just a detached house in the street, five bays, two storeys, with the centre bay slightly projecting and a normal domestic doorway.

METHODIST CHURCH, Dovecot Street, 1823. Five bays with arched windows and three-bay pediment. Narrow W porch. Red brick. Behind the church, in William Street, the METHODIST SUNDAY SCHOOL of 1824. The two buildings together and the houses attached to them make up a frontage of eleven bays, all with arched first floor windows.

METHODIST CHURCH, Norton Road, 1824. Simple brick building with some stone trim. Part of a symmetrical terrace of houses (*see* p. 223).

UNITARIAN CHURCH, Wellington Street (formerly ST PAUL) 1885, by *Pritchett*. Red brick and of no interest.

PUBLIC BUILDINGS

One group only need be mentioned, on an island site in the
60b middle of the High Street. The TOWN HALL was built in 1736, a red brick cube with arched main floor windows, a hipped roof and a tower whose upper storey has detached timber columns. It ends in a pretty spike. Immediately to the N of the Town Hall the MARKET CROSS, a Tuscan column of 1768, and behind this the SHAMBLES, one-storeyed, of nine by five bays, built in 1825.

PERAMBULATION

The HIGH STREET is impressive in its general appearance, wide and well proportioned. But if one looks at individual houses there is hardly anything to hold one's attention. The best old house is the disused BOROUGH HALL of 1851 (by *Clephan*), but still entirely Georgian in looks; the best building altogether the remarkably chaste and carefully detailed NATIONAL PROVINCIAL BANK by *Gibson*, 1877. CHURCH ROAD runs E from the High Street. Here are the finest Georgian houses of Stockton, Nos 70–82. They were originally known as PARADISE ROW. No. 72 in particular, a six-bay house, is distinguished by a beautiful staircase with Venetian window and sets of three thin balusters of different shape to each tread. The date probably *c.* 1730. No. 80 has an entertaining doorway in which Roman Doric columns turn Gothic (trefoil instead of circular section). Opposite this terrace of houses and all along the E side off the High Street there is a good deal of squalor, although such streets as FINKLE STREET contain old houses which were once no doubt quite commodious (e.g. the Custom House Hotel, 1730). To the w of the High Street all minor early C19 terraces, doorways with Roman Doric demi-columns or Tuscan pilasters. Examples, for instance, in John Street, Albert Road, Regent Street, Brunswick Street (the names date them). In BRUNSWICK STREET again Roman Doric columns going Gothic, this time by the application of shaft rings. More interesting in DOVECOT STREET the former LITERARY AND PHILOSOPHICAL INSTITUTION of 1839, stone, with giant pilasters and arched windows, but an inscription in black letter ('Age quae justa sunt, Confide recte agens'), and further on No. 32, a specially wealthy Georgian house, five bays, three storeys, quoins, broad Ionic door-piece with pediment. – To the N in NORTON ROAD all is early C19: North Terrace and No. 4 and further on Nos 66–82 opposite with heavy unfluted Ionic porches. Albert Place opposite the church of St Mary is more graceful, with doorways decorated by fluted columns and segmental pediments. Nos 437–445 form one composition with the Methodist Chapel of 1824. Rich High Victorian merchants or manufacturers preferred to live further out and houses of theirs can, for example, be seen at PRESTON (Woodside Hall, now Cleveland School, of 1876, and Southfield, coarse and picturesque, with heavy-handed detail).

(In addition the MHLG lists the following which ought to be mentioned: 48 BRIDGE STREET, a brick cottage facing the railway line. It is of no architectural value but memorable as having been the original booking office of the Stockton–Darlington Railway. In BISHOPTON ROAD WEST Stockton Farm Grange, attractive C17 house, re-windowed in the C18, and Holstone House Farm, six bays wide, C18.)

The NORTH TEES POWER STATION near Stockton, not yet complete at the time of writing, was designed by *Sir Giles Gilbert Scott* (the designer of the Battersea Power Station in London), a brick structure on an impressive scale.

STOTLEY HALL
1½ m. E of Middleton-in-Teesdale

Probably Jacobean, two-storeyed, with mullioned and hood-moulded windows.

STRANTON

ALL SAINTS. W tower Perp, with diagonal buttresses (rare in County Durham) and battlements. The body of the church is earlier but almost entirely renewed. In the chancel traces of C12 E windows. The N chancel chapel of two bays probably C15. C14 and C15 windows, re-used in C19 walls. Are the shapes correct? The nave arcades of two bays differ. S side with arches which die into the piers: C14 (cf. Newcastle Cathedral). The N arches are clearly C19. – PLATE. Chalice of 1639.

STREATLAM CASTLE

In ruins. Only the most inadequate fragments remain to remind one of this fine large symmetrical mansion which was begun in 1718. Blakiston Bowes for whom it was built called it 'very near finished' in 1720, and 'the best in our Northern parts'. Yet it was completed only in the second third of the C19. It had a thirteen-bay front (nine-bay centre and two projecting two-bay wings), French-looking banded rustication, plain windows (on the ground floor segmentheaded), balustraded top, and three symmetrically arranged identical little cupolas.

STUBB HOUSE
1 m. NE of Whorlton

To a simple house of 1690 a larger and more representational mansion was added at r. angles in 1750. This is of buff stone; five-bay, two-and-a-half-storey front with quoins and flat roof. The ground floor windows have Gibbs surrounds, the doorway a broken pediment on Tuscan demi-columns. Short wings of 1816 to the l. and r.

SUNDERLAND

Although the first charter of Sunderland dates from 1274 and both shipbuilding and the coal trade were in existence before the year 1400, Sunderland now (with the exception of a few defaced monuments and one arch) possesses no medieval remains. The present County Borough comprises, of course, Monkwearmouth with its venerable church, but that is treated separately. It also comprises Bishopwearmouth, which is roughly speaking the part of to-day's Sunderland w of the bridge, but Sunderland proper was situated at the far NE tip of the south bank of the river Wear, and it is there, between wharves, slums, war damage, and new council flats that one has to look for the historic monuments of the town, and none of them dates back further than the early C18. By then Sunderland had about 3,000 inhabitants; by 1800 it had grown to nearly 25,000. This remarkable growth is due to the Industrial Revolution, that is progress in coal mining, shipbuilding, and coal shipping. The River Wear Commissioners were appointed in 1787. Two years later the first Sunderland church was built to mark the independence of the town from Bishopwearmouth, which during the C19 became just the w part of the new city. In 1793 the Bridge was begun, a triumph of the new metallurgy and engineering ingenuity. It was of cast iron and spanned the river in one sweep of 236 ft. It was designed for Philadelphia by *Thomas Paine*, the author of *The Rights of Man*. The castings were made by *Walker's* of Rotherham under the direction of *Thomas Wilson* as Clerk of the Works. Then, however, the scheme was given up and Rowland Burdon took over what had been done, in order to get a bridge for Sunderland. The bridge was a structure of superb elegance, and it is a great pity that it had to be replaced by a more solid one by *Robert Stephenson* in 1858, and again by the uninteresting present bridge in 1929. The North Pier was built in 1787–1802. Its LIGHTHOUSE was moved bodily to a position further out, when the pier was lengthened in 1841. In 1856 the South Pier followed; in 1848 the South Dock was begun. By then the population had reached 65,000. In 1901 it was 146,000. It is now 182,000.

CHURCHES

HOLY TRINITY. The parish church of Sunderland. It now lies surrounded by slums, but still with a churchyard as large as that of a country town with one church. It was built in 1719 and enlarged by the odd, nearly circular, apse in 1735. Red brick with stone dressings. w tower with quoins and a big rusticated doorway. The w front is emphasized by giant Tuscan pilasters. The body of the church has seven large arched windows on each side. Nice staircase balustrades. The interior with tall giant Corinthian columns supporting a flat roof, remodelled at the end of the c18 by *Thomas Wilson* of the iron bridge (*see* above). When the apse was added it was partly screened off from the nave by a reredos-like structure with coupled columns and three little open pediments. The apse has a Venetian window. The whole of this work of 1735 is rather in the spirit of Hawksmoor, even if not on his scale. – WEST SCREEN, 1724, with thin Roman Doric columns. – COMMUNION RAIL of a design like the staircase balustrade. – FONT. Pretty baluster-shape with a very handsome cover, decorated by cherubs' heads; looking rather earlier than 1719. – PLATE. Chalice, 1705;

Chalice, 1724; Almsdishes, 1724 and 1725; two Flagons, 1708 (?). – MONUMENT. Robert Gray † 1838, former Rector, a surprisingly magniloquent display by *Chantrey*. More than life-size standing statue with, on the l. and r., reliefs of Faith and Charity, both young women with children.

CHRIST CHURCH, Ryhope Road, 1862–4, by *James Murray* of Coventry (GR). Big, rockfaced edifice in the geometrical style, with SW spire. Interior with circular piers with the typically High Victorian elaborately carved foliage capitals. Quite a different note is brought in by the STAINED GLASS of the E window, by *Morris & Co*. As in much early *Morris* glass the figure work, apart from the angels in the tracery, consists of smallish square panels with scenes beautifully drawn and in colours of a quite un-Victorian clarity: much red and brown.

ST JOHN THE EVANGELIST, Chapel Street. The second church of Sunderland, after Holy Trinity. In the same decayed NE district, and still in the same style. The date is 1769, the architect *John Thornhill*, the material brick. Three-staged W tower, nave with three tiers of windows, narrower chancel. The galleries have been taken out, but their supports remain, shapeless on the ground floor, but with pairs of Ionic columns (set at r. angles to the main direction of the church) on the upper floor. All this wood-work is altered. Nice contemporary PULPIT. The setting of the church from some angles appears decidedly Dutch. – PLATE. Chalice, Almsdish, Cruet, Bread Dish; all made in London, 1770–1.

ST MARY (R.C.), Bridge Street, 1835 (additions 1852). Front to the street E.E. and attached to houses on the l. and r.

ST MICHAEL, High Street West. The parish church of Bishopwearmouth. C18 tower, transepts of 1849, the rest 1933–5 by *W. D. Caroë*. Quite a remarkable effort in a free Neo-Perp. Nothing like the strong individuality of Prior (*see* Roker), but a sensitive handling of period material, and on a scale not often demanded in C20 churches. Nave and double aisles. Pretty piers, polygonal with concave sides, depressed arches. Transepts screened off by the w–e continuation of the arcades. Nice roofs. – PLATE. Chalice and Cover, London-made, 1574; Cover inscribed 1608; Chalice and Cover, London-made, 1718; two Flagons, 1725; large Chalice inscribed 1826. – EFFIGY of a Knight, C14, severely damaged (s transept).

ST GEORGE (Presbyterian), Ashmore Street, 1890, by *J. B. Pritchett*. Red sandstone with a very original tall tower whose upper part, below the pyramid roof with turrets, is all open, the openings being extremely long uprights.

UNITARIAN CHAPEL, Bridge Street, 1830. White brick with Greek Doric entrance *in antis*, and upper windows with Grecian frames with sloping sides.

METHODIST CHURCH, Whitburn Street, 1826.* The front five bays wide, with pediment. The inside with galleries on Corinthian cast-iron columns.

FRIENDS MEETING HOUSE, Nile Street, 1822 and later. Red brick. The front with big pediment screened from the street by a wall. An addition towards Borough Road polygonal with a flat dome. It contains a room for smaller meetings.

PUBLIC BUILDINGS

Sunderland is not fortunate in its public buildings. None really call for special mention. The MUNICIPAL BUILD-INGS of 1890 and the PUBLIC LIBRARY AND MUSEUM of 1879 are both by *Tiltman,* hardly one of the ornaments of the Victorian era. The Gothic STATION is not of interest and so closely surrounded by buildings as to be scarcely visible. Other big buildings at Sunderland also suffer from lack of open space around.

PERAMBULATION

On a plan of 1817 Sunderland still covers only a small area by the mouth of the river. On the N side is Monkwear-mouth church and untidy housing between it and the bank. On the s side Sunderland itself is just the NE tip of the present town, and Bishopwearmouth a small growth

* No longer in use.

by the church. Between the two runs the High Street. The Iron Bridge leads to what is called the Pann Field, that is the salt-making field. Urban growth has started s of High Street East by Coronation Street and Prospect Row and N and s of High Street West with King Street, Queen Street, etc. After 1820, however, the speed of development increased rapidly, and its marks are still visible in many parts of the town.

The present-day axis of Sunderland is BRIDGE STREET and FAWCETT STREET, now all commercial and with nothing of note except the handsome Sunderland Club of c. 1835–40 (with attached Ionic columns) and perhaps the extremely debased and just thereby remarkable pub-Gothic premises of Messrs Burton's of 1873–7 at the corner of HIGH STREET. High Street is the main W–E axis. Here, near the E end (No. 197 High Street East), the Sunderland EXCHANGE by *Stokoe*, 1812, with a ground floor arcade now blocked up and the ARCADE, Late Classical of c. 1840, in the style of Dobson at Newcastle. Between them examples of commercial architecture of all dates from the NATIONAL PROVINCIAL BANK of 1876 by *Gibson*, tasteful Late Classical, with arched, rusticated ground floor and an upper giant Ionic order carrying blank arches (cf. Durham, Market Place), to MARITIME BUILDINGS and SUNNISIDE CHAMBERS (St Thomas Street and West Sunniside) of 1902–3, and to the new parts of Messrs JOPLING'S in the International Modern with rounded corner and bands of horizontal windows around.

Parallel with Fawcett Street to the E runs JOHN STREET, the best street of Sunderland to look at. Chronologically the start is No. 66, a good five-bay, three-storey brick house of 1827 with the usual Tuscan demi-column doorway with broken pediment. Further s and in the streets to the E of John Street all is Neo-Greek of c. 1830. In John Street the houses have doorways with Greek Doric columns and handsome honeysuckle friezes. The motif repeats in FOYLE STREET, where another pretty house, at the corner of Athenaeum Street, has in addition now windows. ATHENAEUM STREET, FREDERICK STREET, etc., have doorways with pilasters with slight incised ornament.

Further E in the old Sunderland there is also still a certain amount to be seen close to the two C18 churches. In the NE corner of the churchyard of Holy Trinity the DONNISON SCHOOL, small, one-storey, brick, founded *c.* 1770, enlarged 1827. Opposite TRINITY PLACE, decayed early C18 cottages. Of wealthy early C18 houses a group remains in a desperate condition in CHURCH STREET, N of the church, five-bay, three-storey mansions. S of the church the ASSEMBLY GARTH MERCHANT SEAMEN'S HOUSES of 1727. The Hall with arched windows and a broad Tuscan doorpiece up some steps and the Governor's House (of two bays) to its r. remain in the original state. The composition is round three sides of a court. The same was chosen for the MERCHANT SEAMEN'S ALMSHOUSES of 1840 in Church Walk, next to the Donnison School. The architecture is completely plain. Much building of council flats (with the typical heavy long balconies) has recently taken place in this area to replace war losses. At the time of John Street, Sunderland also grew to the W of the original nucleus to reach the new fashionable part, and in such streets as, for example, NICHOLSON STREET, cottages with the typical Tuscan pilasters at the doors remain. The development of this area began in 1820.

The same style in the SE in GRAY TERRACE off Hill Street, and then at Hendon in WARD TERRACE of 1835, ADDISON STREET and others, and in the S in DOURO TERRACE, Burdon Road.

Of BISHOPWEARMOUTH not much need be said. The medieval church has gone; of the medieval Rectory one solitary arch is preserved in the most incongruous context near the S end of MOWBRAY PARK. It appears as the opening to a cave at the foot of rocks. At Bishopwearmouth itself the GREEN and its neighbourhood, though much come down in the world, still deserve a glance. On the W of the Green the RECTOR'S ALMSHOUSES of 1721 the prettiest feature of which, the three-light Gothic windows, seem to date from the restoration of 1878. On the E side FENWICK LODGE, red brick, early C18, once a mansion of some consequence. Nos 17 and 18 on the S side also still betray their more genteel past. A little to the E in MARITIME TERRACE off Crowtree Road, the MARITIME ALMSHOUSES of 1819, a row with centre doorway with depressed rusticated arch and centre pediment.

The old BRIDGE lies between a singularly characterless new one and one of the typical Durham railway viaducts of numerous red brick arches. Both are high up compared with the medieval structure. This has four round arches, the two middle ones original (C13?) and ribbed, and triangularly projecting breakwaters. It was widened in 1822 but is still narrow.

ST BARTHOLOMEW, 1843–6, by *Pickering* (GR), and later enlarged. In the Neo-Norman style specially popular in England at that particular moment.

CROXDALE HALL (*see* p. 69).

TANFIELD

ST MARGARET. The W tower may be on C13 foundations. Rebuilt 1853. The nave is of 1749 (inscription). The arcades and Neo-Perp windows from the remodelling of 1878. Chancel of 1864. – PLATE. Chalice, 1725; of London make. – MONUMENT to Dorothea Methold † 1857, by *Bedford*; mourning husband leaning against a sarcophagus with the medallion portrait of his wife.

TANFIELD HALL, C17, refronted early C18. Five bays, three storeys. Thickly rusticated gateposts by the side. The large garden gates to the walled front garden are the finest work that early C18 blacksmiths have done in the county. (Good staircase inside; MHLG.)

THORNTON HALL
2 m. NE of Piercebridge

A handsome and interesting small manor house. Two building periods can be distinguished, early C16 and later C17.

Of the first the carved beams in the kitchen with Flamboyant Gothic tracery decoration, the windows in the two main gables (three lights, straightheaded, each light with a round-arched top), and the heraldic frieze between them, which, no doubt, was once the crowning motif of the porch, of the second the mullioned and transomed windows with their various pediments (scrolly open, steep triangular, semicircular), especially on the E side, and the staircase. Most of the S windows have been Georgianized.

THORPE THEWLES
1½ m. SSE of Grindon

VENN ARMS. Brick, with shaped brick friezes and an asymmetrically placed shaped gable with a horizontal oval window at its foot. Probably early C18.

TOW LAW

SS PHILLIP AND JAMES, 1869, by *Hodgson Fowler*. E.E., and with a sensitive handling of materials and style characteristic of his work. In the church a SCREEN which, one hopes, will one day be drawn by Miss Barbara Jones: Gothic forms represented by blackened fir cones, pine cones, walnuts, chestnuts, acorns, set closely together and glued on to a wooden frame. The work was done in their spare time by the then Vicar, the *Rev. T. H. E. C. Espin*, *Mr W. Work*, and *Mr J. Harrison*. It took fourteen months.

TRIMDON

ST MARY MAGDALENE. Unusually and very attractively placed, with its churchyard an island in the green. Chancel Norman, as proved by the depressed roundheaded chancel arch and a low side window. The nave masonry medieval too, inclusive of the bellcote, though all the windows are C19. N aisle 1873.

TUDHOE

1 m. NE of Spennymoor

HOLY INNOCENTS, 1866, by *Hodgson Fowler* (GR). Neo-E.E.

ST ANDREW, Tudhoe Grange, 1884, by *Hodgson Fowler* (GR). Neo-Perp. Both churches have thin towers with polygonal tops and spirelets.

TUDHOE OLD HALL. With some blocked mullioned windows.

TUDHOE HOUSE. Built as a girls' school *c.* 1825 (H. Conyers Surtees). Stuccoed front with Tudor windows with hood-moulds.

(NORTH FARM, 'an ancient house'; H. C. Surtees.)

(COLDSTREAM FARM, 'an old building'; H. C. Surtees.)

At TUDHOE GRANGE Mr Marmaduke Salvin built a colony of workers' houses in 1865–70 (dates on some of the houses). These are placed along four parallel streets, but instead of being in long terraces are semi-detached and arranged chequer-board-wise so loosely that no house overlooks another at its front or back. In addition a quarter of an acre belongs to each pair—considering the date a remarkably far-seeing contribution to the problem of working class housing.

UNTHANK HALL *see* STANHOPE

USHAW

ST CUTHBERT'S COLLEGE, Ushaw, is the resurrection of the Douai seminary. This was abolished by the French republican army. The refugees first went to Crook Hall near Lanchester and then, in 1803 started building at Ushaw. In 1808 they were able to enter into the first completed part of the new establishment. 1812 is the date on the clock above the S front. The original plan provided for three ranges, the front facing S and the other ranges running N along the W and E sides of a back courtyard. The front is two and a half storeys high and fifteen bays wide, of rubble and ashlar. All windows and the central

doorway have rusticated surrounds of alternating sizes.
There is a pediment over the three middle bays. While
thus the original appearance of the college was classical,
the numerous and extensive additions made between *c.*
1840 and *c.*1885 are Gothic throughout. With the earlier
of them *A. W. N. Pugin* had much to do. He designed
the college CHAPEL in 1840. It was built from 1842 to
1848, but has since been rebuilt more grandly and lavishly
by *Dunn & Hansom*. Consecration took place in 1885.
Reports call the new chapel 'in most respects a repro-
duction of the old'. It consists of an antechapel separated by a screen of the verandah type from the chapel
proper. Nearly all the STAINED GLASS round the Sanctuary is from Pugin's chapel. So is the present W window,
which was originally the E window. This was made by
Oliphant and called by Pugin 'the finest work of modern
times'(Mrs Stanton).The STALLS also are Pugin's design.
So is some of the metalwork, such as the tall PASCHAL
CANDLESTICK, which was exhibited at the 1851
Exhibition.

Close to the chapel are various smaller oratories. Of these
the CHAPEL OF ST JOSEPH, 1852–3, is by *Pugin* himself (completed by *E. W. Pugin*, the son). It is a lofty
four-bay room with a five-light E window. All the
stained glass was made by *Hardman*. Statue by *Karl Hoffmann*. By *E. W. Pugin* the CHAPEL OF ST CHARLES
BORROMEO, 1857, the CHAPEL OF ST MICHAEL (or
Mortuary Chapel), 1858, and the CHAPEL OF THE HOLY
FAMILY, 1852–3. In this an Adoration of the Magi by
von Roden. The same painter painted the Crucifixion in
E. W. Pugin's CHAPEL OF ST ALOYSIUS in the College
for Junior Students of 1857. The Statue of the Virgin is by
Hoffmann. Other domestic extensions and alterations:
Library and Museum 1839–40, Refectory gothicized (by
the elder *Pugin*) 1846 and enlarged 1873, Exhibition
Room 1853–4 (by *Joseph* and *Charles Hansom*), Great
Library and Study Hall 1849–51 (also by the *Hansom*
brothers), Infirmary and Museum 1856, the latter 180 ft
long (by *E. W. Pugin*).

USWORTH

HOLY TRINITY, 1832, by *John Green*, the chancel later.
E.E., with bellcote, like many others of *Green's* churches.
USWORTH HALL, *c.* 1800, five bays, two storeys, ashlar,
with broken pediment over the middle three bays. The
porch probably an imitation or alteration.

WALWORTH CASTLE

A remarkable, too little known mansion of *c.* 1600. The S 53a
front of three storeys has thick semicircular angle towers.
The windows mostly Georgianized, but still mullioned
and transomed on the top floor. This three-storeyed part
has to the N in its centre a spectacular porch with three
superimposed orders of coupled columns: Tuscan, Ionic,
and Corinthian. The porch was originally at the far end
of an entrance court flanked to E and W by two-storeyed
wings. The court was later closed by a lower N wing. The
N ends of the wings have two-storeyed bay windows. On
the E side of the E wing is another well preserved two-
storeyed bay. Inside, the groundfloor Hall and the
Saloon above have mid C18 decoration. Of the same date
the Venetian window on the N side of the main range.
Walworth village was reported as decaying in 1626.

WASHINGTON

HOLY TRINITY, 1833, by *John Green* of Newcastle. In the
usual E.E. style, without tower.
The RECTORY of 1720 was burnt out recently and is now
being replaced by the Urban District Offices, incorporating parts of it and, alas, imitating its style. The new façade
is stone-faced.
WASHINGTON HALL. A good medium-sized early C17
house with a symmetrical front towards the church. Central door, a four-light mullioned window on each side,
three-light windows above, and short projecting wings
with gables and also four- and three-light windows. A

similar projection at the back and a staircase projection. The house was in a bad state and is now being restored with funds from the United States, as it was in the C14 the house of the ancestors of George Washington. There is indeed a C13 or C14 fragment of an arch still in the internal wall between Hall and Kitchen.

(NORTH BIDDICK HALL, ½ m. S. Georgian stone house with bow window; MHLG.)

WEST AUCKLAND

Houses along a large village green, notable amongst them the following:

WEST AUCKLAND HALL, C17, on an H-plan; gabled. The front has still a few windows of Tudor type left (straight-headed under hood-moulds, with the individual lights roundheaded; some also transomed), but the central door-way has an open segmental pediment. This and some of the younger windows may belong to alterations of after 1670. A higher part at the back of the house looks older than the rest. Behind the house the old brick buildings of a BREWERY. The house would amply reward closer study.

NO. 115. Long, two-storeyed, early C17 front with central porch and mullioned and hood-moulded windows. The porch is crowned by a pretty gable of stepped quarter-circle pieces.

NO. 64. Also early C17, also with a central porch, but smaller and at the time of writing very neglected.

NO. 65. Again early C17, with a canted bay window.

WEST BOLDON

16b ST NICHOLAS. The W tower with its spire is not high, yet, as the church lies on an elevation, it is visible from far away, and it is in addition of considerable architectural interest. It appears to be entirely of the early to mid C13, and early to mid C13 spires are a rarity. Ground floor with one lancet on each side, first floor with six lancets and dogtooth. Heavy clasping buttresses to support the spire with its heavy broaches. The dormer windows right at the foot have single-chamfered jambs and arches. While the spire was still in construction, it seems, the aisleless church (the nave walls have left their marks on the E walls of the tower) was enriched by aisles, and these were taken as far W as the W face of the tower. The old lancets of the tower to N and S remain. The aisles have lancet W windows with dogtooth. The other aisle windows are C19, as are all chancel windows. Some head-stops of hood-moulds, however, are original. The S porch also belongs entirely to the C13, with its inner and outer doorways. The nave is divided from the aisles by arcades of three bays with octagonal piers with moulded capitals (with a little occasional nailhead) and double-chamfered arches. The chancel arch is contemporary. So are the Piscina in the S aisle and the two recesses for tombs. – PLATE. Chalice inscribed 1672; Cover inscribed 1681; Flagon, 1740; Dish, 1745. – MONUMENTS. Two effigies of Priests, both early C14, one in a S wall recess, the other in the chancel.

WEST BOLDON HALL. A stately stone house of 1709, five bays, two storeys, doorway with open segmental pediment on corbels. Big gateposts and corner posts of the walled front garden.

RECTORY. The front is *c.* 1840, stone, with two canted bay windows; behind it older parts.

ST NICHOLAS TERRACE. N of the church; C18 stone cottages, one dated 1771.

BANK HOUSE, Gateshead Terrace, an early C18 cottage with a doorway embellished by a thick scrolly pediment.

SCOT'S HOUSE, 1½ m. W. A distinguished building. Its front is 1798 (rainwater head). Ashlar, five windows width, two storeys, with a broken three-bay pediment and a similar pediment on Tuscan columns for the porch. The stables to the W are earlier C18. At the back of the mansion far projecting wings, probably older still in their structure.

WEST HARTLEPOOL *see* **THE HARTLEPOOLS**

WESTERNHOPEBURN
1¼ m. WSW of Eastgate

The house has an inscription with the date 1606 over the door. This is new but probably represents an original one. Long, two-storeyed, with symmetrically arranged mullioned windows under hood-moulds. The front is all covered by ivy and appears behind fine old trees.

WESTERTON

WESTERTON FOLLY. A circular, medieval-looking tower in the village, built *c.* 1780–90 (H. C. Surtees: *c.* 1765) as an observatory by *Mr Wright*, a local mathematician and astronomer. Among the windows the cross-shaped slit is typical of C18 Gothic Revival.

WESTGATE

ST ANDREW, 1869, by *R. J. Withers*. E.E., with polygonal apse and a circular bellcote with conical roof.

PARK HOUSE, E of the village. One hood-moulded window left and the porch. All now one-storeyed.

WESTHOLME HALL
1 m. N of Winston

A very complete example of its date, 1606, as marked on the large fireplace in the Hall. H-plan, with the Hall in the centre, the Kitchen in one wing, a large parlour (now subdivided) in the other, and the staircases (altered) at the back. Three-light and four-light mullioned and transomed windows, except for the Hall window which has six lights. The Hall was originally single-storeyed. The room above (Great Chamber?) had the same size. Its handsome plaster frieze with putti, foliage, etc., survives. Also original several doorways with four-centred heads. The house is described by Surtees as 'a good specimen of the domestic architecture of the middle gentry in the age of James I'.

WESTOE

St Michael (South Westoe), 1881–2, by *Austin, Johnson, & Hickey*; the aisles of 1895. Large and prosperous, red brick and stone dressings. N and S porches to the l. and r. of the w baptistry. Isolated polygonal Campanile at the NE. Inside, low heavy hammerbeam roof, octagonal piers, and arches dying into them.

Westoe Village 'consists chiefly of one respectable street, inhabited by successful maritime adventurers who have retired hither from active life' (Dugdale, *The New British Traveller*, 1819). The street is like a long Green and has quite a number of nice C18 and early C19 houses, although punctuated by higher and showier houses of the 1870s and 1880s, some of them, it seems, by *J. J. Stevenson*. Of the earlier buildings the following deserve notice: No. 1 and Nos 5–8 on the S, Ivy House and Meadow Croft on the N side. These have the characteristic Late Georgian doorways with broken pediments on Tuscan demi-columns or pilasters. No. 8 is dated 1810. Further w No. 17, with lozenge-shaped glazing bars and crenellation. At the w end of the village across the end of the Green Westoe House, early C18, five-bay front of two storeys, brick, with the pedimented doorway on Roman pilasters. On the N side a porch with an odd pedimented gable, in a style which one connects with the mid C17, yet apparently original.

WEST RAINTON

St Mary. A proud High Victorian church by *E. R. Robson*, 1864 (GR). The broach spire is visible from far away and also the tall high-pitched nave roof. Late C13 detail. N of the N transept two arches from Domican Priory at Newcastle have been re-erected, when that building was demolished in 1868 (*cf.* Whitburn House). Inside the church a plaque which formed part of the Great Pyramid of Gizeh.

WHESSOE

A stone building by the side of the farmhouse with C16 two-light windows and a fireplace must be part of the original manor house. It is now a pig-sty.

WHICKHAM

A relatively unspoilt village on a hillside close to Gateshead.

ST MARY. Lying back from the Green, up some steps. Short w tower, buttressed only at the foot, battlemented and with C13 twin bell-openings. All windows new, but the Priest's Door in the chancel probably Norman or Transitional. Norman chancel arch with thick demi-columnar responds with big scalloped capitals (that on the l. with demi-rosette decoration of the scallops). The arch is slightly double-chamfered. Arcades of four bays, that on the s original, in the Transitional style, with slightly single-chamfered arches and very flat moulded capitals with stylized leaves or sprigs at the upper corners to support the abaci. N aisle and outer N aisle C19. But at the E end of the outer N aisle two re-erected late C13 two-light windows with pointed trefoils in the spandrels. Very plain single-chamfered tower arch. – SCULPTURE. Two foliated cross tomb-lids in the s porch. – PLATE. Elizabethan Chalice and Cover inscribed 1622; Paten, 1692; two Flagons of London make, 1722.

In the main street, slightly above, and looking down on, the church, is the former RECTORY (Cottage Hospital) of 1713, of five bays and two storeys, with an oversized, flat, semicircular pediment on the door and a coat of arms in it, then WHICKHAM CHASE, also of five bays and two storeys, with a less formal wing to the r., and WHICKHAM LODGE, lying further back. This is a fine C18 five-bay two-storey house, also with a less formal wing to the r. The main part has a broad doorway with Tuscan pilasters.

Outside the village towards the E DUNSTON HILL (now a hospital), dated on a rainwater-head 1740; a plain, substantial stone mansion of seven bays and two and a half storeys with hardly any embellishments.

WHITBURN

ST ANDREW (?). E.E. W tower, unbuttressed, unembattled (upper part C15), with the upper floor openings with an early type of hood-moulds. All other windows of the church renewed, except for the interesting small W window of the S aisle, in the shape of a vesica. The chancel S lancets, and one on the N, are correctly restored. The moulded rear arches are original. Five-bay arcade, that is a long nave. Relatively low, with short circular piers, the simplest moulded C13 capitals, and only slightly double-chamfered arches. All this points to the early C13, and that date can most probably be accepted, although the restoration of 1865 has done much to obscure the original state of affairs. – BELLS. Two of the C14. – MONUMENTS. Two foliated cross tomb-lids (outside W wall, S aisle). – Michael Mathew † 1689, the anachronism of a recumbent effigy on a tomb-chest, looking slightly ridiculous with his broad, heavy face, periwig, and contemporary clothes.

The village of Whitburn is uncommonly attractive. To the W of the church the stately former RECTORY, built in 1818. It is a three-storeyed stone mansion with a S front of three central windows and three ample bow windows to their l. and r. The house looks over towards the sea. From the sea front looking NW Whitburn appears all embedded in trees.

To the N of the church runs the GREEN, beautifully shaded by two rows of trees. A specially successful feature is the considerably elevated position of the houses on the N side of the Green. No individual house need be mentioned specially, except for Whitburn Hall and Whitburn House.

WHITBURN HALL, on the N side, is a long rambling building composed of different parts of different ages, from the two-storeyed part which may be c.1600 to the old Drawing Room and W tower of c.1800, the large new Drawing Room and Entrance Hall at the W end of 1856, the centre wing on the N side of 1881, and the curious balustrading and statuary of the Edwardian decade.

WHITBURN HOUSE is Victorian, but in the garden is re-erected a fragment of St John's Church, Newcastle, taken to Whitburn in 1869. It contains a four-light Perp window.

WHITFIELD HOUSE *see* WOLSINGHAM

WHITFIELD PLACE *see* WOLSINGHAM

WHITWORTH

CHURCH. 1850, in the E.E. style. In front of the W side two MONUMENTS: cross-legged Knight with cylindrical helmet entirely covering his face, sandstone, late C13. – The other effigy has become wholly unrecognizable. So much of the stone has weathered away that the head is now as small as if it were carved by Henry Moore. – PLATE. London-made Chalice, Paten, and Flagon, 1721.

WHITWORTH HALL. Five-bay garden front with one-storeyed porch on coupled columns, one-bay pediment. In the Late Georgian style, but apparently rebuilt after a fire in 1892. – In the garden an iron arbour, called the Rose Temple. This was bought in Italy by the owner of Burn Hall.

WHORLTON

ST MARY, 1853.

SUSPENSION BRIDGE of 1829 across the river Tees.

WILLINGTON

ST STEPHEN, 1857 (?), by *J. A. Cory*, enlarged 1869–73 (GR). The W tower looks as if it might be left over from the medieval church. It has diagonal buttresses, that is Perp. The roof is now pyramidal.

WILLINGTON HALL. A pretty Gothick front of three bays was added probably in the later C18. The windows have depressed ogee arches. The C19 used this form no longer. The back of the house is obviously older.

Hall and church lie outside the present-day colliery village or town of Willington.

WINDLESTONE HALL
3½ m. E of Bishop Auckland

By *Bonomi*, called 'nearly completed' in 1834. Large, two-storeyed, with banded rustication of the walls and a top balustrade. The main front has a long colonnade of coupled Tuscan columns. To the N handsome stables with a gateway the big clock tower of which has an open drum of Tuscan columns. The gate lodge with a temple front with four-column Tuscan portico.

WINGATE

HOLY TRINITY, 1840, by *George Jackson* of Durham (GR). E.E., without tower. Quite pretty, partly owing to the decay of the stonework.

WINLATON

ST PATRICK, 1828. – PLATE. Plain Early Elizabethan Cup and Cover, London-made in 1570, both given in 1842.

WINSTON

ST ANDREW. In an isolated position outside the village and above the bank of the river Tees. A beautiful very wide C13 chancel with lancet windows, the two nearest the W end on the N and S shorter than the others and with an inner roll-moulding. The rest of the exterior (no tower) rebuilt in 1848. Inside, a three-bay arcade of which the first is separated from the others by a piece of solid wall (as at St Helen Auckland). The others have a circular pier and double-chamfered arches. All responds are keeled. – SCULPTURE. Saxon cross-head with figures (in the porch). – Tomb-lid with foliated cross and shaft with birds; C13. – FONT. An exceedingly puzzling piece. Circular, with two tracery motifs of typical late C13 character, but in addition a sprig of oak with leaves, so realistic that they look more C16 than C13, and the oddest of combats between two dragons. Their heads are clearly Celtic or Saxon in design, and their tails wriggle accordingly. But the tails sprout out into a realistic acorn and between the beasts is a flower with stem, neither early nor high medieval. Is the whole an Elizabethan or even a romantic piece of revivalism? Or just a retooling? Or an early fake? – PLATE. Chalice, 1632.

BRIDGE. Stone, one arch of 111 ft span; 1764; designed by *Sir Thomas Robinson*.

WITTON GILBERT

The monuments of the village lie together and on their own amid trees close to the river Browney.

ST MICHAEL AND ALL ANGELS. Chancel walls and s side of the nave Norman (*see* the small, deeply splayed, round-headed windows). The rest 1863, but with the use of two C14 windows (E end and nave SE end). – PLATE. Chalice and Cover, London, 1570; Flagon, London, 1773.

LEPER HOSPITAL. Some masonry and one fine late C12 or early C13 window-head (pointed, with a ball motif in the outer voussoirs and a blank quatrefoil in the spandrel; cf. Darlington and Ripon) remain in the building of Witton Hall.

CHAPEL OF ST JOHN. Some insignificant fragments of walls close to the river.

WITTON-LE-WEAR

SS PHILIP AND JAMES. The s doorway plain, undecorated Norman, the N aisle arcade C13 on circular piers with double-chamfered arches and capitals as at Stanhope, altered when the church was rebuilt by *Hodgson Fowler* in 1902 in a pleasant buff stone and pleasant Neo-Perp forms straightheaded windows and a bellcote.

WITTON TOWER (formerly Witton Hall), an extremely interesting fragment of a medieval house, still with its chapel with a Norman window and later diagonal buttresses, and with a tall broad tower with Late Perp win-

dows, remodelled in the C17 (*see* the quoins and parapet).
The staircase with heavy balusters belongs to this remodelling.

WITTON CASTLE. The history of this remarkable building
is not sufficiently known. Licence to crenellate was obtained in 1410, after building had begun, and from that
time date the big tower-house on the N side, to which large
additional living quarters were added on the W side in *c.*
1790–5, and the curtain wall (except for the NW parts)
with its angle turrets (or bartizans). Of these three survive: SW, SE, NE. Two of them are round, the third is
square. On the SE turret two figures as at Hylton, Raby,
Alnwick, etc. The details of the turrets are as instructive
as those of the curtain wall. The house, however, has been
so much altered in the C19 that little of interest can now
be seen. Its basement is tunnel-vaulted (cf. Lumley, Hollinside, Ludworth, etc.). Entrance to the courtyard is by
the E and W gates. The S tower in the curtain wall has C16
windows and is not original.

WOLSINGHAM

SS MARY AND STEPHEN. W tower late C12; all the rest
1848, in the E.E. style, and according to GR probably by
Gilbert Scott & Moffatt. The baptistery was added by
Hodgson Fowler in 1896 (GR). In it a STAINED GLASS
window with Jacob's Ladder which must be by *Burne-
Jones* and made by *Morris & Co.* – PLATE. Foreign Plate,
C17; Paten, 1705; Flagon, 1772–3.

ST THOMAS OF CANTERBURY (R.C.), 1854, by *J. A.
Hansom* (GR).

CHAPEL WELLS. The scanty remains of an undated house
of the Bishop of Durham, demolished in the C17.

TOWN HALL. A pretty, free-standing little building of
classical forms, dated 1861.

WHITFIELD HOUSE and WHITFIELD PLACE. Two neigh-
bours, the taller and younger House of six bays and three
storeys, with quoins and top parapet, beautifully half-
hidden by two ilex trees, seems to be of *c.* 1700; the older
Place, dated 1677, long and low, still with mullioned and

hood-moulded windows and two bay windows. (In the House some panelled rooms and a good staircase; the remains of a pulpit used by Wesley in the garage.)

BISHOP OAK, 1½ m. NW. With a summer-house apparently of the late C17, quoined and with a pyramid roof and finial.

BRADLEY HALL *see* p. 58.

WOLVISTON

ST PETER, 1876, by *Austin, Johnson, & Hicks* (GR). Red brick, in the E.E. style, with a pretty flèche. – PLATE. Elizabethan Chalice; Paten of 1637.

The village has a handsome spacious GREEN with a number of nice Georgian houses, e.g. the Rectory, Manor Farm House, Wolviston Hall (altered, but four-column Roman Doric porch towards the garden), the Parochial School of 1836, and the Londonderry Almshouses of 1838.

WOODLANDS HALL
3 m. W of Lanchester

'A neat structure' recently built, say *The Beauties of England and Wales* in 1803.

WYNYARD PARK

The most splendid C19 mansion in the county, and entirely unaffected by the romantic picturesque leanings of the age. It was begun in 1822 by *Benjamin Wyatt* for the third Marquess of Londonderry, the coal magnate and founder of Seaham Harbour. Building went on for nineteen years and was then nearly complete. However, in 1841, a fire gutted the mansion. It was somewhat later remodelled inside. The chapel was again burnt out later, redone by *Brooks*, and once more in 1903–5.

The façades are clearly of the 1822 design. The entrance side is thirteen windows wide, with a grand six-column giant Corinthian portico and, near the angles, a tripartite window on each side. Opposite these on the garden front are bow windows. Otherwise the garden side is quite plain. The entrance hall is still in the Adam-Wyatt tradition of 1800, with a coffered segmental tunnel-vault and apses at both ends. The other ground floor rooms all look *c.* 1850, with their classical canons debased by detail going somewhat Baroque or Frenchy. Thus the main octagonal centre room with its dome lit by lantern-light and sky-light has caryatids and other figures about the dome, but the suite of rooms towards the terrace and gardens have Rococo bits and other dixhuitième elements. Some fire-places, on the other hand, show the High Victorian liking for naturalistic detail. The most impressive thing about the rooms is their size. Only a few decades later a rich nobleman's mansion might have had still as many rooms as Wynyard, or more, but the house would have been asymmetrical and a few large rooms would be connected by many of more manageable size. Here there are still on the whole ground floor (with the exception of one guest suite) nothing but state rooms. Yet there were never on the upper floor more intimate family living rooms either. So everyday life in 1850 was actually carried on in these saloons. Now it is a training establishment for county council school teachers.

In the grounds OBELISK to commemorate the visit of the Duke of Wellington in 1827; 127 ft high.

BLAKESTON HALL *see* p. 58.

GLOSSARY

ABACUS: flat slab on the top of a capital (q.v.).

ABUTMENT: solid masonry placed to resist the lateral pressure of a vault.

ACANTHUS: plant with thick fleshy and scalloped leaves used as part of the decoration of a Corinthian capital (q.v.) and in some types of leaf carving.

ACHIEVEMENT OF ARMS: in heraldry, a complete display of armorial bearings.

ACROTERION: foliage-carved block on the end or top of a classical pediment.

ADDOSSED: two human figures, animals, or birds, etc., placed symmetrically so that they turn their backs to each other.

AEDICULE, AEDICULA: framing of a window or door by columns and a pediment (q.v.).

AFFRONTED: two human figures, animals, or birds, etc., placed symmetrically so that they face each other.

AMBULATORY: semicircular or polygonal aisle enclosing an apse (q.v.).

ANNULET: see Shaft-ring.

ANTIS, IN: see Portico.

APSE: vaulted semicircular or polygonal end of a chancel or a chapel.

ARABESQUE: light and fanciful surface decoration using combinations of flowing lines, tendrils, etc., interspersed with vases, animals, etc.

ARCADE: range of arches supported on piers or columns,

free-standing; or, BLIND ARCADE, the same attached to a wall.

ARCH: round-headed; i.e. semi-circular pointed, i.e. consisting of two curves, each drawn from one centre, and meeting in a point at the top; Segmental, i.e. in the form of a segment; pointed; four-centred, *see* Fig. 1(*a*); Tudor, *see* Fig. 1(*b*); Ogee, *see* Fig. 1(*c*); Stilted, *see* Fig. 1(*d*).

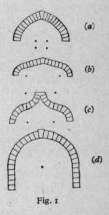

Fig. 1

ARCHITRAVE: lowest of the three main parts of the entablature (q.v.) of an order (q.v.) (*see* Fig. 11).

ARCHIVOLT: undersurface of an arch (also called Soffit).

ARRIS: sharp edge at the meeting of two surfaces.

ASHLAR: masonry of large blocks wrought to even faces and square edges.

ATRIUM: inner court of a Roman house, also open court in front of a church.

ATTACHED: see engaged.

ATTIC: topmost storey of a house, if lower than the others.

AUMBREY: recess or cupboard to hold sacred vessels for Mass and Communion.

BAILEY: open space or court of a fortified castle.

BALDACCHINO: canopy supported on columns.

BALLFLOWER: globular flower of three petals enclosing a small ball. A decoration used in the first quarter of the C14.

BALUSTER: small pillar or column of fanciful outline.

BALUSTRADE: series of balusters supporting a handrail or coping (q.v.).

BARBICAN: outwork, constructed like a gateway, defending the entrance to a castle.

BARGEBOARDS: projecting decorated boards placed against the incline of the gable of a building and hiding the horizontal roof timbers.

BASILICA: in medieval architecture an aisled church with a clerestory.

BASTION: projection at the angle of a fortification.

BATTER: wall with an inclined face.

BATTLEMENT: parapet with a series of indentations or embrasures with raised portions or merlons between (also called Crenellation).

BAYS: internal compartments of a building; each divided from the other not by solid walls but by divisions only marked in the side walls (columns, pilasters, etc.) or the ceiling (beams, etc.). Also external divisions of a building by fenestration.

BAY-WINDOW: angular or curved projection of a house front with ample fenestration. If curved also called bow-window; if on an upper floor only also called oriel or oriel window.

BEAKHEAD: Norman ornamental motif consisting of a row of bird or beast heads with beaks pointing downwards and biting usually into a roll moulding.

BELL-COTE: turret usually on the W end of a church to carry the bells.

BILLET: Norman ornamental motif made up of short raised rectangles placed at regular intervals.

BLOCK CAPITAL: Romanesque capital cut from a cube by having the lower angles rounded off to the circular shaft below (also called Cushion Capital) (Fig. 2).

Fig. 2

BOND, ENGLISH or FLEMISH: see Brickwork.

BOSS: knob or projection usually placed to cover the intersection of ribs in a vault.

BOW-WINDOW: see Bay-Window.

BOX PEW: pew with a high wooden enclosure.

BRACES: *see* Roof.

BRACKET: small supporting piece of stone, etc., to carry a projecting horizontal.

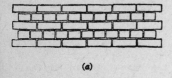

(a)

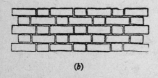

(b)

Fig. 3

BRICKWORK: *Header:* brick laid so that the end only appears on the face of the wall. *Stretcher:*

brick laid so that the side only appears on the face of the wall. *English Bond:* method of laying bricks so that alternate courses or layers on the face of the wall are composed of headers or stretchers only (Fig. 3a). *Flemish Bond:* method of laying bricks so that alternate headers and stretchers appear in each course on the face of the wall (Fig. 3b).

BROACH: *see* Spire.

BROKEN PEDIMENT: *see* Pediment.

BUTTRESS: mass of brickwork or masonry projecting from or built against a wall to give additional strength. *Angle Buttresses:* two meeting at an angle of 90° at the angle of a building (Fig. 4a). *Clasping Buttress:* one which encases the angle

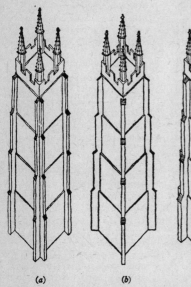
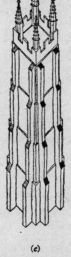
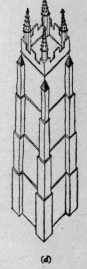

(a)   (b)   (c)   (d)

Fig. 4

(Fig. 4*d*). *Diagonal Buttress:* one placed against the right angle formed by two walls, and more or less equiangular with both (Fig. 4*b*). *Flying Buttress:* arch or half arch transmitting the thrust of a vault or roof from the upper part of a wall to an outer support or buttress. *Setback Buttress:* angle buttress set slightly back from the angle (Fig. 4*c*).

CABLE MOULDING: moulding imitating a twisted cord.

CAMBER: slight rise or upward curve of an otherwise horizontal structure.

CAMPANILE: isolated bell tower.

CANOPY: ornamental covering above an altar, pulpit, niche, etc.

CAP: in a windmill the crowning feature.

CAPITAL: head or top part of a column (q.v.).

CARTOUCHE: tablet with an ornate frame, usually enclosing an inscription.

CARYATID: human figure used instead of a column.

CASTELLATED: decorated with battlements.

CEILURE: panelled and adorned part of a wagon-roof above the rood or the altar.

CENSER: vessel for the burning of incense.

CENTERING: wooden framework used in arch and vault construction and removed when the mortar has set.

CHALICE: small cup used in the Communion service or at Mass.

CHAMFER: surface made by cutting across the square angle of a stone block, piece of wood, etc., at an angle of 45° to the two other surfaces.

CHANCEL: that part of the E end of a church in which the altar is placed, usually applied to the whole continuation of the nave E of the crossing.

CHANCEL ARCH: arch at the W end of the chancel.

CHANTRY CHAPEL: chapel attached to, or inside, a church endowed for the saying of Masses for the soul of the founder or some other individual.

CHEVET: French term for the E end of a church (chancel, ambulatory, and radiating chapels).

CHEVRON: sculptured moulding forming a zigzag.

CHOIR: that part of the church where divine service is sung.

CIBORIUM: box or container for the consecrated bread. Also used to mean a baldacchino (q.v.).

CINQUEFOIL: *see* Foil.

CLAPPER BRIDGE: bridge made of large slabs of stone, some built up to make rough piers and other longer ones laid on top to make the roadway.

CLASSIC: here used to mean the moment of highest achievement of a style.

CLASSICAL: here used as the term for Greek and Roman architecture and any subsequent styles copying it.

CLERESTORY: upper storey of the nave walls of a church, pierced by windows.

COADE STONE: artificial (cast) stone made in the late C18 and the early C19 by Coade and Seely in London.

COB: walling material made of mixed clay and straw.

COFFERING: decorating a ceiling with sunk square or polygonal ornamental panels.

COLLAR-BEAM: *see* Roof.

COLONNADE: range of columns.

COLONNETTE: small column.

COLUMNA ROSTRATA: column decorated with carved prows of ships to celebrate a naval victory.

COMPOSITE: *see* Orders.

CONSOLE: bracket (q.v.) with a compound curved outline.

COPING: capping or covering to a wall.

CORBEL: block of stone projecting from a wall, supporting some horizontal feature.

CORBEL TABLE: series of corbels, occurring just below the roof eaves externally or internally, often seen in Norman buildings.

CORINTHIAN: *see* Orders.

CORNICE: in classical architecture the top section of the entablature (q.v.). Also for a projecting decorative feature along the top of a wall, arch, etc.

COVE, COVING: concave undersurface in the nature of a hollow moulding but on a larger scale.

COVER PATEN: cover to a Communion cup, suitable for use as a paten or plate for the consecrated bread.

CRADLE ROOF: *see* Wagon-roof.

CRENELLATION: *see* Battlement.

CREST, CRESTING: ornamental finish along the top of a screen, etc.

CROCKET, CROCKETING: decorative features placed on the sloping sides of spires, pinnacles, gables, etc. in Gothic architecture, carved in various leaf shapes and placed at regular intervals.

CROCKET CAPITAL: *see* Fig. 5.

Fig. 5

CROSSING: space at the intersection of nave, chancel, and transepts.

CRUCK: big curved beam supporting both walls and roof of a cottage.

CRYPT: underground room usually below the E end of a church.

CUPOLA: small polygonal or circular domed turret crowning a roof.

CURTAIN WALL: connecting wall between the towers of a castle.

CURVILINEAR: *see* Tracery.

CUSHION CAPITAL: *see* Block Capital.

CUSP: in tracery (q.v.) the small pointed member between two lobes of a trefoil, quatrefoil, etc.

DADO: decorative covering of the lower part of a wall.

DAGGER: tracery motif of the Dec. style. It is a lancet shape rounded or pointed at the head, pointed at the foot and cusped inside (*see* Fig. 6).

Fig. 6

DAIS: raised platform at one end of a room.

DEC ('DECORATED'): historical division of English Gothic architecture covering the first half of the C14.

DEMI-COLUMNS: columns half sunk into a wall.

DIAPER WORK: surface decoration composed of square or lozenge shapes.

DOG-TOOTH: typical E.E. ornament consisting of a series of four-cornered stars placed diagonally and raised pyramidally (Fig. 7).

Fig. 7

DOMICAL VAULT: see Vault.

DONJON: see Keep.

DORIC: see Orders.

DORMER (WINDOW): window placed vertically in the sloping plane of a roof.

DRIPSTONE: see Hood-mould.

DRUM: circular or polygonal vertical wall of a dome or cupola.

E.E. ('EARLY ENGLISH'): historical division of English Gothic architecture roughly covering the C13.

EASTER SEPULCHRE: recess with tomb-chest usually in the wall of a chancel, the tomb-chest to receive an effigy of Christ for Easter celebrations.

EAVES: underpart of a sloping roof overhanging a wall.

EAVES CORNICE: cornice below the eaves of a roof.

ECHINUS: quarter round moulding carved with egg and dart pattern, used in classical architecture.

EMBATTLED: see Battlement.

EMBRASURE: small opening in the wall or parapet of a fortified building, usually splayed on the inside. See Loop.

ENCAUSTIC TILES: earthenware glazed and decorated tiles used for paving.

ENGAGED COLUMNS: columns attached to, or partly sunk into, a wall.

ENGLISH BOND: see Brickwork.

ENTABLATURE: in Classical architecture the whole of the horizontal members above a column (that is architrave, frieze, and cornice) (see Fig. 11).

ENTASIS: very slight convex deviation from a straight line; used on Greek columns and sometimes on spires to prevent an optical illusion of concavity.

ENTRESOL: see Mezzanine.

EPITAPH: hanging wall monument.

ESCUTCHEON: shield for armorial bearings.

EXEDRA: the apsidal end of a room. See Apse.

EXTRADOS: outer surface of an arch.

FAIENCE: decorated glazed earthenware.

FAN TRACERY: see Tracery.

FAN VAULT: see Vault.

FERETORY: place behind the High Altar, where the chief shrine of a church is kept.

FESTOON: carved garland of flowers and fruit suspended at both ends.

FILLET: narrow flat band running down a shaft or along a roll moulding.

FINIAL: in Gothic architecture the top of a pinnacle, gable, or bench-end carved into a leaf or leaf-like form.

FLAGON: jug for the wine used in the Communion service.

FLAMBOYANT: properly the latest phase of French Gothic architecture where the window tracery takes on wavy undulating lines.

FLÈCHE: slender wooden spire on the centre of a roof (also called Spirelet).

FLEMISH BOND: see Brickwork.

FLEURON: decorative carved flower or leaf.

FLUSH WORK: Decorative use of flint in conjunction with dressed stone so as to form pattens: tracery, initials, etc.

FLUTING: vertical channelling in the shaft of a column.

FLYING BUTTRESS: see Buttress.

FOIL: lobe formed by the cusping (q.v.) of a circle or an arch. Trefoil, quatrefoil, cinquefoil, multifoil, express the number of leaf shapes to be seen.

FOLIATED: carved with leaf shapes.

FOSSE: ditch.

FOUR-CENTRED ARCH: see Arch.

FRATER: refectory or dining hall of a monastery.

FRESCO: wall painting on wet plaster.

FRIEZE: middle division of a classical entablature (q.v.) (see Fig. 11).

FRONTAL: covering of the front of an altar.

GALILEE: chapel or vestibule at the w end of a church enclosing the porch. Also called Narthex (q.v.).

GALLERY: in church architecture upper storey above an aisle, opened in arches to the nave. Also called Tribune (q.v.) and often erroneously Triforium (q.v.).

GARGOYLE: water spout projecting from the parapet of a wall or tower; carved into a human or animal shape.

GAZEBO: lookout tower or raised summer house in a picturesque garden.

'GEOMETRICAL': see Tracery.

'GIBBS' SURROUND: of a doorway or window. A surround with alternating larger and smaller blocks of stone, quoin-wise, or intermittent large blocks, sometimes with a narrow raised band connecting them up the verticals and along the extrados of the arch (Fig. 8).

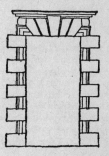

Fig. 8

GROIN: sharp edge at the meeting of two cells of a cross-vault.

GROINED VAULT: see Vault.

GROTESQUE: fanciful ornamental decoration: see also Arabesque.

HAGIOSCOPE: see Squint.

HALF-TIMBERING: see Timber Framing.

HALL CHURCH: church in which nave and aisles are of equal height or approximately so.

HAMMER-BEAM: see Roof.

HANAP: large metal cup, generally made for domestic use, standing on an elaborate base and stem; with a very ornate cover frequently crowned with a little steeple.

HEADERS: see Brickwork.

HERRINGBONE WORK: brick, stone, or tile construction where the component blocks are laid diagonally instead of flat. Alternate courses lie in opposing directions to make a zigzag pattern up the face of the wall.

HEXASTYLE: having four detached columns.

HIPPED ROOF: see Roof.

HOOD-MOULD: projecting moulding above an arch or a lintel to throw off water (also called Dripstone or Label).

ICONOGRAPHY: the science of the contents of works of art.

IMPOST: brackets in walls, usually formed of mouldings, on which the ends of an arch rest.

INDENT: shape chiselled out in a stone slab to receive a brass.

INGLENOOK: bench or seat built in beside a fireplace, sometimes covered by the chimney breast, occasionally lit by small windows on each side of the fire.

INTERCOLUMNATION: the space between columns.

IONIC: see Orders (Fig. 11).

JAMB: straight side of an archway, doorway, or window.

KEEL MOULDING: moulding whose outline is in section like that of the keel of a ship.

KEEP: massive tower of a Norman castle.

KEYSTONE: middle stone in an arch.

KING-POST: see Roof (Fig. 13).

LABEL: see Hood-mould.

LABEL STOP: ornamental boss at the end of a hood-mould (q.v.).

LANCET WINDOW: slender pointed-arched window.

LANTERN: in architecture, a small circular or polygonal turret with windows all round crowning a roof (see Cupola) or a dome.

LANTERN CROSS: churchyard cross with lantern-shaped top usually with sculptured representations on the sides of the top.

LEAN-TO ROOF: roof with one slope only, built against a higher wall.

LESENE or PILASTER STRIP: pilaster without base and capital.

LIERNE: see Vault (Fig. 20).

LINENFOLD: Tudor panelling ornamented with a conventional representation of a piece of linen laid in vertical folds. The piece is repeated in each panel.

LINTEL: horizontal beam or stone bridging an opening.

LOGGIA: recessed colonnade (q.v.).

LONG AND SHORT WORK: Saxon quoins (q.v.) consisting of stones placed with the long sides alternately upright and horizontal.

LOUVRE: opening, often with lantern (q.v.) over, in the roof of a room to let the smoke from a central hearth escape.

LOZENGE: diamond shape.

LUNETTE: tympanum (q.v.) or curved opening in a vault.

LYCH GATE: wooden gate structure with a roof and open sides placed at the entrance to a churchyard to provide space for the reception of a coffin. The word lych is Saxon and means a corpse.

MACHICOLATION: projecting gallery on brackets constructed on the outside of castle towers or walls. The gallery has holes in the floor to drop missiles through.

MAJOLICA: ornamented glazed earthenware.

MANSARD: see Roof.

MERLON: see Battlement.

METOPE: in classical architecture of the Doric order (q.v.) the space in the frieze between the triglyphs (Fig. 11).

MEZZANINE: low storey placed between two higher ones.

MISERERE: see Misericord.

MISERICORD: bracket placed on the underside of a hinged choir stall seat which, when turned up, provided the occupant of the seat with a support during long periods of standing (also called Miserere).

MODILLION: small bracket of which large numbers (modillion frieze) are often placed below a cornice (q.v.) in classical architecture.

MOTTE: steep mound forming the main feature of C11 and C12 castles.

MOUCHETTE: tracery motif in

Fig. 9

curvilinear tracery, a curved dagger (q.v.) (Fig. 9).

MULLION: vertical post or upright dividing a window into two or more 'lights'.

NAILHEAD: E.E. ornamental motif, consisting of small pyramids regularly repeated (Fig. 10).

Fig. 10

NARTHEX: enclosed vestibule or covered porch at the main entrance to a church (see Galilee).

NEWEL: central post in a circular or winding staircase; also the principal post when a flight of stairs meets a landing.

OBELISK: lofty pillar of square section tapering at the top and ending pyramidally.

OGEE: see Arch (Fig. 1c).

ORATORY: small private chapel in a house.

ORDER: (1) of a doorway or window: series of concentric steps receding towards the opening; (2) in classical architecture: column with base, shaft, capital, and entablature (q.v.) according to one of the following styles: Greek Doric, Roman Doric, Tuscan Doric, Ionic, Corinthian, Composite. The established details are very elaborate, and some specialist architectural work should be consulted for further guidance (see Fig. 11).

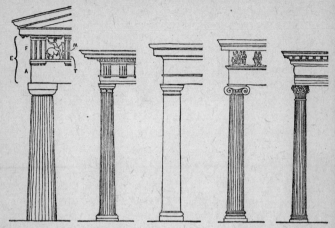

Fig. 11 – Orders of Columns (Greek Doric, Roman Doric, Tuscan, Ionic, Corinthian)
E, Entablature; F, Frieze; A, Architrave; M, Metope; T, Triglyph

ORIEL: *see* Bay Window.

OVERHANG: projection of the upper storey of a house.

OVERSAILING COURSES: series of stone or brick courses, each one projecting beyond the one below it.

PALIMPSEST: (1) *of a brass:* where a metal plate has been re-used by turning over and engraving on the back; (2) *of a wall painting:* where one overlaps and partly obscures an earlier one.

PALLADIAN: architecture following the ideas and principles of Andrea Palladio, 1518–80.

PANTILE: tile of curved S-shaped section.

PARAPET: low wall placed to protect any spot where there is a sudden drop, for example on a bridge, quay, hillside, house-top, etc.

PARGETTING: plaster work with patterns and ornaments either in relief or engraved on it.

PARVISE: room over a church porch. Often used as a school-house or a store room.

PATEN: plate to hold the bread at Communion or Mass.

PATERA: small flat circular or oval ornament in classical architecture.

PEDIMENT: low-pitched gable (q.v.) used in classical, Renaissance, and neo-classical architecture above a portico and above doors, windows, etc. It may be straight-sided or curved segmentally. *Open Pediment:* one where the centre portion of the base is left open. *Broken Pediment:* one where the centre portion of the sloping sides is 'broken' out.

PENDANT: boss (q.v.) elongated so that it seems to hang down.

PENDENTIF: concave triangular spandrel used to lead from the angle of two walls to the base of a circular dome. It is constructed as part of the hemisphere over a diameter the size of the diagonal of the basic square (Fig. 12).

Fig 12.

PERP (PERPENDICULAR): historical division of English Gothic architecture roughly covering the period from 1350 to 1530.

PIANO NOBILE: principal storey of a house with the reception rooms; usually the first floor.

PIAZZA: square open space surrounded by buildings, in c17 and c18 English sometimes used to mean a long colonnade or loggia.

PIER: strong, solid support, frequently square in section or of composite section (compound pier).

PIETRA DURA: ornamental or scenic inlay by means of thin slabs of stone.

PILASTER: shallow pier attached to a wall.

PILLAR PISCINA: free-standing piscina on a pillar.

PINNACLE: ornamental form crowning a spire, tower, buttress, etc., usually of steep pyramidal, conical, or some similar shape.

PISCINA: basin for washing the Communion or Mass vessels, provided with a drain. Generally set in or against the wall to the s of an altar.

PLAISANCE: summer-house, pleasure house near a mansion.

PLATE TRACERY: *see* Tracery.

PLINTH: projecting base of a wall or column, generally chamfered (q.v.) or moulded at the top.

POPPYHEAD: ornament of leaf and flower type used to decorate the tops of bench or stall-ends.

PORTCULLIS: gate constructed to rise and fall in vertical grooves; used in gateways of castles.

PORTE COCHERE: porch large enough to admit wheeled vehicles.

PORTICO: centre-piece of a house or a church with classical detached or attached columns and a pediment. A portico is called *prostyle* or *in antis* according to whether it projects from or recedes into a building. In a portico *in antis* the columns range with the side walls.

POSTERN: small gateway at the back of a building.

PREDELLA: in an altar-piece the horizontal strip below the main representation, often used for a number of subsidiary representations in a row.

PRESBYTERY: the part of the church lying E of the choir. It is the part where altar is placed.

PRINCIPAL: see Roof (Fig. 13).

PRIORY: monastic house whose head is a prior or prioress, not an abbot or abbess.

PROSTYLE: with free-standing columns in a row.

PULPITUM: stone rood screen in a major church.

PURLIN: see Roof (Figs. 13, 14).

PUTTO: small naked boy.

QUADRANGLE: inner courtyard in a large building complex.

QUARRY: in stained-glass work, a small diamond or square-shaped piece of glass set diagonally.

QUATREFOIL: see Foil.

QUEEN-POSTS: see Roof (Fig. 14).

QUOINS: dressed stones at the angles of a building. Sometimes all the stones are of the same size; more often they are alternately large or small.

RADIATING CHAPELS: chapels projecting radially from an ambulatory or an apse.

RAFTER: see Roof.

RAMPART: stone wall, or wall of earth surrounding a castle, fortress, or fortified city.

RAMPART-WALK: path along the inner face of a rampart.

REBATE: channel or small recess cut into a piece of wood or stone longitudinally to receive the edge of some member that is to be secured in it. The depth of the channel is equal to the thickness of the member to be let into it.

REBUS: pun, a play on words. The literal translation and illustration of a name for artistic and heraldic purposes (Belton=bell, tun).

REEDING: decoration with parallel convex mouldings touching one another.

REFECTORY: Dining hall; see Frater.

RENDERING: plastering of an outer wall.

REPOUSSÉ: decoration of metal work by relief designs, formed by beating the metal from the back.

REREDOS: structure behind and above an altar.

RESPOND: half-pier bonded into a wall and carrying one end of an arch.

RETABLE: altar-piece, a picture or piece of carving, standing behind and attached to an altar.

RETICULATION: see Tracery (Fig. 19).

REVEAL: that part of a jamb (q.v.) which lies between the glass or door and the outer surface of the wall.

RIB VAULT: see Vault.

ROCOCO: latest phase of the Baroque style, current in most Continental countries between c. 1720 and c. 1760.

ROMANESQUE: that style in architecture which was current in the C11 and C12 and preceded the Gothic style (in England often called Norman).

ROOD: cross or crucifix.

ROOD LOFT: singing gallery on the top of the rood screen, often supported by a coving.

ROOD SCREEN: see Screen.

ROOD STAIRS: stairs to give access to the rood loft.

ROOF: *Hipped:* roof with sloped instead of vertical ends. *Mansard:* roof with a double slope, the lower slope being larger and steeper than the upper. *Saddleback:* tower roof shaped like an ordinary gabled timber roof. The following members have special names: *Rafter:* roof-timber sloping up from the wall plate to the ridge. *Principal:* principal rafter, usually corresponding to the main bay divisions of the nave or chancel below. *Wall Plate:* timber laid longitudinally on the top of a wall. *Purlin:* longitudinal member laid parallel with wall plate and ridge beam some way up the slope of the roof. *Tie-beam:* beam connecting the two slopes of a roof across at its foot, usually at the height of the wall plate, to prevent the roof from spreading. *Collar-beam:* tie-beam applied higher up the slope of the roof. *Strut:* upright timber connecting the tie-beam with the rafter above it. *King-post:*

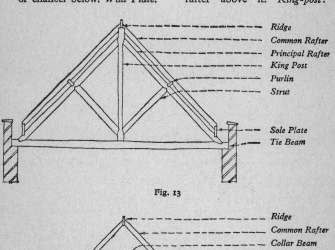

Ridge
Common Rafter
Principal Rafter
King Post
Purlin
Strut

Sole Plate
Tie Beam

Fig. 13

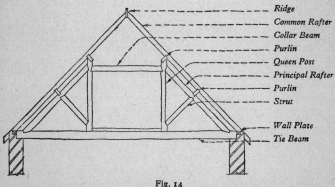

Ridge
Common Rafter
Collar Beam
Purlin
Queen Post
Principal Rafter
Purlin
Strut

Wall Plate
Tie Beam

Fig. 14

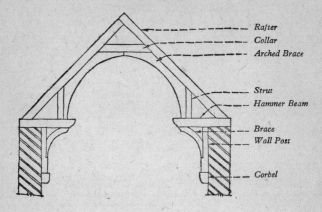

Fig. 15

upright timber connecting a
tie-beam and collar-beam
with the ridge-beam. *Queen-
posts:* two struts placed symmetrically on a tie-beam or
collar-beam. *Braces:* inclined
timbers inserted to strengthen
others. Usually braces connect
a collar-beam with the rafters
below or a tie-beam with the
wall below. Braces can be
straight or curved (also called
arched). *Hammer-beam:* beam
projecting at right angles,
usually from the top of a wall,
to carry arched braces or struts
and arched braces (*see* Figs.
13, 14, 15).

ROSE WINDOW (or WHEEL
WINDOW): circular window
with patterned tracery arranged to radiate from the
centre.

ROTUNDA: building circular in
plan.

RUBBLE: building stones, not
square or hewn, nor laid in
regular courses.

RUSTICATION: Ashlar-work of
blocks with the margins only
wrought and the faces rough or
specially rock-faced: or ashlar-
work of smooth-faced blocks
with the joints greatly emphasized (smooth rustication).
If only the horizontal joints are
emphasized it is called banded
rustication.

SADDLEBACK: *see* Roof.

SALTIRE CROSS: equal-limbed
cross placed diagonally.

SANCTUARY: area around the
main altar of a church (*see*
Presbytery).

SARCOPHAGUS: elaborately
carved coffin.

SCAGLIOLA: material composed
of cement and colouring matter
to imitate marble.

SCALLOPED CAPITAL: development of the block capital (q.v.)
in which the single semi-
circular surface is elaborated
into a series of truncated cones
(Fig. 16).

Fig. 16

SCARP: artificial cutting away of the ground to form a steep slope.

SCREEN: *Parclose screen:* screen separating a chapel from the rest of a church. *Rood screen:* screen at the W end of a chancel. Above it on the roodbeam was the rood (q.v.).

SCREENS PASSAGE: passage between the entrances to kitchen, buttery, etc., and the screen behind which lies the hall of a medieval house.

SEDILIA: seats for the priests (usually three) on the S side of the chancel of a church.

SEGMENTAL ARCH: see Arch.

SET-OFF: see Weathering.

SEXPARTITE: see Vaulting.

SGRAFFITO: pattern incised into plaster so as to expose a dark surface underneath.

SHAFT-RING: ring round a circular pier or a shaft attached to a pier.

SILL: lower horizontal part of the frame of a window.

SLATEHANGING: the covering of walls by overlapping rows of slates, on a timber substructure.

SOFFIT: see Archivolt.

SOLAR: upper drawing-room of a medieval house.

SOPRAPORTE: painting above the door of a room, usual in the C17 and C18.

SOUNDING BOARD: horizontal board or canopy over a pulpit. Also called Tester.

SPANDREL: triangular surface between one side of an arch, the horizontal drawn from its apex, and the vertical drawn from its springer, also the surface between two arches.

SPIRE: tall pyramidal or conical pointed erection often built on top of a tower, turret, etc. *Broach Spire:* spire which is generally octagonal in plan rising from the top or parapet of a square tower. A small inclined piece of masonry covers the vacant triangular space at each of the four angles of the square and is carried up to a point along the diagonal sides of the octagon. *Needle Spire:* thin spire rising from the centre of a tower roof, well inside the parapet.

SPIRELET: see Flèche.

SPLAY: chamfer, usually of the jamb of a window.

SPRINGING: level at which an arch rises from its supports.

SQUINCH: arch or system of concentric arches thrown across the angle between two walls to support a superstructure, for example a dome (Fig. 17).

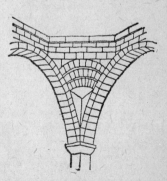

Fig. 17

SQUINT: hole cut in a wall or through a pier to allow a view of the main altar of a church from places whence it could not otherwise be seen (also called Hagioscope).

STALL: carved seat, one in a row, made of wood or stone.

STEEPLE: the tower or spire of a church.

STIFF-LEAF: E.E. type of foliage of many-lobed shapes (Fig. 18).

Fig. 18

STILTED: see Arch.

STOUP: vessel for the reception of holy water, usually placed near a door.

STRAINER ARCH: arch inserted across a room to prevent the walls from leaning.

STRAPWORK: C16 decoration consisting of interlaced bands, and forms similar to fretwork or cut and bent leather.

STRETCHERS: see Brickwork.

STRING COURSE: projecting horizontal band or moulding set in the surface of a wall.

STRUT: see Roof.

STUCCO: plaster work.

STUDS: Upright timbers in timber-framed houses.

SWAG: festoon formed by a carved piece of cloth suspended from both ends.

TABERNACLE: richly ornamented niche (q.v.) or free-standing canopy. Usually contains the Holy Sacrament.

TAZZA: shallow bowl on a foot.

TERMINAL FIGURES (TERMS, TERMINI): upper part of a human figure growing out of a pier, pilaster, etc., which tapers towards the base.

TERRACOTTA: burnt clay, unglazed.

TESSELATED PAVEMENT: decorative floor or wall covering made up of tesserae or small coloured cubes of stone, fitted into a bed of cement.

TESTER: see Sounding Board.

TETRASTYLE: having four detached columns.

THREE-DECKER PULPIT: pulpit with Clerk's Stall and Reading Desk placed below each other.

TIE-BEAM: see Roof (Figs. 13, 14).

TIERCERON: see Vault (Fig. 20).

TILEHANGING: see Slatehanging.

TIMBER-FRAMING: method of construction where walls are built of timber framework with the spaces filled in by plaster or brickwork. Sometimes the timber is covered over with plaster or boarding laid horizontally.

TOMB-CHEST: chest-shaped stone coffin, the most usual medieval form of funeral monument.

TOUCH: soft black marble quarried near Tournai.

TOURELLE: turret corbelled out from the wall.

TRACERY: intersecting ribwork in the upper part of a window, or used decoratively in blank arches, on vaults, etc. *Plate tracery:* early form of tracery where decoratively shaped openings are cut through the solid stone infilling in the head

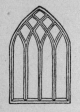  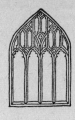 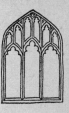

(a)   (b)   (c)   (d)

Fig. 19

of a window. *Bar tracery:* intersecting ribwork made up of slender shafts, continuing the lines of the mullions of windows up to a decorative mesh in the head of the window. *Geometrical tracery:* tracery consisting chiefly of circles or foiled circles. *Intersected tracery:* tracery in which each mullion of a window branches out into two curved bars in such a way that every one of them runs concentrically with the others against the arch of the whole window. The result is that every light of the window is a lancet and every two, three, four, etc., lights together form a pointed arch (Fig. 19*a*). *Reticulated tracery:* tracery consisting entirely of circles drawn at top and bottom into ogee shapes so that a net-like appearance results (Fig. 19*b*). *Panel tracery:* tracery forming upright straight-sided panels above lights of a window (Fig. 19, *c* & *d*).

TRANSEPT: transverse portion of a cross-shaped church.

TRANSOME: horizontal bar across the opening of a window.

TRANSVERSE ARCH: *see* Vaulting.

TRIBUNE: *see* Gallery.

TRICIPUT, SIGNUM TRICIPUT: sign of the Trinity expressed by three faces belonging to one head.

TRIFORIUM: arcaded wall passage or blank arcading facing the nave at the height of the aisle roof and below the clerestory (q.v.) windows. (*See* Gallery.)

TRIGLYPHS: blocks with vertical grooves separating the metopes (q.v.) in the Doric frieze (Fig. 11).

TROPHY: sculptured group of arms or armour, used as a memorial of victory.

TRUMEAU: stone mullion (q.v.) supporting the tympanum (q.v.) of a wide doorway.

TURRET: very small tower, round or polygonal in plan.

TUSCAN: *see* Order.

TYMPANUM: space between the lintel of a doorway and the arch above it.

UNDERCROFT: vaulted room, sometimes underground, below a church or chapel.

VAULT: *Barrel vault: see* Tunnel vault. *Cross-vault: see* Groined vault. *Domical vault:* square or polygonal dome rising direct on a square or polygonal bay, the curved surfaces separated by groins (q.v.). *Fan vault:* vault where all ribs springing from one springer are of the same length, the same distance from the next, and the same curvature. *Groined vault* or *Cross-vault:* vault of two tunnel vaults of identical shape intersecting each other at right angles. *Lierne:* tertiary rib, that is, rib which does not spring either from one of the main springers or the central boss. *Quadripartite vault:* one wherein one bay of vaulting is divided into four parts. *Rib vault:* vault with diagonal ribs projecting along the groins.

Ridge-rib: rib along the longitudinal or transverse ridge of a vault. *Sexpartite vault:* one wherein one bay of quadripartite vaulting is divided into two parts transversely so that each bay of vaulting has six parts. *Tierceron:* secondary rib, that is, rib which issues from one of the main springers or the central boss and leads to a place on a ridge-rib. *Transverse arch:* arch separating one bay of a vault from the next. *Tunnel vault* or *Barrel vault:* vault of semicircular or pointed section (Fig. 20).

VAULTING SHAFT: vertical member leading to the springer of a vault.

VENETIAN WINDOW: window with three openings, the central one arched and wider than the outside ones.

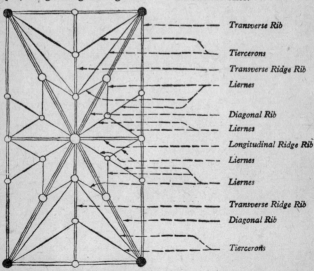

Transverse Rib

Tiercerons
Transverse Ridge Rib
Liernes

Diagonal Rib
Liernes
Longitudinal Ridge Rib
Liernes

Liernes

Transverse Ridge Rib
Diagonal Rib

Tiercerons

Fig. 20

VERANDAH: open gallery or balcony with a roof on light, usually metal, supports.

VESICA: Oval with pointed head and foot.

VESTIBULE: ante-room or entrance hall.

VILLA: according to Gwilt (1842) 'a country house for the residence of opulent persons'.

VITRIFIED: made similar to glass.

VOLUTE: spiral scroll, one of the component parts of an Ionic column (*see* Orders).

VOUSSOIR: wedge-shaped stone used in arch construction.

WAGON-ROOF: roof in which by closely set rafters with arched braces the appearance of the inside of a canvas tilt over a wagon is achieved. Wagon-roofs can be panelled or plastered (ceiled) or left uncovered.

WAINSCOT: timber lining to walls.

WALL PLATE: *see* Roof.

WATERLEAF: leaf shape used in later C12 capitals. The waterleaf is a broad, unribbed, tapering leaf curving up towards the angle of the abacus and turned in at the top (Fig. 21).

Fig. 21

WEATHER-BOARDING: overlapping horizontal boards, covering a timber-framed wall.

WEATHERING: sloping horizontal surface on sills, buttresses, etc., to throw off water.

WEEPERS: small figures placed in niches along the sides of some medieval tombs (also called Mourners).

WHEEL WINDOW: *see* Rose Window.

INDEX OF PLATES

INDEX OF ARTISTS

INDEX OF PLACES

The references in brackets indicate the square in which the place will be found on the map preceding the title-page